Cyberpower

The culture and politics of cyberspace and the Internet

Tim Jordan

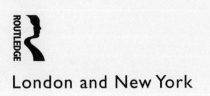

London and New York

First published 1999
by Routledge
11 New Fetter Lane, London EC4P 4EE

Simultaneously published in the USA and Canada
by Routledge
29 West 35th Street, New York, NY 10001

Typeset in Goudy by Routledge
Printed and bound in Great Britain by
Redwood Books, Trowbridge, Wiltshire

British Library Cataloguing in Publication Data
A catalogue record for this book is available from the British
Library

Library of Congress Cataloging in Publication Data
A catalogue record for this book has been requested

ISBN 0–415–17077–X (hbk)
ISBN 0–415–17078–8 (pbk)

Cyberpower

Cyberspace and the Internet are becoming increasingly important in today's societies and yet there has been little analysis of the forces and powers that construct life there. This book presents for the first time a wide ranging introduction to the politics of the Internet, covering all the key concepts of cyberspace. Subjects analysed include the collective imagination in cyberspace, the virtual individual and power and society as created by the Internet. The author uses examples ranging from cross-gendered virtual selves to the meaning of Bill Gates.

In his questioning of who actually governs cyberspace and what powers the individual can control there, Tim Jordan presents a vast range of material, using case studies and original research in interviews as well as statistical and theoretical analysis. Organised around key concepts and providing an extensive bibliography of cyberspace-speak, *Cyberpower* will appeal to students as the first complete analysis of the politics and culture of the Internet. It will also be essential reading for anyone wondering how cyberspace is remaking global society and where the superhighway might be leading us.

Tim Jordan is Senior Lecturer in the Department of Sociology, University of East London.

Contents

Illustrations

Figures

Table

Acknowledgements

Sincere and very grateful non-cyberspatial thanks to all the following.

Four generations of students in my third year unit 'Cyberpunks' helped form these ideas. Interviews with Mike Godwin, John Gilmore, Stanton McCandlish, John Perry Barlow, Lori Fena and Jonah Seiger provided a rapid education. Siraj Izhar and the Stalk provided helpful comments, as did Jordan Crandall and Eyebeam's online discussion 'Artistic Practice in the Network'. Paul Taylor taught me about hackers. Anonymous referees provided useful comments. Tony Higgins provided talk about all things computer and Alan Gavin about all other things. Stepping Stones provided a real-world counterpoint as this was written. Colleagues at UeL offered an always-exciting intellectual context. Funding from the Sociology Department at the University of East London meant teaching never overwhelmed research and allowed a sabbatical in which this book was completed. Barbara Harrison solved a sudden bout of technological determinism when, right at the end, all my computer resources failed. Rod Home and the Ashworth Centre for Social Theory provided an institutional home for six months at the University of Melbourne. Geraldine Williams and Joanne Mattingly at Routledge were always extremely helpful. Most of all, the Reds won again. And, of course, thanks to those I've forgotten.

Thanks to Mari Shullaw at Routledge who took a chance with these ideas, shepherded a decent book proposal and provided excellent comments and support.

Thanks to Mum, Jason, Gayle, Emerald, Denis, Mandy, Stewart, Georgy, Mark, Kim, Olivia and Mary for houses and fun in Melbourne. Thanks to Mum for all her support.

But most of all, thanks to Kate and Matilda, especially for starting a second great adventure.

May 1998

Chapter I

Power and cyberspace

Key concepts

Virtuality
> Cyberspace can be called the virtual lands, with virtual lives and virtual societies, because these lives and societies do not exist with the same physical reality that 'real' societies do. With the emergence of cyberspace, the virtual becomes counterposed to the real. The physical exists in cyberspace but is reinvented. Virtuality is the general term for this reinvention of familiar physical space in cyberspace.

Power
> Power is the name applied to that which structures culture, politics and economics. Power has many forms and there are many theories of power, but each draws its relevance from the sense that power names the things that determine how a life may be lived.

Introduction

Cyberspace now touches all lives. For some it has become as essential as the telephone or the letter. For others it is still a fearful whisper of technological promise. Sometimes we look on bemused, uncertain why all those little addresses that begin 'http://' appear in advertisements, and sometimes we are shocked by the possibilities, when a friend sends letters instantly across the globe through the telephone. When cables and phone lines are allied to computers, this parallel world of cyberspace is created. It is often called a virtual world because it does not exist in tangible, physical reality but in the light and electronics of communications technology. In the virtual world people live virtual lives, alongside their real lives, that may be as substantial as marriage and as insubstantial as checking a television guide. Even those uninterested in the virtual world are affected, often without their knowing. An automated bank teller gives us money because its communications in cyberspace authorise it to; after we have given our password and told an ATM what we want, it then uses a phone line to call a computer that decides whether our request is legitimate.

Virtuality, whether chosen by us or not, has grown parallel to reality and encompasses us all. Cyberspace and its virtual lives need their cultural, political and economic shapes analysed for their social consequences and meaning.

Cyberpower provides this analysis by investigating the nature of power in cyberspace. To do this the nature of cyberspace must first be defined. Chapter 2 does this by exploring the interrelations between science fiction visions of virtuality's possibilities and the reality of networked computers. On the basis of this broad understanding of where cyberspace came from and how it works, three regions of power in cyberspace will be analysed by defining in turn the types of power typical of individual lives in cyberspace (Chapter 3), of virtual communities or societies (Chapters 4 and 5) and of virtual imaginations that unify dispersed individuals as members of the virtual world (Chapter 6). With these three types of power defined their interrelations will be explored to create an overall characterisation of power in cyberspace (Chapter 7). Cyberpower will emerge as a complex form of power in which a digital grassroots find and use tools to gain greater choice of action in their lives but whose use of tools also fuels the increasing domination of a virtual elite over the nature of cyberspace and its capabilities. The power and paradox of cyberspace is its ability to liberate and dominate simultaneously.

Cyberpower

Virtual lives are different to the lives we all know. For a start, nobody takes their physical body there. Each of us might sit at a computer screen, conversing online with others, and our actions occur 'out there' in virtuality while our bodies remain seated at the terminal. We can travel the world meeting people, yet remain forever seated in our home. Certainly, we often have to wait in cyberspace and this gives a sense of distance, of the time needed to traverse a particular part of cyberspace, but this sense of distance has nothing to do with physical distance. Virtually meeting someone in Australia from London can be quicker than virtually meeting someone in New York, depending on the speed of the networks. And though we transgress the physical as we have known it, we do not eliminate our bodies from cyberspace but reinvent them. Nothing tells us this more clearly than sex in cyberspace. Whether someone is idling over to playboy/girl.com to see the latest 'unpublished nude photograph' or furiously typing climax after climax in online dangerous liaisons, it is clear that cyberspace is not purely a realm of the mind. We may not go there physically but we certainly have bodily desires there. There are many such transformations in cyberspace; sex and the body are merely the most often and most lasciviously discussed. Virtual space is the paradox of non-physical space. And virtual societies mean the reinvention of all that is familiar.

Every society achieves a pattern to its politics, technology and culture. Virtual societies are marked by political, technological and cultural patterns so intimately connected as to be nearly indistinguishable. For example, a virtual discussion may allow all to speak and all to be heard at once. Each participant types their contributions and places them in a centrally held discussion, accessible to all other participants. In this way, all contributions are always available, no one can be silenced because their voice is the quietest and no one can be heard with more effect simply because they are more aggressive. Such distinctive forms of computer-mediated discussion give rise to the hope that, perhaps, virtual technology creates a more politically egalitarian debate. The technology, culture and politics of virtual discussions are inextricable. Virtual societies have also become increasingly important, taking over the central functions of existing societies and inventing their own. Ask yourself, 'where is my money?'[1] If it is in a shoe-box under your bed or if you know the numbers of your gold bars in a Swiss vault, then you are exceptional; for nearly everyone else money is virtual, held electronically as numbers in computer databases. Alchemists would look on us wistfully, as we turn plastic cards into gold at every automated teller through the magic of computer communication. Virtual societies have endured now for at least a quarter of a century and it is time their regular patterns of politics, technology and culture were described and analysed.

Many analogies between real and virtual societies have been offered to grasp the meaning of cyberspace – railroads, minds, highways – but few, if any, analyses allow the overall patterns of politics, technology and culture in the virtual lands to be made out. Some say this is because the virtual life changes so fast that perpetual change is the only pattern we can find, and this is a pattern that tells us little except that any insight we have found is useless because it is bound to change (or already has changed). Many glorify virtuality's ability to change and believe that shifts occur so quickly that discerning patterns is a fool's game. But 'Societies exist where normative order exists' (Barnes, 1988: 44). The claim that there is perpetual change in cyberspace denies there can be a normative order, of any sort, in virtual communities and this is tantamount to saying virtual communities cannot exist, but they manifestly do. It is time to outline the normative orders of cyberspace. It is time to put aside the fear of appearing to be 'out of date' with virtual lives' newest playthings.

The patterns of a virtual life are clear enough to be mapped. The virtual world and its social order can be traced now in its entirety, from pole to pole. This does not mean all areas are perfectly known. Sometime in the future we will probably look back at this map and see where it has equivalents to the dragons and sea monsters faithfully represented on early maps of the world. However, we can produce an overview of all of cyberspace's multifarious life, the first globe of cyberspace. This book is such a globe. It is a cartography of the powers that circulate through virtual lives, a chart of the forces that pattern the politics, technology and culture of virtual societies. These powers set the basic conditions of virtual lives. They are the powers of cyberspace and together they constitute cyberpower.

Yet, a vast range of cultural, political and technical matters need to be analysed to discern the structures that govern cyberspace. The notion of virtual communities needs to be examined and the particular forms of communication that create a certain culture need to be drawn out. For example, we need to examine emoticons. These are the use of characters to indicate a picture that relates an emotion, such as ;-), seen side-on as a smiling wink. The technology that allows all messages to be broken down into small digital parcels and then sent out across wires to their destination, with no single pre-planned route, and then to be reassembled into the emails, pictures and conversations that make up cyberspace, needs to be analysed and related to culture and society. The politics of a place where all can speak and all can be heard needs to be explored. The range of material demands some ordering principles that allow theories of power to be applied and conclusions to be drawn. First, power itself needs some definition (later in this chapter). Second, cyberspace needs to be defined (Chapter 2). Following this power can be explored in cyberspace by analysing three interconnected regions: power from the viewpoint of the individual (Chapter 3), power from the viewpoint of the social (Chapters 4 and 5) and power from the viewpoint of the collective imagination (Chapter 6). In conclusion, the relations between these different cyberpowers will be defined and the overall nature of cyberpower summarised (Chapter 7). These regions of the map of cyberpower will now be briefly outlined.

What is power? It can seem the simplest concept, understood and used by nearly everyone. Yet, it can also be the most elusive and difficult concept, consuming book after book. Before plunging into the complex field of power, it is important to remember that this book's task is to outline the stable forms of power in cyberspace. If the question 'what is cyberpower?' can be answered without answering the question 'what is power?', then there is no need to define power in the abstract. Instead, a number of provisional definitions of power can be given that can be used as tools to analyse cyberspace. The nature of power can be safely left to other writers, even as theories of power are used to prise open the nature of cyberspace. Three theories of power will be outlined in the second half of this chapter: Max Weber's common sense theory of power as the possession of individuals, Barry Barnes' theory of power as the constituent of social order and Michel Foucault's analysis of power as domination. A reader may find this analysis somewhat abstract and dry compared with the anecdote and evidence-laden analyses of cyberspace, and there is no reason why the theories of power cannot be put to one side while the definition and analysis of cyberspace are explored. Understanding the theories of power will undoubtedly help the reader because they are useful tools for grasping the nature of societies, but this can be done either when the reader feels it is necessary or after all other analyses have been read. The theories of power inform the analysis of cyberpower and are contained in the second half of this introductory chapter, but the reader can also take this section as self-contained, to be read when necessary.

The nature of cyberspace will be outlined in Chapter 2. Simple questions need answers, such as: Who goes there? What do they do there? How does it work? These questions will be considered before beginning the analysis of power in cyberspace. To provide such an introduction two constituent parts of cyberspace must be outlined. First, there are the conceptions of cyberspace that have been produced in science fiction, specifically cyberpunk science fiction. Here will be found many ideas that have provided a visionary framework within which really existing computer networks have developed. The work of writers such as William Gibson, Bruce Sterling, Pat Cadigan or Neal Stephenson will be explored. Two components of cyberpunk are particularly relevant to cyberspace and will be analysed. These are the images cyberpunk writers create of cyberspace and their explorations of cyborgs. The development of computer networks in reality forms the second part of a definition of cyberspace. First, a broad history of the technology that creates and maintains cyberspace is provided. Here the emergence of government-funded networks such as ARPANET and the Internet, as well as co-operative networks such as FidoNet and Usenet, are examined. Particular attention is paid to the emergence of the World-Wide Web. Following this the size of the Internet and the nature of its users are defined. In conclusion, interaction between the two parts is explored to create a definition of the cyberspace that currently exists. Here we find a cyberspace in which fictional ideas inspire the construction of real computer interaction, which constitutes new networks that, in turn, inspire new fictions. With a clear and detailed definition of cyberspace, it will be possible to turn to cyberpower and its nature.

Cyberpower will be broken down into three distinct levels: the individual, the social and the imaginary. Each of these levels results from a particular perspective on the nature of cyberspace and creates certain questions from which a map can be developed. Each of these perspectives is derived from certain compelling ideas about the nature of cyberspace that appear repeatedly both in online life and in discussions about the nature of virtual space. In Chapter 3, power at the level of the individual is defined as resulting from the perception many have that they enter cyberspace as individuals. For nearly all users of cyberspace, the repetitive moment is of sitting down at a computer terminal and confronting their individuality as they enter passwords to gain access. This basic, inescapable fact often means people assume that cyberspace is constituted of many different individuals, who may or may not come together to construct virtual communities. Beginning from this perception means that three elements of cyberpower at the level of the individual come to the fore: identity fluidity, the remaking of hierarchy and spaces made out of information. Taken together these three constitute cyberpower as an individual possession and result in a form of politics that has the two axes of access to cyberspace and the defence of individual rights in cyberspace. Within this cyberpolitics can be found all the typical political issues that have arisen in and about cyberspace: the financial and cultural barriers to access, privacy, encryption, copyright and censorship. Understood this way, cyberspace offers powers to the individual.

A second fundamental perception often follows from understanding cyberspace as individualist, because after some time in cyberspace many users feel a commitment to their communities that transcends the rights of individuals. Some begin to assume that their communities have both rights over individuals and set the conditions for individuals' virtual lives. This shift is explored in Chapters 4 and 5, with Chapter 4 focusing on the social *in* cyberspace and Chapter 5 on power *in between* online and offline societies. Beginning from the perception that cybersocieties offer a limited set of possibilities from which individuals construct virtual lives leads to an analysis of the technology that underpins cyberspace. From this perspective, the fundamental fact of cyberspace is that it is made possible by forms of technology that are constructed according to social values but are used and experienced by those online as inert things. Power here flows from the ability to act within networks of technology, and this ability is determined by expertise. The conclusion from this perspective is that an expertise-based elite has far greater freedom of action within cyberspace, to the extent that they can determine the fabric of virtual lives. Cyberpower of the social is a power of domination analysed in two parts. First, cyberpower of the social is explored for societies within cyberspace. Here a particular direction to cyberpower is identified in the continual demand for more complex technology to allow easier and more complete access to cyberspace's almost infinite amount of information. This greater elaboration of technology fuels increasing opportunities for the elite to govern cyberspace. Second, cyberpower of the social is explored in the conjunction between online and offline life. Here the services cyberspace offers to offline life, and which alter offline life, are identified and the role of the online elite in meeting the demands offline life make are defined. A particular form of information management and control is created in cyberspace, called the informational space of flows, and it contains the resources offline interests demand from cyberspace. These analyses point to the ongoing emergence of online elites and the interests of offline elites in cyberspace. Taken together, analysis of social cyberpower allows a battle between online elites, who also mediate the demands of offline elites, and online grassroots to be identified as a key constituent of cyberspace.

A third fundamental perception follows from the realisation that people become committed to cyberspace not only in terms of the immediate communities they participate in, but also in the types of interaction and tools they gain in cyberspace. In Chapter 6, the collective imagination or imaginary of cyberspace is analysed. The struggle for online rights, typical of cyberpower of the individual, is a struggle on behalf of all users of cyberspace, not just those who happen to know each other. The demand for more elaborate technology to allow more complex communities in cyberspace, typical of cyberpower of the social, is a demand for all communities in cyberspace, not just those articulating technological needs. The binding together of individuals and societies as members of cyberspace points to a collective imagination through which people, who may never know each other, become committed to the same imagined community. The collective imagination of cyberspace is constructed around the twin fantasies of heaven and hell. Some hope cyberspace will bring immortality and the final ascension of humanity into the godhood that has always been its potential. Some fear cyberspace will make possible the total surveillance of individuals and create the ultimate totalitarian society. In hoping and fearing, people come to recognise their membership, even citizenship, of a digital nation. Cyberpower of the imaginary is a power through which virtual social order is constituted.

Cyberpower as a map of cyberspace's fundamental social and individual forces will be complete when the interrelations of the three levels of cyberpower are articulated in Chapter 7. It will become clear that the powers of the individual and the social connect to each other in ways that constantly feed each other, creating ongoing instability and a drive for constant change in cyberspace. The powers of the imaginary permeate through both other levels, binding individuals and societies together as part of the larger, imagined community of cyberspace. The final conclusion is that cyberspace at the end of the twentieth century has at its heart a constant battle between the empowerment of individuals and the propagation of an ever more powerful virtual elite. By providing ever more powerful tools to the individual, cyberspace seems to offer power in various virtual possessions. Yet, the reliance on these tools ensures individuals become ever more dependent on an expertise-based elite who create and maintain those tools. Cyberpower is a cartography of power in cyberspace that makes clear that the virtual lands host a constant, complex conflict between grassroots and elites.

This introduction to cyberpower is a preliminary chart of the terrain that will be explored in subsequent chapters. To assist the exploration of this terrain two further tools have been provided. Nine myths of the electronic frontier are spread throughout the book and there are key concepts for each chapter. The myths of the electronic frontier are tall tales, sometimes true, that are repeated across the virtual lands and they establish some of the fundamental morals of cyberspace. These stories are introduced when the moral they offer is relevant to the analysis of cyberpower. The lists of key concepts for each chapter provide a shorthand for the fundamental points made in each chapter. Put another way, the key concepts provide a set of signposts to the conceptual journey needed to grasp cyberpower. A glossary also provides some help in dealing with the dense thicket of acronyms that is all too familiar to anyone exploring cyberspace. With these additional helpers and supported by the three concepts of power discussed next, it will be possible first to define cyberspace and then to distil out of it the essential forces that construct virtual lives and societies in the virtual lands.

Power

As already noted above, the following explanation of three theories of power is a self-contained section, in the sense that it focuses on power and puts aside cyberspace. The concepts explored are all then used in the subsequent analysis of cyberpower, but it may help some readers to return to these theories after having explored the object, cyberspace, to which they are applied. The reader can determine when they need to understand Weber's, Barnes' or Foucault's theory of power. These understandings of power have been included because they will help the reader to understand cyberpower. They are effective and easily grasped theoretical tools that will help the reader understand power in cyberspace.

Power is something we all intuitively understand, because we all use power to explain and understand our lives (Barnes, 1988; Clegg, 1989). President Clinton is powerful, children are powerless, that car is more powerful than this, one advertisement is more powerful than another – the list could go on for ever. These everyday uses of power nearly always refer to the different abilities people or objects have to 'do things', to take action. President Clinton is more powerful than I am because he can order the US Army to invade, but I am more powerful than my students are because I mark their exam papers. Power is a belief or theory we use in everyday interactions that allows us to grasp the different ability people and objects have to act. At its most general, power is a word we use to indicate differences about abilities. Understood in this way, the nature of power seems intuitively clear. The concept of power also looks like a good tool to take with us to cyberspace. Power can link political, cultural and technological objects and this is a great help when examining a land where it is often hard to see the gap between the social, the cultural and the technological. Power also focuses discussion on differential abilities to take actions: Who can do what and who cannot? Who has power and who does not? Power will be our tool because it allows us to begin with the assumption that sociological, cultural and political analyses of technologically based societies are intimately linked.

But for all these advantages there is a problem. Our everyday theories will always seem clear, simply because they are the taken-for-granted ideas we use to live hour by hour and minute by minute. Using power in its everyday sense might then mean we never move beyond the detail of our minute-to-minute lives and our social theory would be effectively limited by our everyday lives. Anything more complex than whatever can be grasped by the individual would disappear. Power would become an impossible concept that refers equally to the ability of the President of the USA to invade another nation and to the speed a car's engine can produce. Common sense and everyday theories can be important places to begin, because we all understand what is being talked about, but common sense cannot be where our theories end. Some further development of power is needed to take with us the advantages of our intuitive understanding of power, but also ensure we can develop counter-intuitive understandings of technological, cultural and political aspects of cyberspace. Some further theoretical development is needed, but not so much that we lose sight of our starting point. This will be done by examining three different understandings of power: power as a possession, power as the result of patterned interactions between individuals, and power as networks of dominated and dominator. The explanations of these three powers that follows will be largely uncritical because the aim is to apply these conceptions to cyberspace to see how they fit and because such discussions are widely available elsewhere.[2] The first of these provides a bridge to more complicated understandings of power because it is, essentially, a developed version of our common sense conception of power.

Max Weber: power as a possession

We intuitively talk of power as though it were a possession, an object that can be passed from one to another and which enables the possessor to force actions on others. If am sitting in Dry Gulch saloon holding a gun, I can enforce my desire to see someone dance, but if I then lose the gun I will easily be subjected to a similar demand to pick up my feet. To develop the common sense view, a number of elements of this intuition need to be separated. First, power is intentional; someone wills something to be done and it is done. 'I' want to see someone dance and 'I' have the power to make dancing happen, so dancing occurs. Somebody intends the effects of power; they are willed. But we don't understand power as existing only at the specific moment that someone forces an action to occur. President Clinton is powerful even when he is asleep and a gun makes me powerful even if no one is dancing. Power is not only the actions that are produced but, perhaps more importantly, the capacity to produce them. Someone or something is powerful to the extent that they, or it, are capable of defining an action or objective and have the ability to enforce or create that action or objective. Anybody or anything that possesses such ability is powerful. Power is not itself described but is imputed from its effects. When I make someone dance, I would be considered powerful because I have that ability and no discussion of the particular nature of my gun is necessary. This is clear from robberies accomplished with replica guns that cannot fire bullets; these guns still ensure certain actions are taken because it is assumed they have the same ability to fire bullets as real guns. We do not need to examine in detail the exact nature of power within this theory because we know it exists from its effects. Similarly, we can say a flame is hot because a thermometer measures its heat without having to know the details of combustion. Power understood as a possession essentially addresses the effects of power. If we can see an effect or if we know with confidence that an effect could be obtained, then we know power is present, even if we do not know exactly how this effect is produced.

Second, power understood as a possession needs resistance. If no one resisted my request for dancing, for example if I called for more dancing while in the bar during half-time at the ballet rather than asking Butch Cassidy in Dry Gulch saloon to dance, then no power would be involved. No one would believe I had made the ballerina dance in the second half and they would be right. Power as a possession needs resistance to manifest itself and unless power manifests itself we have no idea that it exists. When power is only known because its effects are known and its effects are only known when there is resistance, power is absent when someone willingly does whatever is requested. Power is a negative phenomenon; it forces actions that are against the will of someone. We need power to be exercised for us to know that it exists; it can then become a capacity that need not be exercised, only threatened. If I make Butch Cassidy dance, and the word gets around, I may not have to show my gun to make the Sundance Kid dance. One interpretation of Saddam Hussein's actions in the Gulf War was that he did not believe President Bush actually had the power to launch war, despite Bush's position as head of the US military. Hussein may have seen Bush as merely a titular military leader because US public opinion would not allow dead US soldiers. Bush's power to invade, to be able really to unleash the US Army, had to occur in reality to re-establish this power as a capacity.

Third, if power concerns the ability to overcome resistance then stable patterns of power can be equated with forms of domination. The picture so far is that to have power is to be able to overcome resistance and enforce a will. Power is the ability to make someone or something do what you want them to, even when they do not want to. If we think of patterns of such occurrences then we can see not just individual moments of domination but systems of domination, like the outlawing of a certain form of music (such as techno or music the law defines by its repetitive beat[3]). If all disc jockeys who play techno music in a particular society are subject to a threat of imprisonment, fines and loss of their sound systems, then we do not have here individual moments of power but a system of musical domination. Such systems will depend not on power's capacities' being realised on every subject – not all DJs need to be imprisoned – but must manifest themselves to an extent that establishes that power as a capacity – some DJs must be successfully prosecuted. Power becomes domination when repressions are not individual and may even merely be threatened.

Power understood as a possession, our basic common sense view of power, leads to a theory of power that has three main components. Power is the ability to impose an intention or a will on someone or something. Power is only realised against resistance. Systems of domination occur when there are patterned relations of power. This theory of power is close to the one found in the work of German sociologist Max Weber. 'In general, we understand by "power" the chance of a man or of a number of men to realize their own will in a communal action even against the resistance of others who are participating in the action' (Weber, 1952: 180; 1986: 29). Weber also notes that domination is a 'special case of power', as has been outlined. If further development of this theory of power were needed by anyone, they could begin with Weber (Mommsen, 1989; Clegg, 1989). However, the central concern of this text is to establish a number of views of power that can be used to analyse cyberspace, rather than a detailed analysis of power for its own sake. We can now turn to two further conceptions of power and both these begin from a similar criticism of the common sense understanding of power.

The theory of power as possession just outlined leaves some questions unanswered. Most important, what is it that enforces obedience to the powerful will? By reading power from its effects and ignoring the substance of power the common sense view fails to grasp the most important feature of power. What is it that ensures compliance? What overcomes resistance? If I were to haul out a gun at the ballet and demand that the ballerinas dance, I might experience a momentary power but would likely end up in jail. If I slouched in Dry Gulch saloon, drinking champagne, eating smoked salmon sandwiches and discoursing on the perfect pirouette, I might find it harder to convince Butch Cassidy that he dance to the tune of my gun, no matter how real my gun was. Clearly, contexts for obedience to power are important. Perhaps instead of beginning from individual instances of power from which systems of domination are built, block by block, the existence of collective structures should be presumed. Perhaps, we should recognise that the common sense version hides exactly what we should be seeking because, by beginning from individual instances of power, it obscures the social relations that already exist that make sense of individual instances. There are two other understandings of power that begin from just such a criticism of power understood as a possession: power understood as the result of interactions between knowledgeable individuals and power understood as strategies that situate subjects as dominated or dominator. We will look at these in turn and then our theoretical toolbox will be full.

Barry Barnes: power as social order

To understand power's basis in the interactions between people we can begin with an example. Why do cars stop at red lights?[4] Why do red lights, only certain red lights of course, have the power to stop traffic? If you are the first car at a red light there is often nothing physically preventing you moving out and you would have the advantage of moving sooner. Two restraining factors spring to mind. First, there is the fear of a car you cannot see obeying its green light and running into you. Second, there may be a police car or camera, unseen, which will stop you and extract the appropriate penalty. On the one hand, knowledge of a certain routine or common understanding between all car drivers enforces the situation it describes (that red means stop and green means go) and, on the other, sanctions that penalise certain behaviours prevent those behaviours. Properly understood, these two are actually of the same type because both are knowledge of sanctions. In one we know and fear the sanction of a car crash and in the other we know and fear the law's sanctions.

The power of a traffic light derives from various routines of social life that we know about. It is the very real power to stop cars and punish those who disobey with violence and fines. The two aspects, routine and knowledge, are crucial and the second far more important. In fact it is impossible to think of an effective social routine without there being generalised knowledge of that routine. Say an unfortunate Martian comes to Earth because, having been conversing with Elvis, they desperately want to drive a red Chevrolet with tail fins. Unfortunately, the king of rock and roll has talked a lot about cars and burgers but never about road rules and the results we can all imagine. It is the Martian's ignorance that leads to an accident. Collective knowledge ensures the vast range of routines that make up a society or community persists and so that society persists. From behaviour at traffic lights to the solidity of institutions like banks, the persistence of all these social forms is based on each member of a community knowing about the routines that constitute those social forms. Think of what happens when routines change. For example, when investors decide a bank is no longer a safe place for their investments and start to withdraw them, the institution changes. In this case, the bank collapses, revealing its previous objectivity and solidity to have been based solely on the persisting patterns of investors.

Understood this way, societies and communities are nothing more nor less than the knowledge that members of those communities hold about their societies. If we all know what happens at red lights we can be confident that red lights hold the power to stop cars. However, if we are transported to Lisbon, at 3 a.m. 1979 then we will find those Portuguese red lights only having the power to slow down cars because, despite the Australian cowering in the back of the car who has different expectations, the Portuguese collectively understand this is the case. Social objects and social structures exist on the basis of persisting routines of behaviour of individuals and these persisting routines are based on common, collective knowledge of those routines. These routines then feel like external, objective elements of society. This is one of the paradoxes of this view of power that needs to be stressed. Even though power is based on patterns of interactions between individuals, it is not subject to each individual's actions. If enough people act in a certain way, then a pattern is not subject to any one person's actions. If we think of a bank again, one person suddenly withdrawing their funds will not affect the bank at all. It is only if many people suddenly do so that a run occurs and the bank's dependence on all these patterns of action is revealed. Language is another example: it is possible for anybody to invent their own words but impossible for them to have those meanings immediately accepted. We know what bad and good mean and anyone advising us that this egg is bad, while meaning it is good, will be misunderstood. The meaning of good and bad is objectively established by the ongoing use of these words in a linguistic community. Of course, this does not mean that individuals cannot change the world, but they can only do so when many others repeat their actions. If I am sitting in a 1950s jazz club and someone tells me the saxophonist is bad tonight, I might know that this means the saxophonist is good. If such a usage becomes widespread among a linguistic community then that community can operate with the ambiguity that bad might mean good or bad. In short, while social structures appear external and objective to the individuals who constitute them, such structures are wholly internal to the collective or group. Social structures can change but only through concerted collective action.

The structures that constitute a society can now be understood as the result of the knowledge individuals have of those structures and of the consequences actions will probably have. This knowledge is self-referring, it is knowledge about what others do, and it is self-validating – the more knowledge is used the more valid it becomes. The more I know that others will not stop at a red light, the more likely it is that I will not stop and the more I do not stop or see others not stopping, then the more valid my knowledge is that red lights do not necessarily mean stop. The most vivid memory of a Portuguese night might just be the lesson that power is the result of the knowledge we all have of each other's knowledge.

But what is power and where does it reside? It appears as if our common sense notion of power, which is based on power wielded by individuals or objects, is completely irrelevant. However, the present theory of power encompasses the common sense version because it shows us how individualised power necessarily relies on collectively constituted structures. Red lights have no inherent power to stop traffic but do so because of the common knowledge drivers' hold of their significance, because of common knowledge each individual red light does, in fact, stop traffic. The power each driver experiences on a day-to-day level is of individual red lights stopping them, but this power relies on collectively constituted knowledge that is validated again and again at each red light. When that knowledge no longer remains valid, as found in Portugal, then the red light ceases to have the power to stop traffic. The same can be said for banks. We think of banks as stable institutions but if we hear on the radio that our bank may be in trouble, perhaps through a massive fraud, our knowledge is altered. If we then hurry to the bank and find hundreds of others queuing to remove their savings then we might swiftly reassess our understanding of the bank's solidity and join in its demolition. These distributions of knowledge confer on all of us the capacity for certain actions – to stop at red lights, to rush to our bank – and these individual capacities are very much like power in the common sense version. The connection is that the distribution of knowledge across society creates certain capacities for action that can be taken up as individual instances of power.

It is further possible for power to be delegated in various ways. So far a red light has been used as the main example, but though it stops cars it seems slightly odd to think of a metal pole, coloured glass and electricity as wielding power and it would be anthropomorphic to think the red light 'intends' to stop traffic. The answer is that human actors have delegated power to the red light that wields power on behalf of all of us. Intuitions of being more or less powerful can also be understood as the various ways power is delegated through society. There is no greater symbol of this than representative governments that must beg for votes once every four or five years and are restrained very little by the electors in between. Governments can so enrage their populations that they withdraw the power they have delegated, and this shows that the delegated capacity for action is still dependent on the collective routines that create that capacity, but most government decisions are not going to trigger revolution no matter how unpopular they are. Power can be delegated. Any theory of power should be able to grasp that President Clinton and Prime Minister Blair are powerful, and this theory does that while, at the same time, pointing towards the sources of delegated power.

Power can be the possession of individuals or objects. The latter fact may be especially useful when investigating a place, like cyberspace, that is heavily dependent on technology. But such possession is never inherent in the individual or object but is dependent on the distribution of knowledge across society. The final key point about this theory emerges here because, unlike the common sense belief that power makes mad and that power and knowledge are separate things, power in this theory is a form of knowledge. Power is the capacity for action that is created by collectively held knowledge. The ability to bank money and feel relaxed is constituted by our collectively held belief that banks are stable institutions that will look after our savings. The power of banks is based on their ability to reassure savers that their money is safe; it is dependent on our individual knowledge of banks. As already noted, this does not mean that any one individual can bring down a bank because it is collective knowledge that produces power, just as one person running a red light does not destroy the power of that red light to stop cars. Power is essentially the same thing as knowledge.

By examining the red light we come to a theory of power as the result of collectively held knowledge. This theory reconciles the individual possession of power with the collective constitution of power as capacities for action. It is a theory based in the tradition of interactionism, of understanding society as the result of interactions between individuals, but in this form it is essentially the work of UK sociologist Barry Barnes:

> In a stable normative order knowledge that an action is normal and routinely done encourages the performance of the actions, so that the general dissemination of the knowledge suffices to validate it in practice. I drive up to a red light. I am free to stop or go, but I know that it is normal to stop....Any specific distribution of knowledge confers a generalised capacity for action upon those individuals who carry and constitute it, and that capacity for action is their social power, the power of the society they constitute by bearing and sharing the knowledge in question. Social power is the added capacity for action that accrues to individuals through their constituting a distribution of knowledge and thereby a society.
>
> (Barnes, 1988: 56–7)

Barnes' theory has three features that will be useful when examining cyberspace: it explains individuals' power and its source, social power can be embodied in objects, and knowledge and power are essentially the same thing. Barnes' account also has the strength of focusing attention on the day-to-day maintenance of power as part of social order. He notes that many theories focus on 'the use of power against opposition and resistance, so that there is a tendency for the negative aspects of power relations to be dwelled upon and emphasised' rather than seeing that power 'may be sustained by genuinely co-operative social interaction' (Barnes, 1988: x). For Barnes, power is constitutive of social order and is neither good nor bad, though different powers may be good or bad. The problem of power for Barnes is the more general problem of how social order is maintained (Barnes, 1995). This puts aside the common use of power that often assumes it is a bad or negative thing, used to repress and dominate. However, this produces a problem because, for many people, the most important forms of power are the ones that create inequalities or oppressions. We talk about power in many forms – car engines, red lights, Presidents – but it is the forms of power that repress large numbers of people that are the most important to understand. In the previous examples, the issue of criminalised music sat alongside Butch Cassidy's dancing feet – something that may have caused some readers to pause – and for many this is too general an analysis. We are often interested in power because it is the word we use to examine all sorts of inequalities and these should be our focus, not power itself as a theoretical concept but power as the term for whatever it is that generates inequalities and oppressions. A focus on domination is not a criticism of Barnes' theory, as there is no reason why repression cannot be understood as a particular form of delegated power. However, to fill our toolbox for the investigation of cyberspace it will be useful to take up another theory, one that also begins from a criticism of the common sense notion of power but rather than forming a theory of social order examines power as domination. Whereas Barnes' theory is directed towards the analysis of any social order, we can also look at a political interpretation of power: power as the analysis of social inequalities. We can make our central problem power as the forcible suppression of people. Such a move involves a shift from a theory of exactly what power is to an analysis of how power represses. We will still need to make some general comments about power but these will be more like methodological principles for studying power than the truth about power. Such an approach to power will constitute an analytics of power that defines which features of society we must investigate in order to force power out from hiding and see its entire dimension.[5] The difference of this approach to both Weber and Barnes is that it has no pretension to deciding the nature of power in the abstract, but sees power as only existing in certain forms in particular times and places. Comments about the nature of power are still needed but only to define how we go about the analysis of specific forms of power.

Michel Foucault: power as domination

The first principle of this third theory of power is that power is a force that generates structures of inequality between people. As with Barnes, power's effects are created in relations between people and, against Weber, power is not a possession. This might seem mildly confusing; if we are dealing with inequalities aren't we dealing with some people who have power and some that do not? But having and having not, whether it is money, free speech or the right to play certain forms of music, is the effect of power. The example of jailing DJs who play certain music is of an action, imprisonment, whose significance is clear only as an effect or exercise of power within relations between lovers of a certain musical style, called ravers, and of a nation-state who declared this musical style a danger. It makes little sense to try and understand the criminalisation of repetitive beats as a purely musical gesture, as if the UK government wished to dictate the nature of pop music. The full significance of this power is only clear within a number of other relations which tell us that techno music was part of a transgressive social movement that opposed many of the cultural values held by the UK government. Rave valued drug use and ecstatic moments over hard work. Ravers made connections to other oppositional movements, such as squatters. Rave was a political battle and the criminalisation of techno only makes sense when the general relations it is part of are understood (Huq, 1998). Power is a relation, not a possession. It is a relation that is part of many social relationships as that which creates inequalities. Power is not exercised by the elite or the superior over their inferiors but traverses across all people. It might be said that power comes from below not because we live in perfectly democratic societies, but because power enmeshes all of us. Power's effects then become clear in a multitude of minor and major instances. A minor example of sexual harassment, a wolf whistle, may be insignificant considered by itself but gains greater meaning as an instance of the differential relations of power between men and women. A whistle becomes the reminder of other, less musical and more forceful acts. As an analytic principle we should look for the relations between people that underpin instances of power.

Much of this is close to Barnes' conception of power, but focusing on power as the process of oppression allows a more politically acute version to emerge. Some of its consequences are also paradoxical. Most important, a form of power both intends to produce certain effects but is not driven by any one will. What this means is that power is akin to the strategy employed by an army. Different elements move in a way that fulfils an overall purpose and which is served by a number of tactics common to different micro-parts of the army. For example, the overall strategy might be swinging through the north-western regions of France, as Germany did in 1914 and 1939, and to effect this strategy each small unit will have been taught forms of operation. In the same way, there are grand strategies of social power that rely on micro-tactics to work. If we look at the construction of economic inequality we can identify education as one strategy that helps maintain divisions of rich and poor and we can note the micro-tactic of exams, which are everywhere present in the education system and everywhere similarly shaped. The different micro-elements construct major strategies that have a direction but are also not directed by any single centre. The analogy of an army is helpful when understanding the relationship between a grand strategy and micro-tactics but, unfortunately, also misleading because it implies a commander whose will infuses and directs strategy. But strategies of power are not like military strategies in this respect, because strategies of power do not have an overall commander. If we think, in the most general terms, of the strategy of power that produces inequality between men and women then there is no individual or group of individuals directing this strategy. There may be individuals who are more important than others, the legislators who determine the legal status of divorce for example, but there is in no sense a commander or ruling council for patriarchy and the same could be said of all the strategies of power that produce domination. The methodological principle for studying power that results is: assume tactics purposefully implement a strategic design of domination but that no will creates or directs this design.

Domination implies both dominated and dominator and power as a relation implies both powerful and powerless. The understanding of power as the day-to-day tactics and micro-instances that underpin a grand domination assumes some sort of relationship; the exertion of male power assumes females, the invasion of an army assumes an enemy. It is often easily assumed that this means the relationship of power is two sided, that each great strategy of power is binary, but the diffuse mesh-like nature of micro-tactics means that no such assumption should be made. Strategies of power will hardly ever appear with the clarity that uniforms give armed forces. There is no reason why strategies of power cannot interrelate several forms of domination and different mixtures of dominator and dominated, producing forms of power that create multiple positions individuals occupy in the strategies of power. Rather than a straight fight, power relations of domination imply subjection and resistance. They imply many interactions of seemingly different importance that continually add up to broad strategies. Further, it would be a mistake to think that such a relationship is always repressive, that it continually prevents certain actions. Far more powerful and subtle is the ambiguity that subjecting individuals produces subjects, individuals who themselves produce the effects of power. Power is both repressive and productive. Resistance is not only implied but necessary to engage individuals in strategies of power. Resistance is implied by the claim that power is a relation but it is made essential by power's subtler means of attempting to form subjectivities appropriate to a form of power. The ongoing attempt to convince women that their role is as a support to their husbands may produce women who take on that subjectivity, who become the loyal wife in the background. Economic power has an interest in persuading us that our needs both change, requiring further purchases, and are often unknown to us, requiring advice on our purchases through advertising. When examining power we must not assume that it is binary or that it is only repressive, we must pay attention to the way power embeds itself in subjectivities. Finally, analysis of power in this way is the analysis of forms of governance, not of government. Governance is the analysis of the many forms, not just the institutionalised forms, by which we govern our

daily conduct. This is then not just, or even primarily, the analysis of bureaucracies or the state but analysis of the ways people act in relation to each other. If
we assume power has a hand in forming our individual nature, our needs and
desires, then the examination of power produces an analysis of the typical
conduct of individuals and how that conduct contributes to, produces or resists
forms of power.

Power is manifested in great strategies of inequality. Power is not something
that can be defined completely in the abstract but an analytics of power or a
methodology for studying power can be defined, which then allows the analysis
of different strategies of power. The principles of any such analysis are, first, that
power is a relation, not a possession, as with Barnes we should direct our attention to what makes individual acts possible. Second, power is constituted in
tactics that insinuate everyday life and that create an overall strategy, but for
which there is no overall guiding will, either individual or organisational.
Finally, power must not be understood as a battle between two sides or as merely
repressive – power is multiple and productive. This theory of power is based on
work most closely associated with the French philosopher and historian Michel
Foucault:

> power applies to immediate everyday life which categorises the individual,
> marks him by his own individuality, attaches him to his own identity,
> imposes a law of truth on him which he must recognise and which others
> have to recognise in him. It is a form of power which makes individuals
> subjects. There are two meanings of the word *subject*: subject to someone
> else by control and dependence, and tied to his own identity by a
> conscience or self-knowledge. Both meanings suggest a form of power
> which subjugates and makes subject to.
>
> (Foucault, 1983: 212)

Foucault's theory directs attention to power as it exists in different societies at
different times and provides analytic principles for examining these powers. It
also assumes that in examining power, the analyst also examines the forms of
domination and subjection in societies. Here Foucault extends the Weberian
intuition that power is about 'power over', power is about subjugation, but redefines what this means to capture a more complex view than the common sense
one. Foucault also diverges from Barnes, because Barnes sees power as essentially neutral, capable of underpinning dominating and non-dominating social
structures, but Foucault assumes the study of power is the study of domination.
Of the three theories of power two address the intuition many have that power
concerns inequalities and oppressions, while one explores a seemingly deeper
possibility by arguing power is actually the basic constituent of social order.
Whereas Foucault and Weber look darkly on power, seeing in it the means by
which domination is created and maintained, Barnes is neutral seeing in power
the elements of order.

In a different way, Foucault's approach is similar to Barnes' and different to Weber's, in that it focuses on the relations between subjects that create the basis for power to be displayed as a possession. Weber develops the common sense version of power, as that which some people 'have' that enables them to force other people to do things they would prefer not to do. Power is a negative force that can be handed around, just as a gun, powerful car or even a presidency can be passed on. Foucault and Barnes look beneath this seemingly obvious approach. They ask under what conditions is a gun produced and given to certain people? And what about those conditions ensure they can use the gun to enforce their will? For something to be possessed, it must first be constituted and then be able to be made someone's property; what are the rules that govern these processes? For Foucault and Barnes, social relations exist underneath the individualism of power as property and make the common sense understanding possible. Weber remains close to the most obvious interpretation of power, perhaps reflecting the fact that he developed his theory of power nearly a hundred years before Foucault and Barnes.

Finally, Foucault argues that attempting to define power in the abstract is not necessary; instead a methodology for studying power is needed and only then can specific forms of power that exist in particular times and places be analysed. For Foucault, it is these really existing forms of power that are the most important topic for analysis. Weber and Barnes more directly address the nature of power, attempting to define its fundamental characteristics. This last distinction is finer than the previous two because Foucault's analytics of power requires some discussion of power to be able to justify its methodological validity. Foucault considers whether power should be studied as a relation or as a possession, whereas Barnes and Weber analyse whether power is a relation or a possession. The essential difference is that Foucault claims theories of the nature of power only have use as a preliminary to studying historically variable forms of social, whereas Barnes and Weber see power as an essential object in itself.

Weber, Barnes and Foucault are different and similar around three issues. Is power neutral or the cause of domination? Is power a relation or a possession? Is the object of study power or particular forms of power? The three theories that have been examined all agree and disagree. All three provide three frameworks through which power can be analysed. All three will be applied to the forms of power that circulate in cyberspace to ensure a complex analysis of the bases for virtual lives and societies.

Chapter 2

Cyberspace and the matrix

Key concepts

Gibsonian cyberspace

William Gibson coined the phrase 'cyberspace'. Gibson's fictional conception of cyberspace was of a place that collated all the information in the world and could be entered by disembodied consciousnesses. Disembodiment took place through a computer. Gibsonian cyberspace offers power to those who can manipulate information in cyberspace, either individual hackers relying on expertise or large institutions relying on corporate muscle.

Cyberpunk

Cyberpunk is a genre of science fiction that emerged in the 1980s. It analysed current society and technology by making them appear fictional and strange. Cyberpunk was a movement that contained such authors as William Gibson, Bruce Sterling, Pat Cadigan and others. It had its own magazines, tropes and social networks. Cyberpunk became a general cultural term for an outlaw or critical attitude to the effects of information technology on society.

Computer networks

Computers process information and provide tools for doing this, from word processors to databases. Computers can communicate with each other, either to send information or to offer remote access to tools one computer has but another does not. This access is organised via dedicated cables or telephone lines and is governed by rules usually called protocols. Any computer organised to communicate with another is part of a network and any computer may be part of many networks.

Barlovian cyberspace

When cyberspace is understood as the space computer networks create, it can be called Barlovian cyberspace (as opposed to Gibsonian cyberspace, understood as a fictional and visionary conception of cyberspace). This space can be understood as a vastly more complex version of the space people enter when they talk on the phone. The emergence of global networks serving millions has seen the emergence of a complicated and seemingly infinite Barlovian cyberspace. Barlovian cyberspace is named after John Perry Barlow, who many credit for using Gibson's term 'cyberspace' in relation to existing computer networks.

Introduction

Millions of computers across the world speak to each other because they are connected to networks that speak to each other. These connections support an infinite creativity. Anyone with a minimum of equipment and knowledge can not only read what is already there, take copies of information already there and participate in communal activities already there, but can also build there. Anyone can open a bulletin board, create an alternative world, post their thoughts or just exist as a 'net.lurker'. Analysis of this world-wide interconnection of computers and the forms of power circulating on it is caught between the reality of communications between computers across wires and the science fiction image of a way of interpreting data. To see this we can compare the leading network taxonomist's description of the world-wide network with a fictional network created by a leading cyberpunk science fiction writer:

> Networks may be classified according to their purposes. Two strong groupings are readily visible in the real world: noncommercial and commercial. Most commercial networks are closely interconnected into a metanetwork that allows electronic mail to pass between almost any pair of them....All of the networks and conferencing systems that are interconnected for mail transfer form a worldwide metanetwork, the *matrix*.
>
> (Quarterman, 1990: 125)

Quarterman focuses on realities that define which computers are or are not connected, electronic mail being the test here. The matrix is a world of people sending typed messages to each other. William Gibson's description of a science fiction cyberspace, on the other hand, looks to possibilities. In this extract from his key novel *Neuromancer*, the character Case is listening to a history of cyberspace:

> 'The matrix has its roots in primitive arcade games,' said the voice-over, 'in early graphics programs and military experimentation with cranial jacks.' On the Sony, a two dimensional space war faded behind a forest of mathematically generated ferns, demonstrating the spacial possibilities of logarithmic spirals; cold blue military footage burned through, lab animals wired into test systems, helmets deeding into fire control circuits of tanks and war planes. 'Cyberspace. A consensual hallucination experienced daily by billions of legitimate operators, in every nation, by children behind taught mathematical concepts....A graphic representation of data

abstracted from the banks of every computer in the human system. Unthinkable complexity. Lines of light ranged in the nonspace of the mind, clusters and constellations of data. Like city lights, receding.'

(Gibson, 1984: 67)

Gibson's possibilities are still distant. They include cranial implants that allow a physical connection between computer and person, all the world's data collected and pictured and access to this data through virtual reality. In Gibson's world, individuals immerse themselves totally in cyberspace, rather than in Quarterman's where people look simultaneously at cyberspace on their screen and at their 'normal' offline life in the rest of their room. However, the two are coming closer together. For example, Sandia National Laboratories has been one of the homes of US research into nuclear arms and here methods of grasping data graphically or visually are already developed. A system using a head-mounted virtual reality that immerses the viewer in an alternative world includes

a gorgeous scale model of our solar system...planets and moons too tiny to be seen in true scale are visibly wheeling through their correct orbits. Once elusive facts – for example, that the Uranian system is perpendicular to the orbit of every other planet – are plain as the nose on your face.

(Rapaport, 1995: 75)

In the system just described data is grasped by flying through it and seeing it, dancing in the solar system, much as Gibson envisaged. A further example of the gap between fact and fiction closing is German research that establishes a connection between thought and computer commands. This work includes success in an experiment where a person with wires attached to their head moves a dot on a computer screen solely by thought (Hardman, 1995). But caution is needed because too enthusiastic a connection between such developments and Gibson's vision can misdirect us from the really existing matrix, within which cyberspace has emerged. Such a mistaken reading of the actuality of the virtual lands from the fiction of Gibson, and others, is all the more seductive because this genre of science fiction has been read as social and cultural theory. One of the harder headed Marxist analysts of current urban environments, Mike Davis, cites Gibson's vision as 'prefigurative social theory' – as an already existing theory of a yet to exist society – and Burrows and Featherstone affirm that cyberpunk science fiction can be read simultaneously as fiction and as 'social and cultural theory' (Davis, 1992: 3; Burrows and Featherstone, 1995: 6; Burrows, 1997). When the fictional dreams of one man and his typewriter[1] assume the status of theoretical prophecy, the temptation is to turn away from what is actually occurring because we have seen the future.

This chapter will define cyberspace by exploring, in turn, the science fiction of online life and networked worlds of wires and computers. The analysis of science fiction, first, establishes the way science fiction may act as prefigurative

social theory by creating fictional worlds that make familiar elements of current
societies strange and thereby open them to criticism. A particular school of
science fiction relevant to cyberspace is identified in cyberpunk and its two
main roles in imagining cyberspace are discussed. These roles are creating
pictures of cyberspace and exploring the human/machine figure of the cyborg.
Following this exploration of the meaning of science fiction for cyberspace, the
reality of networked computers is analysed. First, a history of the technologies
that create cyberspace is given. This explores the emergence of government-
funded networks such as ARPANET, of co-operative networks like FidoNet and
of the protocols, computers and wires that allow networks to exist. The emergence of the Internet and the World-Wide Web are explored; in particular the
way they are absorbing all the resources of different networks is analysed.
Second, the demographics of cyberspace are explored. A definition of the size
and current rates of change in the Internet are given and the typical user and
uses of cyberspace are defined. Finally in this chapter, the two components of
cyberpunk images and networked realities are discussed together to provide a
definition of the cyberspace that currently exists.

Cyberspace is with us but it is an emergent form of cyberspace: elements
appear before our eyes without any certainty they will eventually coalesce into
the fictional visions. Millions live in versions of cyberspace and the social structures these millions are generating will have profound effects on any future
cyberspace. Certain circuits of power are already in existence and no matter
how much the look and feel of cyberspace changes, even if it becomes a fully
realised four-dimensional virtual reality, these circuits will continue to flow in
the societies created there. The facts of existing cyberspace weigh like a nightmare on the brains of future cyberspace. But neither can fictional visions be
ignored, because many are fired to work towards them. Visions provide an
essential intellectual framework within which cyberspace is being shaped,
because they allow us to grasp the significance of some changes as steps on the
road to 'somewhere' rather than just as aimless steps. To grasp the nature of
cyberspace the dream of Gibson must be described and related to the reality of
the matrix. If either is ignored we may fail to see the real conditions of
computers, phone lines and code that create cyberspace or fail to recognise the
possibilities that are dawning. This chapter will take up, in turn, the science
fiction vision, the reality of the matrix and finally the combination of the two
that is cyberspace.

Cyberspace: the science fiction vision

Even for lands as strange as the virtual lands, it is perhaps odd to begin the
description of somewhere where people live out tangible, material lives with
fictional texts. Even if we were to accept that all texts are fictional, even those
of academic sociology and politics, they are at least fictions that address the
society we live in, but science fiction addresses societies that have never and

often can never exist. Interestingly, much of the attraction or repulsion people feel for science fiction stems from this need to initiate the reader into each science fictional world, as does much of science fiction's ability to articulate visions of cyberspace. Here are the opening words of Greg Bear's 1983 story *Petra*:

> I'm an ugly son of stone and flesh, there's no denying it. I don't remember my mother. It's possible she abandoned me shortly after my birth. More than likely she is dead. My father—an ugly beaked, half winged thing, if he resembles his son—I have never seen.
>
> (Bear, 1985: 105)

The first sentence could be read as metaphorical but by the last the reader knows they are dealing with a world that includes winged, semi-stone people. Through things unknown to our societies, science fiction possesses the power to make our societies and ourselves strange to us by representing our societies in fantastic forms. The reader has to learn the fictional world to enjoy the story and this can only be done by reading the story. Further, the world will have to be largely inferred from the language of the story; science fiction writers rarely systematically set out the nature of the world they are discussing by telling us its rules and regulations. Instead, they tell a story and the reader has to learn of the world, people and its strangeness as they read (Bukatman, 1993a: 10–12).[2] We can think here of the opening words to Neal Stephenson's *Snow Crash*:

> The Deliverator belongs to an elite order, a hallowed subcategory. He's got esprit up to here. Right now, he is preparing to carry out his third mission of the night. His uniform is black as activated charcoal, filtering the very light out of the air. A bullet will bounce off its arachnofibre weave like a wren hitting a patio door, but excess perspiration wafts through it like a breeze through a freshly napalmed forest. Where his body has bony extremities, the suit has sintered armorgel: feels like gritty jello, protects like a stack of telephone books.
>
> (Stephenson, 1992: 1)

What on earth is 'sintered armorgel'? When we learn that the Deliverator delivers pizza, we know the world Stephenson is presenting must be strange and will have to be learned. Science fiction's basic premises allow readers' selves and societies to be re-presented back to readers as strange, thereby establishing a distance that can be used to criticise or comment. Science fiction's basic technique is language that can never have its meaning fully closed down, because it implies more than it explains. The excess of new terms (arachnofibre) dislocates the reader and involves them in a journey of the construction of meaning, through which comment can be made on really existing societies. Here is the fundamental importance of science fiction to cyberspace, because these techniques provide characterisations through which virtual selves and societies have been understood. The science fiction genre most involved in imagining cyberspace is called cyberpunk (Bukatman, 1993a; Sterling, 1985).

If any genre of science fiction fulfils its potential for social criticism through linguistic excess, then cyberpunk does (Clark, 1995: 114). Like all intellectual movements cyberpunk is both a set of ideas and styles and a particular group of people writing and thinking at a particular time. As a movement of individuals, cyberpunk emerged in the early 1980s and was quite possibly over by the late 1980s. Its history is yet to be written but it is important not to forget that behind the ideas existed individuals who typed and created, companies that published, phones that rang and the momentum people gain from realising they are, unexpectedly or not, part of a group or movement. Such a history will have at its centre writers loosely organised around Bruce Sterling's fanzine *Cheap Truth*, which included Gibson, Pat Cadigan, Lewis Shiner and others, and will have to examine the role particular magazines, such as *Interzone*, played in publishing early cyberpunk stories (Dery, 1993b: 755). Cyberpunk arrived as a movement in 1984, when Gibson published *Neuromancer*, which received science fiction's highest awards (Hugo and Nebula). By 1985, Sterling's preface to his edited collection *Mirrorshades: the cyberpunk anthology* was already looking back on a movement whose existence could be taken for granted and whose principles could be confidently outlined (Sterling, 1985). He argued that central to cyberpunk's self-conception is that it blends fiction and social criticism:

> The cyberpunks are perhaps the first SF generation to grow up not only within the literary tradition of science fiction but in a truly science fictional world. For them, the techniques of classical 'hard SF'—extrapolation, technological literacy—are not just literary tools but an aid to daily life. They are a means of understanding, and highly valued.
>
> (Sterling, 1985: xi)

Or, as Gibson said, 'When I write about technology, I write about how it has *already* affected our lives' (Cited in McCaffery, 1991a: 274). If science fiction is at least partially constituted around social criticism, then cyberpunk is the genre of science fiction that takes this possibility to heart. From the emergence of cyberpunk as a particular group of people in the 1980s, the cyberpunk ethos or style has spread into films, music, journalism and more, until R.U. Sirius could casually state, in 1992, that 'Cyberpunk escaped from being a literary genre...into cultural reality.' (Rucker *et al.*, 1992: 64; Dery, 1996) While it is clear that cyberpunk was a movement, its ideas have had a much broader effect than on just science fiction. Two ideas in particular were prefigured in cyberpunk science fiction that have had a lasting effect on cyberspace: the organisation of information as virtual spaces and the nature of virtual bodies. Other ideas and styles have been important to cyberpunk but these two are central when trying to grasp the vision that has affected the virtual lands.[3] The first is the most significant because it attempts to directly describe, picture, dissect and understand cyberspace. The second explores the consequences for humans of the electronic realms. They will be examined in turn, but with emphasis on the first, as the central contribution of cyberpunk to the emergence of cyberspace.

Cyberspace has been conceptualised as a net, matrix, metaverse and, universally, as a place constructed out of information. The place of cyberspace appears as a non-place because it is where physically separated individuals meet and it is made tangible in cyberpunk fiction. Bukatman points out that electronic space is itself imperceptible. Each virtual individual experiences a terminal screen whereas interaction occurs somewhere beyond everyone's terminal and cyberpunk attempts 'to redefine the imperceptible (and therefore absent to consciousness) realm of the electronic era in terms of the physically and perceptibly familiar' (Bukatman, 1993a: 117; Clark, 1995: 114). By developing elaborate metaphors and analogies with familiar spaces, cyberpunk began to teach what cyberspace might mean as a place. It is not necessary to survey all these visions to grasp this. Examining two of the more important will establish how cyberpunk helped define cyberspace. These are William Gibson's 'cyberspace' from the trilogy *Neuromancer, Count Zero* and *Mona Lisa Overdrive*, and Neal Stephenson's 'metaverse' from *Snow Crash*.

Gibson's cyberspace is a four-dimensional representation of the sum of human knowledge, which is experienced as a virtual reality and is used by 'moving' through it. Gibson's vision of cyberspace has four key parts: bodiless consciousnesses live there, it is described with familiar images such as flying through skyscrapers or across grids, it is made of information offering great power to those who can manipulate information, and it is possible immortality will be attained there. First, Gibson's descriptions are of human consciousnesses that have become bodiless in cyberspace and which 'fly' in it, finding and using data by seeing and moving to it. In most cases, these consciousnesses also exist as corporeal bodies but become disembodied by entering, or 'jacking into', cyberspace. By the end of the trilogy several characters forsake their bodies, their 'meatspace', for a pure existence as spirits or angels in cyberspace. Gibson's first premise of cyberspace is, then, a loss of physicality, of flesh, blood and bone, when individuals enter cyberspace. Being in cyberspace is then described as a continuous, never-ending grid on which different constructions emerge. These constructions sometimes appear as large buildings (drawing on images of flying between grids of skyscrapers), sometimes appear as tangled knots of lines and sometimes appear as something new, never seen. Each construction indicates a centre of data. The following are some of Gibson's descriptions of cyberspace:

transparent 3D chessboard extending to infinity. Inner eye opening to the stepped scarlet pyramid of the Eastern Seabord Fission Authority burning

beyond the green cubes of Mitsubishi Bank of America, and high very far
away he saw the spiral arms of military systems forever beyond his reach.

(Gibson, 1984: 68–9)

They found their paradise, a 'pirate's paradise,' on the jumbled border of a
low-security academic grid. At first glance it resembled the kind of graffiti
student operators sometimes left at the junctions of grid lines.

(Gibson, 1984: 101)

Gibson's cyberspace is a vision of information organisation, one all the more
seductive for only being described allusively in his novels where most action
takes place in the 'real world' (Bukatman, 1993a: 146–54). Politically,
cyberspace is not conceived as free and equally open, rather it is an economi-
cally divided space. 'Walls of data, rather than walls of brick and glass, divide
a hardwired, or postorganic, humanity into economic protagonists' (Tomas,
1991: 44). Access to the citadels of knowledge held by large corporations and
the military is available only to those who work for or control those organisations or to those who can illegally find a path through cyberspace to them.
The second possibility allows that an exceptionally talented individual could
gain enormous power, equalising the dystopian social structures Gibson's
novels describe in collapsed urban life. The figures of such hackers, a word
with a long history,[4] allow individual action to effect enormous change. In
Neuromancer, it is hacker Case's ability to crack a seemingly impregnable
computer system in cyberspace that allows the organisation of information to
become sentient and then, by the third volume of the trilogy, this results in
the living, self-conscious cyberspace becoming aware of life on another planet.
However, while offering enormous potential power for lone hackers, Gibson
also enmeshes hackers in institutionalised webs of power, of which they are
often unaware. Case's ability to crack the impregnable system is based on his
use of software passed to him by the institution that has hired him, while not
revealing its own nature to him. In Gibson's worlds, it is unclear whether
there are any nations; the most relevant social entities are, on the one hand,
large corporations and, on the other, cities or urban sprawls that appear as
vast, semi-militarised zones. Structures of power and dominance are not
destroyed by cyberspace but are rearticulated within it.

Gibsonian cyberspace draws on a number of familiar images to create a
vision of a totally new place constructed out of information. Descriptions of
cyberspace close to those that would describe flying through a city of skyscrapers
draw on the familiarity of film or personal experience of flight and the familiarity of city centres. 'He punched himself down a wall of primitive ice
belonging to the New York Public Library, automatically counting potential
windows' (Gibson, 1984: 72). Hacker Case is here counting windows of opportunity, gaps in the software security that is called ice (intrusion countermeasures
electronic), but the familiarity of counting windows in New York refers to

skyscraper life. The oddity of a world made from information through which human consciousness can fly is made familiar and can be grasped.

The final element of Gibson's vision of cyberspace is that it raises the possibility of immortality. 'Silicon doesn't wear out; microchips were effectively immortal' (Gibson, 1986a: 120). As people effectively enter their consciousnesses into the silicon world when they enter cyberspace, the possibility emerges of someone uploading their consciousness into cyberspace and becoming immortal. Gibson underlines this possibility in *Neuromancer* by introducing a captured consciousness called the Flatline who exists immortally on silicon but confined to a particular ROM[5] cassette and who happens to be a famous hacker that Case knew before Flatline died. Case finds it 'disturbing to think of the Flatline as a construct, a hardwired ROM cassette replicating a dead man's skills, obsessions, knee-jerk responses' (Gibson 1984: 97). The immortality of Flatline is underlined when he/it demands his/its payoff for the mission.

> 'Hey asshole,' the Flatline said, when Finn had gone a dozen paces. The figure paused, half turned. 'What about me? What about my payoff?'
> 'You'll get yours,' it said.
> 'What's that mean?' Case asked, as he watched the narrow tweed back recede.
> 'I wanna be erased,' the construct said. 'I told you that, remember?'
> (Gibson, 1984: 246)

In addition, at the end of the trilogy, the reader is confronted with several characters who appear to have entered cyberspace totally and may have become immortal. With these 'angels' and the Flatline, Gibson both tells us immortality in silicon is a potential of cyberspace and asks us whether immortality will really be much fun.

While Gibson's vision offers us an alien place that he struggles to make familiar, Stephenson's metaverse presents cyberspace through the familiarity of urban space and sometimes struggles to make virtual life seem strange. Stephenson calls cyberspace the metaverse and first describes it as a mundane place of work for the central character of *Snow Crash* – Hiro Protagonist. Stephenson describes it as a street populated by recognisably human forms and Protagonist first goes there after losing his job as a pizza deliveryman for the Mafia, in the course of which he loses a Mafia car and is as a result in desperate need of money. Protagonist then falls back on his part-time job as a freelance information collector for the merged Central Intelligence Agency and Library of Congress. The previous sentences will, perhaps, already be creating the strangeness that science fiction trades on; they should also be conveying the more playful nature of Stephenson's novel against the darker language Gibson employs. The greater emphasis on comedy in Stephenson is despite the fact that his world is every bit as dystopian as Gibson's. In *Snow Crash*, nation-states have collapsed or merged with mega-corporations, law enforcement is a private and pecuniary affair, a key character is allowed to do what he wants because his death would cause the explosion of a nuclear device attached to his motorcycle and the plot's central drama comes from a struggle against the destruction and enslavement of all computer programmers to religious fundamentalists. Purely from the point of view of plot, *Snow Crash* is even more serious than *Neuromancer*, but from the point of view of style, of the language and analogies that convey science fiction's underlying message, *Snow Crash* is far lighter and funnier. Here is Stephenson's first description of the metaverse:

> Hiro is approaching the Street. It is the Broadway, the Champs Élysées of the Metaverse. It is the brilliantly lit boulevard that can be seen, miniaturized and backward, reflected in the lenses of his goggles. It does not really exist. But right now, millions of people are walking up and down it....Like any place in Reality, the Street is subject to development. Developers can build their own buildings, parks, signs, as well as things that do not exist in Reality, such as vast hovering overhead light shows, special neighbourhoods where the rules of three-dimensional spacetime are ignored, and free-combat zones where people can go to hunt and kill each other....Hiro has a house in a neighbourhood just off the busiest part of the Street. It is a very old neighbourhood by Street standards.
>
> (Stephenson, 1992: 23–4)

The strangeness of cyberspace – where people whose bodies are separated by millions of miles can meet – is made familiar by describing it as a street traversed by a monorail and in which people walk using avatars that represent them to each other. There is even pressure towards the closest representation as possible of your real self because 'it takes a lot more sophistication to render a realistic human face than a talking penis' (Stephenson, 1992: 34), sophistication in programming skills that is. The poorer entrants to the metaverse hire or buy off-the-shelf avatars to represent themselves, and end up looking exactly like each other, while the poorest appear in grainy, jerky black and white that means they have logged on from free public terminals. The richest hang out in famous bars, where they can indulge the metaverse's freedom from reality by having the most perfect appearance or the most outrageous hairstyle. The most powerful in the metaverse are those who have written the software that makes the metaverse what it is. When Hiro meets his ex-lover, who programmed the original interface that allowed the metaverse to exist, she says 'you and I are the only two people who can ever have an honest conversation in the Metaverse' (Stephenson, 1992: 62) because they are the only two people who know exactly how the metaverse works.

Stephenson's metaverse, like Gibson's cyberspace, describes a world of information people enter and often work in, but which is outside the rules of the world we normally exist in. The metaverse is, however, far more familiar, almost too familiar as a city street, and Stephenson has continually to throw in comments about things that could not happen on non-virtual city streets to remind the reader that this is the metaverse and not New York. Gibson uses analogies to city space but Stephenson's cyberspace is a city; downtown in the metaverse is 'a dozen Manhattans, embroidered with neon and stacked on top of each other' (Stephenson, 1992: 24). The metaverse also contrasts with Gibsonian cyberspace because in it people have some sort of a body. People travel the metaverse embodied in avatars that represent their real selves who are watching through goggles attached to computers. Once online people in a sense become their avatars, power and prestige can be conveyed simply by looking at someone whose avatar is either spectacular (rock stars with hair cuts they can only dream about in the non-virtual world are prominent) or as close a representation of their real appearance as is possible. 'Hiro's avatar just looks like Hiro, with the difference that no matter what Hiro is wearing in Reality, his avatar always wears a black leather kimono' (Stephenson, 1992: 34). Not only do people aim to look like themselves, or their dreams, but also physical contact is copied. The success of the hero protagonist in saving the world's assembled hackers hinges on his having cut the arms off someone trying to infect him with a virus; his demon-servants then take the virus to a secret work-shop where Hiro invents an antidote. The climactic fight of *Snow Crash* between Hiro and Raven also occurs in the metaverse:

> Raven tries to shove Hiro back. It would work in Reality because Raven has such overpowering strength. But avatars are equally strong, unless you hack them up in just the right way. So Raven gives a mighty push and then pulls his knife back so that he can take a cut at Hiro's neck when Hiro flies away from him; but Hiro doesn't fly away. He waits for the opening and then takes Raven's sword hand off. Then, just in case, he takes Raven's other hand off.
>
> (Stephenson, 1992: 426)

The ambiguity of bodies in the metaverse is that they also have to be programmed. You might look like your real body – as Raven does – but you won't necessarily have your real-world strength – as Raven doesn't – unless you can hack or program the avatars to be different. Bodies, lost in Gibsonian cyberspace, are reinvented in Stephenson's cyberspace.

The metaverse is another vision of cyberspace. Like Gibson, Stephenson pictures cyberspace as a place where our normal, physical bodies are displaced, as a world constructed out of information, as a world in which people work and as a world in which power rests along an axis with corporations and nation-states at one end and individual hackers, often heroes, at the other. The metaverse has many of the same characteristics as Gibsonian cyberspace but also creates a different dimension by playing with bodies in cyberspace far more than Gibson does. There are many other visions of cyberspace in cyberpunk fiction and nearly all take up some or most of the characteristics found in Gibson and Stephenson (Bukatman 1993a). Here is Sterling's description of what he calls the Net from 1988. Fact has caught up so quickly with Sterling that his fictional vision could easily pass for a description of the networked reality that exists less than ten years after he wrote:

> Every year of her life, Laura thought, the Net had been growing more expansive and seamless. Computers did it. Computers melted other machines, fusing them together. Television–telephone–telex. Tape recorder–VCR–laser disk. Broadcast tower linked to microwave dish linked to satellite. Phone line, cable TV, fiber-optic cords hissing out words and pictures in torrents of pure light. All netted together in a web over the world, a global nervous system, an octopus of data. There'd been plenty of hype about it. It was easy to make it sound incredibly transcendental.
>
> (Sterling, 1988: 17)

The essential, underlying characteristic of cyberpunk's cyberspace is the sense that this is a place in which people live and have access to knowledge, but which is also somehow a non-physical place. It is somewhere that bodies do not go, though we need our bodies to get there, and where the physical rules of normal space are transgressed. The loss of a physical body, even if it is replaced with a computer-generated avatar, combined with an intimate relationship with knowledge, creates the belief that what it means to be human is different in cyberspace and that this realisation changes what it means to be human anywhere. These visions, particularly Gibson's, have remained remarkably untouched and active when cyberspace is conceived. The sum of human knowledge will in the future be organised graphically and humans will gain access to it by using a world-wide network of computers to leave their bodies behind and fly or move through it as disembodied consciousnesses or with newly chosen programmed bodies. The really existing cyberspace is often seen simply as a step towards this goal.

Stephenson's play on the body in the metaverse points toward the second key area for cyberpunk in relation to cyberspace. His conceptions certainly come within the framework just outlined – avatars in the metaverse are not bodies in reality and only have a spurious, computer-generated physicality – but there is a more complex story about the body to be told than Gibson's disjunction of consciousness in real space and consciousness free in silicon space. This raises the second recurrent figure of cyberpunk fiction that has had lasting effects on the conception of cyberspace, the cyborg. Simply understood, cyborgs are fusions of human and machine. The two central characters of *Neuromancer* are Case, the hacker and explorer of cyberspace, and Molly, who does what is needed in the real world. Molly is described this way when she and Case first meet:

She wore mirrored glasses. Her clothes were black, the heels of black boots deep in the temperfoam....She shook her head. He realised that the glasses were surgically inset, sealing her sockets. The silver lenses seemed to grow from smooth pale skin above her cheekbones, framed by dark hair cut in a rough shag. The fingers curled around the fletcher were slender, white, tipped with polished burgundy. The nails looked artificial....She held out her hands, palms up, the white fingers slightly spread, and with a barely audible click, ten double-edged, four-centimetre scalpel blades slid from their housings beneath the burgundy nails. She smiled. The blades slowly withdrew.

(Gibson, 1984: 36–7)

These passages demonstrate the science fiction technique of establishing the strange through the familiar in the two transitions from mirrored glasses to implanted lenses and from false nails to hidden blades. We move smoothly from what we know to what we do not, only being surprised when we have arrived. These transitions establish Molly as a cyborg, surgically enhanced in at least the eyes and fingernails, an inextricable mix of woman and machine. Cyberpunk fiction is littered with cyborgs; there are too many examples to mention. The figure of the cyborg offers an exploration of redefined bodies and redefined humanity. It is not that cyborgs have never previously existed. It could be argued that spectacles (or wooden teeth?) inaugurate the first widespread appearance of cyborgs, but in the context of the late twentieth century the addition of mechanical to human is not aiding or recovering known human qualities, as spectacles help recover sight or wooden teeth the ability to chew, but that the meaning of human qualities is being radically redefined. Molly's retractable blades are not enhanced fingernails but a new human possibility that has a faint affinity for previously known attributes.

The nature of the cyborg will be explored in detail in Chapter 6, when it emerges as a key component in the hopes and fears held for and about cyberspace. For present purposes, it is only necessary to grasp that the cyborg is the second key contribution of cyberpunk to cyberspace because its fictional manifestations offer a way to explore the new subjectivities or new humanities many see in cyberspace. Many issues of identity in cyberspace, of the nature of people who exist only as text in the electronic ether, are prefigured in cyberpunk's cyborgs. What new ways of being human might be needed or desirable when the boundary between human and machine is transgressed? Cyborgs allow this question to be posed and explored in fiction, providing further reflections on the selves and societies emerging in really existing cyberspace.

While cyberpunk's exploration of cyberspace allows us to grasp something that might just be entirely new in human history, its obsession with cyborgs is about the reinvention of something humanity has always had. Put together, these two prefigurations establish a vision of the worlds we are moving into and articulate some of the desires and fears the virtual lands create. These visions

have powerfully conditioned understandings of cyberspace; they offer us analogies, metaphors and concepts through which virtual lives have been grasped.
Cyberpunk fiction has become a self-fulfilling prophecy in which we understand
cyberspace through its fantasies but then we find that cyberspace is in fact like
cyberpunk. The importance of cyberpunk for cyberspace is this role it has
played, but it would be a role of limited interest if a real cyberspace used by real
individuals and generated from millions of real computers had not simultaneously come into existence. Ironically, Gibson's consensual hallucination based
on physically separated individuals connected only by computers and wires
existed before Gibson wrote his words. And, doubly ironic, Gibson did not
know about ARPANET as it and other networks began to create in reality what
he and cyberpunk created in fantasy. Before fully grasping the meaning of
fiction, the fact of cyberspace needs to be outlined.

Cyberspace: the matrix of computers

Four questions will be posed to define factual cyberspace. Where did it come
from and how does it work? Here a history of technology is needed. Second,
who goes there and what do they do? Here demographics are required. These
questions will be dealt with in turn creating a comprehensive introduction to
factual cyberspace.

History of a technology[6]

In the late 1960s computers were large, expensive, often specialised and
different to each other. One would be very good at graphics, another at
databases, but unfortunately the two might be thousands of miles apart and be
too expensive for both to be bought for both locations. The obvious answer
was to dial up using a phone line or a dedicated link and use them remotely.
By the mid-1960s such remote use of computers had become, if not common-
place, then at least available. But any user lucky enough to have access to
terminals that could remotely operate a computer would have to learn the
procedure for gaining access to each computer, usually from a terminal devoted
solely to each link, and then learn the peculiarities of each computer. As more
and more defence contractors in the USA asked for computers as part of
defence research, the Department of Defenses' Advanced Research Projects
Agency (ARPA) decided it was time to find a way of allowing researchers to
use each other's computers from a single terminal, no matter where they were
located and no matter what system each target computer was running (Hafner
and Lyon, 1996: 1–3; Quarterman, 1990: 139–41). ARPA defined a project to
network computers and put it out to tender; the result would be the first major
element of cyberspace in a network called ARPANET that led directly to the
Internet.

The network specification ARPA drew up included a number of elements whose effects are still being felt. The difficulty of having many people on many computers all trying to use different computers simultaneously led to the concept of packet switching. When someone is having a telephone conversation it is as if one pipe is opened between the two participants and is kept open exclusively for their use, even if nothing is being said. This poses no problem for phone conversations as people tend to keep up a conversation and then close the link when there is nothing to say, but data tends to be sent in bursts rather than in a steady stream; people sit and think, then work on their data and stop again to contemplate their next move. If a data connection has to be kept exclusively for one exchange then there will be a great deal of wastage, as a line will be open for significant periods when nothing is being sent. It was decided that it would be more efficient if each message were sliced into small sections or packets, each packet were addressed and then sent off, with the message being reassembled when all arrived. If this were done then everyone could use the same lines at the same time (Hafner and Lyon, 1996: 60–2; Minoli, 1997: 8–10) A further advantage is that this system could be extremely robust, as there is no reason why each message or each part of a message has to follow the same path as other messages and parts. This means that if a connection in a network fails, then each section of a message can check its address and route itself a different way. A dynamic form of routing provides assurance that even if part of a network collapsed, all messages, including those in transit, would arrive. By ensuring all connections in such a network are distributed, that is there is no one central point, and that each point made at least three or four connections with other points, an exceptionally high standard of reliability can be created. So high, in fact, that many believe it would survive all-out nuclear war (Hafner and Lyon, 1996: 59, 128–9).

Here we reach the first of the great myths of the electronic frontier that will be used to underline some of the central concepts of cyberspace. These myths are narratives, stories with a moral, that are told and retold on and off the net. They provide some of the founding morality tales of cyberspace and articulate basic values in telling a story accessible to all. Whether the story is accurate or has actually happened is beside the point when looking at such morality tales, because their truth lies in the message they convey, not their accuracy. Of course, no insult is intended by arguing that what has actually happened to some people has become mythical, quite the opposite. What has happened to some people has become relevant to all users of cyberspace and so become mythical. At this early point in the history of computer networking, one of the most important and persistent myths of the electronic frontier was created.

MYTHS OF THE ELECTRONIC FRONTIER 1: THE INTERNET
WILL SURVIVE NUCLEAR WAR

It is often claimed that that when ARPANET was designed one of its
core goals was to be a communication network that would survive
nuclear war. Paul Baran, a researcher at Rand Corporation, was working
in the mid-1960s on the problem of post-nuclear strike communication
and he found that a distributed, non-hierarchical network could flow
around even the damage caused by nuclear strikes. If Philadelphia, New
York and Chicago have been destroyed, then packets from San Francisco
will simply reroute themselves around the destroyed nodes and find
their way to Boston via Detroit and Kansas City. No matter which city
was destroyed, Baran found that a distributed network with dynamic
routing would automatically reach whoever was left alive and able to
contact the network. This design had, however, unintended side effects
because the Internet became uncensorable. Many saw this technical
basis as the reason why John Gilmore said, and has been quoted ever
since, that 'The Internet treats censorship like damage, it routes around
it'.[7] If one part of the Internet removes access to another part then your
request will simply route around that break, as though a nuclear bomb
had caused the break. When prosecutors in Germany sought to have
neo-Nazi sites closed down, because it is illegal in Germany to provide
Nazi material, several free speech advocates simply copied the site to
countries that had no laws preventing neo-Nazi sites. Having done this
Germany's only choice was to sever its connection to cyberspace, a
choice with an almost impossibly high cost, or to accept that the uncensorable and global net had subverted its national laws. Another example
is the claim that during the Gulf War the USA and allied military had
great difficulty destroying Iraq's communication system, despite over-
whelming US and allied military superiority, because Iraq used
cyberspace's technology in a distributed, non-hierarchical communications network. Any damage US aircraft or cruise missiles caused was
simply routed around. The irony that military funding to prosecute the
nuclear arms race resulted in the ultimate weapon of libertarian, grassroots free speech is one enjoyed by many on the net.

The moral everyone takes from this story has two parts, one minor
and one major. The minor moral is that it doesn't necessarily matter
where funding to create technology comes from; networking is an essentially good thing and can even subvert that most rigid of hierarchies, the

military. The major moral is that the Internet is 'rights-bearing tech-nology' which guarantees that certain rights have become inalienable to the net user. Free speech is embedded in cyberspace and it subverts government and media attempts to manage the information people receive. National and regional governments are left trying to monitor all traffic in and out of their territory, an impossible task given the huge amount of data, in order to prosecute those who breach national laws by accessing forbidden material in cyberspace. The only other possibility is severing a nation's connection to cyberspace, but this carries such a high economic and research cost, cyberspace having become central to both, that it is an impossible choice for any nation trying to be at the forefront of the information age. Monitoring is being tried, particularly in Singapore, but safe in the knowledge that the net is stronger than nuclear war many expect Singapore to fail. After all, are the authorities in Singapore really going to break encoded emails? Millions of them?[8]

The belief that the net was designed to survive nuclear war is both a moral-teaching myth and one of the great misunderstandings about cyberspace that was only decisively clarified in Hafner and Lyon's history (Hafner and Lyon, 1996). The truth is more complex and needs to be understood, though it does not under-mine the moral of the myth. It may need repeating that myths carry on teaching their morals, whether their narrative is true or not. The construction of ARPANET as a distributed, packet-switched network had little or nothing to do with nuclear survivability. ARPA wanted reliable communications between computers and opted for distributed packet switching to meet this need. However, while finalising the specification Larry Roberts, head of the division of ARPA responsible for commissioning ARPANET, became aware of two prior discoveries of packet switching, one of which aimed for a communications network that would survive nuclear war. As noted in the preceding myth, in the mid-1960s Paul Baran had taken up the problem of a communications network and nuclear war and come up with the solution of a distributed packet-switched network. However, his attempts to have such a system built were frustrated, first, by the then national telephone company AT&T's failure to understand the idea and, second, by the failure to place the project with an agency Baran felt was competent. He agreed to halt the experiment rather than see it fail, because he hoped for future success. At almost the same time, and also before ARPA became interested in computer communication, the British researcher Donald Davies developed and piloted a small packet-switching network. Like ARPA, Davies worked to improve use of computers not because of the technicalities of mutual assured destruction (Hafner and Lyon, 1996: 63–7). The work of Baran and Davies eventually fed into ARPA's specification for ARPANET but only after packet switching had already been chosen as the appropriate technique and not to make ARPANET nuclear war resistant. Proof that ARPANET was not built to withstand nuclear war is that it was not built with the necessary number of connections for each point of the network. Baran had concluded that three or four connections for every computer to other computers was the minimum needed to survive nuclear war and ARPANET was built with two. In addition, one bomb on one town in the USA would have been (and, at early 1998, was still) enough to disable the net. This is because of the method by which computers find each other. When one computer requests a connection to another, it uses a name to identify the target computer and then makes a request to a central database that looks up the number associated with that name, which allows the connection to be made. There are eight machines that perform this function, but every night the one central master database issues an updated list and its destruction would ensure that within a few days computers could not find each other. A vice-president in the private company that runs this database said of it, in terms that would reassure his shareholders of the importance of his company, 'if you pull the plug out of the back of this baby, everything on the Internet would die in about two days' (cited in Rushkoff, 1997: 11).[9]

The final key element of the specification for ARPANET was the distinction between hosts and servers. Initially it was expected that the computers containing programs and files that were to be accessed remotely would be connected directly to each other. However, there was widespread opposition from all the different agencies whose computers were going to have part of their time dedicated to running the new network. Roberts took the decision that computers specially designed to run the network, pass the packages and route them on open paths would be built and given to each agency. The idea was that these computers would 'serve' the network and their operation would be transparent. Someone using a computer in Boston to connect to one in San Francisco would not have to know that their messages passed through a different computer in Boston and San Francisco, meaning four computers were used for the connection though only two would be apparent to the user. Dedicated network computers, now usually called servers, would serve the computers people wanted to use, now usually called hosts. This meant people with no host computer could connect through a server and use host computers at other places. The agencies that did not want time to be taken away from their computers to run a network became quite enthusiastic about the network when they were offered a free new computer (Hafner and Lyon, 1996: 71–4; Minoli, 1997: 47–60). This arrangement also had the advantage that communications between host and server would be a matter for the agency controlling the host, remembering that there were many different, often incompatible computers that would become hosts. This meant the network had an open architecture, in that any computer, no matter what its peculiarities, could in theory be connected to the network if it could be made to work with a server (Hafner and Lyon, 1996: 143–51).

The contract to build ARPANET went to a Boston firm, Bolt Beranek and Newman (BBN), who produced the promised network on time. ARPANET would grow to over 150 sites by the late 1980s but it remained essentially a US network. ARPANET was built to share access to expensive computers more widely by allowing remote log-in and unifying procedures for log-in. ARPANET was built to eliminate physical distance in the service of economic and research efficiency. But when a survey was conducted in 1973 of the use of ARPANET, it was found that three-quarters of all traffic were for electronic mail. Sending email means sending a message to someone's electronic mailbox, where it waits to be read. Email is similar to normal postal mail (often called snail mail) because it delivers a written message to a specific address, but it is different because it is easier to send email to multiple address, answers can be interpolated into the original message and email is often faster (Quarterman, 1990: 113; Hafner and Lyon, 1996: 193–5). The key point about email is that rather than people using ARPANET to communicate with computers, as the designers expected, people used it to communicate with other people. This was despite the fact that email was not programmed into the system but was added unofficially in an *ad hoc* way. Email emerged spontaneously as the basic resource provided by ARPANET and this has been true of virtually all computer networks. People connect to people using computers, which has given rise to the overarching term computer-mediated communication (Quarterman, 1990: 11–16; Jones, 1995a). ARPANET was finally closed down in 1990, replaced by new high-speed links that supported the Internet (Quarterman, 1990: 143–7).

Developments in other areas of computing meant that by the early 1980s connecting up different networks, of which by this time ARPANET was only one, became possible. The development of these other networks now needs to be outlined, because the emergence of one cyberspace based on one international network of computers does not follow directly from ARPANET. In the late 1970s until even the mid-1990s, it seemed just as possible that a number of networks would develop, each generating a different cyberspace. In these times, the possibility of a corporate or military cyberspace unconnected to poorer grassroots spaces seemed a logical conclusion to the way computer communication was developing. ARPANET does not lead, in a straight unwavering line, to a global packet-switched network on which cyberpunk dreams began to materialise; history, even history of technology, is more interesting and confusing than that. To read this history three different types of networks need to be briefly introduced. These are co-operative networks, corporate networks and Internet service providers (ISPs).

FidoNet is a world-wide network that emerged in 1983 and it makes ARPANET seem like a baroque, military–industrial fantasy of global domination. FidoNet consists of home-based personal computers using freely available software to send electronic mail and online discussions around the world. The building blocks of FidoNet are computer bulletin board services (BBSs).[10] FidoNet grew out of BBS software that allowed mail and then later discussion groups (called echomail) to move from one BBS to another and then another until it reached its target, though in the case of conferences the amount of traffic eventually became so great it was shifted through links dedicated to echomail. This allows messages to move from one corner of the world to the other through small hops, one after the other. At its height in the early 1990s, FidoNet had around 30,000 computer systems connected with an estimated 1.56 million users (Quarterman, 1990: 254–9; FidoNet, 1989; Hardy, 1993). FidoNet is a co-operative grassroots network, built out of free software and shared out telephone bills and avoiding the high cost of laying dedicated communication cables. This co-operative approach has been utilised by a number of other computer networks, the most important of these being Usenet, that used a file-copying program (UUCP) that was part of the UNIX computer system to create the largest computer conference system (Quarterman, 1990: 251–4; Freedman and Mann, 1997: 68–73).[11]

A computer conferencing system allows one of the fundamental innovations of computer-mediated communication because it creates widespread many-to-many communication. Many to many means that many can write and many can read simultaneously with no physical limitation. In a room with a hundred people trying to discuss a topic, it will be impossible for everyone to say all they want to and reply to all they want to. On a computer conferencing system this is simple and potentially creates more inclusive and widespread discussions. This is achieved by creating a topic on which people post messages. All messages appear online in the sequence that they arrive. Some groups are moderated, with a moderator checking all messages (usually called posts) before posting them, but many groups are unmoderated. Usenet is a network devoted to a news-based conference system. It has grown to over 15,000 topics on any subject imaginable; from rec.pets.cats, devoted to cats in all their glory, to alt.tasteless, devoted to tastelessness. Discussions are organised in hierarchies, such as rec. for recreations, rec.pets for pets, rec.pets.cats for cats. Some of the other hierarchies are news., sic., misc. and so on. A key change within Usenet occurred around the refusal of operators to create a group to discuss drugs. In response, a number of participants simply created a new hierarchy of news-groups (the now famous alt. groups that are now the largest component of Usenet) sending traffic around those who did not want to carry it (Hardy, 1993). Initially, Usenet ran using UUCP over telephone lines, resulting in the famous telephone bill for a quarter of a million dollars at DEC which, unknown to its managerial hierarchy, was moving much UUCP traffic around. Eventually a scheme to speed up both Usenet and UCCP resulted in the creation of a set of dedicated lines (Quarterman, 1990: 235–50, 350–9).

FidoNet and Usenet are only two of a number of co-operative networks that emerged, though they are the most spectacular and successful of the world-wide co-operative networks. At the same time as these networks emerged various commercial networks appeared, some also becoming world-wide. These can be divided into those used for internal company purposes, like IBM's VNET or the

XEROX INTERNET, and those that sought profit by offering paid access to individual users, like CompuServe or the now famous WELL. The corporate internal networks focused on serving company interests through communication systems designed to help co-ordination of companies. The access providers created their own conferencing systems that allowed users to log on and create conferences, engage in real-time chat (i.e. the words appear simultaneously on several screens as people type) and over time they have also added world-wide email and access to the Internet (Quarterman, 1990: 260–2, 608; Hafner, 1997; Rheingold, 1994). By the late 1980s the picture of a world-wide network had become complicated, with the networks already mentioned, and others, all existing but with connections between them developing randomly, if at all. To complicate this picture further, local area networks (LANs) had begun to proliferate with universities, local governments, cities, national or regional corporations and bureaucracies, all developing networks that connected computers in different rooms rather than different cities or continents.

By the early 1990s, the development of divided and technically incompatible networks seemed as real a possibility as the creation of a unified world-wide computer network. The situation was exacerbated by the emergence at this time in the USA of a number of large media corporations, for example Time/Warner, and cable companies with an interest in computer networks. The first understanding of many of these companies was to build or buy networks that would be incompatible with their competitors in order to keep customers exclusively to themselves. The first major civil rights organisation for cyberspace, the Electronic Frontier Foundation (EFF), spent a great deal of time campaigning in the early 1990s to prevent cyberspace being balkanised and trying to secure an open network architecture that would ensure all networks could connect to each other and be interoperable (Jordan, 1998). But if cyberspace seemed to be on the verge of splitting into many divided spaces and if some of the darker visions of cyberpunk fiction of secured networks available only to those who could pay seemed to be beginning, then few people had grasped the significance of, first, the Internet that developed out of APRANET and, second, the World-Wide Web (WWW or Web). These two would finally make access to the world-wide network a nearly non-technical matter and would unify most networks into the one matrix. To tell this twist in the story requires returning to the developing ARPANET in the early 1970s.

By 1972 ARPANET was growing and other countries were becoming interested. Networks were developing in both France and the UK and thoughts turned to how networks could be interconnected. The problem was that many networks used fundamentally incompatible systems and could not simply have a new cable strung between them. The solution was to create gateways between different networks, with a computer serving the gateway having the responsibility of taking a packet from one network and transforming it into a style that a different, incompatible network could understand. This is a similar solution to that developed in ARPANET where a computer is placed between other computers that are the actual target of interconnection; this allows all the target computers to be different but not affect the network. Similarly, to connect networks a gateway ensures that each network does not have to communicate directly, which would create enormous translation difficulties. Instead, when a packet reached a gateway and the shift from one network to another occurred, the packet would be placed within a data envelope that could be read by the receiving network. The content of the envelope, which might be incompatible with the network it travelled through, becomes irrelevant because the receiving network reads the data envelope. The ability of a network to communicate with the gateway computer was defined by a protocol, essentially instructions that define what a computer must do to speak to another computer, that was initially called the Transmission Control Protocol (TCP) and later became absorbed into the better known Internet Protocol (IP). The computer that organises the gateway is usually called a router (Hafner and Lyon, 1996: 223–7; Quarterman, 1990: 278–84, Minoli, 1997: 109–16).

If a network implemented TCP/IP then it would be able to send packets to any other network that had also implemented TCP/IP; it would become part of an Internetwork that has become known as the Internet. As the system grew some organisation of names for computers able to use IP to communicate was needed and the Domain Name System (DNS) was developed. To send a message to someone you need to know their address and Internet addresses are characterised by the dot (.) that sits between certain sets of letters, such as eff.org (Electronic Frontier Foundation) or uel.ac.uk (University of East London). Each name is related to a particular number that uniquely identifies that computer, called its IP name. The reason for this duality is that humans more easily use names, whereas numbers are far easier for computers. Naming and numbering is devolved to each level of the hierarchy.[12] To find another computer, a request is sent by the sending computer up the hierarchy of computers it is connected to, eventually reaching the computers that maintain the DNS.[13] The database is then searched and the name's unique IP number found, allowing the sending computer to know where to send its request. As noted above, the distributed and anti-hierarchical nature of the Internet gives way here to a centralised database of IP names and IP numbers.

During the late 1970s and 1980s more and more networks developed. In the USA, ARPANET was superseded by a network set up by the National Science Foundation to connect five supercomputer centres, NSFNET (Quarterman, 1990: 301–9). The Joint Academic Network (Janet) was developed in the UK to consolidate network links already developed and would eventually be overtaken by Super-Janet (Quarterman, 1990: 471–6). France set up FNET and Germany DNET, as did most technologically advanced countries, though it is a mistake to assume an equitable distribution of networks world-wide (see next section on demographics) (Quarterman, 1990). Most countries that developed networking developed networks at the local and national level. At the national level there are usually high-speed dedicated cable and satellite 'backbones' that carry a large amount of traffic at high speed and at the local there are networks of individual personal computers and servers. The local networks (usually called local area networks, LANs) send traffic out to the backbones and receive from it, and the widespread implementation of TCP/IP ensures that whatever networks develop they can be connected to the Internet.

By the early 1990s, a world-wide Internet that was exponentially increasing in size had come into existence. An ever increasing range of things could be done on the Internet: email, transferring files (which means anything that could be turned into a digital file could be transferred: documents, pictures, software, video, etc.), online chat, using other computers remotely and more. The greater difficulty was developing ways of moving around the Internet and finding what might be useful. The University of Minnesota in the USA developed a program called Gopher that organised the Internet's resources as a series of linked tree-like menus. Selecting one topic, like Weather, might lead to another menu of countries; select Australia, then cities, select Melbourne, then weather stations, select Moorabin, which would then display the latest weather and forecast (then remember that it is day in the UK but night in Australia and that is why it seems cold down-under) (Minoli, 1997: 86; Hudson, 1997: 31–3). However, not all resources could be listed in Gopher and not all access offered Gopher. Use of the Internet, for many, remained a formidable technical problem that already technically literate net users tended to underestimate. The problem that prompted the creation of ARPANET had been recreated, with different commands needed to use different parts of the Internet such as email, transferring files or Usenet newsgroups.

With the re-emergence of the problem of incompatibility within and between different networks, we have returned to the early 1990s and the possible mushrooming of different, incompatible systems. Online activist Stanton McCandlish described the state of cyberspace at this time as being like unfermented beer, consisting of three different parts:

> You have the malt, the Internet, the big part that is largely homogenous due to standardisation and history. Then you have the hops, the BBS networks, each one with its own individual flavour, some bitter, some smooth, some large, some small. Lastly you have the water, the 'commercial online services' for lack of a better name.
>
> (McCandlish, 1995)

McCandlish thought of this as an unsustainable situation and when the yeast of grassroots political activism was added a 'stable and enjoyable blend would emerge'. McCandlish's organisation, EFF, certainly added all the weight it could to the maintenance of an open network in the early 1990s but at the same time another source of resolution emerged with the World-Wide Web.[14]

The Web was pioneered in the early 1990s, launched on the Internet around 1992 and had become widely adopted by 1994. The Web provides a unified and simple means of utilising all the resources of the Internet and broadly consists of two parts: a means of organising resources and a means of looking at that organisation. Tim Berners-Lee and colleagues at the physics laboratory CERN in Switzerland developed the first part. Berners-Lee wanted a means of organising his work when collaborating with different groups of people. Initially, he developed a system that organised all his own documents, with internal links that meant if he selected certain references he would be automatically transferred to a new document. He realised that, though this worked, he ultimately needed to include his collaborators' documents as well. The problem was that if you wanted to merge information held in different places so that easy shifts could be made, then the normal practice was to merge all the information into one centrally controlled information source. If there were databases, these would need to be merged, if there were documents these would need to be collated and so on. However, conducting many such large mergers between often incompatible systems is too daunting a task to contemplate. Berners-Lee, Robert Cailliau, Ben Segal and colleagues at CERN turned this assumption inside out and sacrificed the reliability of a centralised system for the openness of a distributed system. They developed a simple procedure by which all resources, of whatever type, could be attached to a short string of characters that indicated where the information resource was. A common space was created between all information resources constituted out of shared compatible addresses. The string of characters was initially called a universal document identifier, but has become one of the symbols of cyberspace: the URL or universal resource locator. It has a similar form to email addresses, such as http://www.uel.ac.uk, where http means hypertext transfer protocol, which tells the computer how to deal with the request, www stands for World-Wide Web and uel.ac.uk has already been discussed. Information resources could then be placed on a specific computer that serves Web requests, a Web server, and would be available across the Internet (Berners-Lee, 1996; Minoli, 1997: ch. 3). The resulting system was one based on hypertext, which means that reading a document, viewing a picture, examining a database or spreadsheet or any other information resource can be done within the one information source and, further, that you can simply point at an interesting piece of information to be taken to further details. For example, if the following sentence were hypertext 'The first part was developed by *Tim Berners-Lee* and *Robert Cailliau* at the *physics* laboratory *CERN* in *Switzerland*.', then you would be able to point to the italicised words and immediately be transported to further information. Perhaps you might like to see a picture of Berners-Lee or find out what CERN does or travel to Switzerland; in each case taking advantage of hypertext would enable a reader to travel through a document to the information they are interested in, rather than being subordinated to the linear logic of a page. A language called hypertext mark-up language (HTML) was developed that converted text, pictures and other resources into hypertext pages that could be read over the Web and found through a URL. Hypertext had been developed as an idea as early as 1945 and several projects had developed, including the Xanadu project, to integrate the world's information into one hypertext (Berners-Lee and Cailliau, 1989; Zeltser, 1995; Bush, 1945; Gromov, 1995; Berners-Lee, 1996).

Berners-Lee, Robert Cailliau, Ben Segal and colleagues at CERN had created a means of organising information on a distributed network, the Internet, utilising hypertext. A computer, usually called a Web server, receives a request that follows a protocol called the hypertext transfer protocol (http), and the server responds to the request. The files or programs that make up Web-based information, usually called Web pages, are then sent to the requesting computer using TCP/IP. The receiving computer then composes the images using the second key component of the Web, a browser (Minoli, 1997: 140–9). To utilise the possibilities of hypertext, it has to appear on someone's computer. To reassemble the information transferred via http a browser is needed; this is something like a window that presents the hypertext to the reader. In 1993 the National Center for Supercomputing Applications (NCSA) released a browser called Mosaic. It developed the first simple graphical user interface (GUI) for the Web, which means it presented the information on the Web as combinations of pictures and text using hypertext. Links could be selected using a mouse that controlled a pointer on the screen and by placing the pointer over the link and clicking. Mosaic also followed in the traditions of the Internet by being released free (Wallace, 1997: 194–8; Hudson, 1997: 41–50). As journalist John Markoff noted in an article in the *New York Times* that was one of the first widely available public explanations of Mosaic and the Web:

> Before Mosaic, finding information on computer data bases scattered around the world required knowing—and accurately typing—arcane addresses and commands like 'Telnet 192.100.81.100'. Mosaic lets computer users simply click a mouse on words or images to summon texts, sound and images from many of the hundreds of data bases on the Internet that have been configured to work with Mosaic.
>
> (Markoff, 1993)

The emergence of Mosaic overcame difficulties in utilising the Internet's resources. Once Mosaic, or its main successors, Netscape's Navigator or Microsoft's Internet Explorer, is running and connected to the net no technical knowledge beyond the ability to point and click with a mouse is needed. The Web also integrates most of the resources available on the Internet. Minoli notes three forms of integration: of documents on different computers because of hypertext, of all the diverse resources of the Internet from software to databases, and of new types of resources, such as video, which can be added to Web pages and browsers. Anybody with access could use virtually any resource available on the Internet (Wolf, 1994; Minoli, 1997: 227–33). In the first year an estimated 2 million users took up Mosaic and it was being downloaded for free at the rate of 1,000 copies a day. Mosaic was released in April 1993 and a survey of the number of http sites found 130 in June 1993 but 623 in December of that year, and Hudson claims an increase of 1,758 per cent in the Web in 1994. If numbers for Internet hosts are looked at (see Figure 2.1 below) the rate of growth of the Internet increases nearly ten-fold in the year following Mosaic's release (Minoli, 1997: 234; Wolf, 1994: 117; 3W, 1994: 32; Hudson, 1997: 42; Markoff, 1993; see next section). While it is true that the Internet was growing prior to the development of the Web, it is also true that this growth dramatically increased following the emergence of the Web:

> It's like the difference between the brain and the mind. Explore the Internet and you find cables and computers. Explore the Web and you find information.
>
> (Tim Berners-Lee, cited in Markoff, 1993)

Following the emergence of the Web, the possibility of the balkanisation of cyberspace receded as the combination of Internet and Web began to absorb other networks. This is not totally due to the Web; a great deal of lobbying occurred in the USA (Jordan, 1998) and prices of computer equipment and of access to the Internet have dropped at exponential rates, but there can be no doubt that the Web's ease of use is the major factor that has led the Internet into widespread public knowledge. McCandlish's beer has resulted, as he expected, in the one major brand of Internet:

> it's all Internet now. There are still BBSs and some small proprietary online services that don't do much Internet but by and large they are gone....FidoNet is doomed. At its peak FidoNet had more than 30,000 people on it but it's really dropped off since then.
>
> (McCandlish, 1996)

The merger between the Internet, corporate and co-operative networks introduced changes in all three. This must be kept in mind when assessing the nature of cyberspace that develops with the Internet, as many find it easy to dismiss the Internet because of its origins in military funding.[15] There are two main social forces that have driven the Internet to its present position. The first is the military–industrial complex, which has provided the main funding for some of the more grandiose projects that make up cyberspace and which provides an important cultural background to certain technological choices that have been made. The second influence is a grassroots and populist attempt to create networks and computers that place the power of computers in the hands of individuals, precisely so that the 'establishment' and elites can be undermined. Here can be found the enthusiasts who created the personal computer, the programmers who have created and shared free software and an ethic of free and open use of networks that still dominates many parts of cyberspace. Neither element of cyberspace's past should be ignored when trying to read its nature from its history (Edwards, 1996; Levy, 1984).

One further trend or fundamental fact concerning the Internet needs to be noted, because embedded in cyberspace's technology is a bias towards particularly English but more generally Roman languages. Analysing a count of Internet hosts reveals that in July 1998, 78 per cent of hosts existed in English-speaking countries[16] and the Internet was largely designed assuming English as the normal language. This has led to the cultural domination of cyberspace by English languages that ensures some cultures feel excluded and marginalised and that makes entry to cyberspace far less attractive for non-English speakers. The fundamental problem is that Internet technology has largely been designed on the assumption that the American Standard Code for Information Interchange (ASCII) is adequate for transmitting language and it provides usually 128 and at maximum 256 characters. This falls far short of the 7,000 needed for modern Japanese or the 15,000 Taiwanese authorities have stated a preference for. ASCII does not even provide full support for languages that use the Roman characters used by English, such as French or German, because other characters like accents are not available (Shapard, 1993: 257, 268; Mason, 1993; Jerman-Blazic, 1996). ASCII is assumed to be standard in the protocols controlling email, which means that sending email in any language but English is made difficult by the fundamental design of email (Bourbonnais and Yergau, 1996). Other Internet services fare little better. Usenet also assumes ASCII as a standard and the Web is effectively English based (not in the language of Web pages, though this is also true, but in the technology needed to access or produce Web pages). Many other Internet services provide little or no support for non-ASCII languages (Bourbonnais and Yergau, 1996; Yong et al., 1996). Various solutions to these problems have been developed. For example, an extension to the HTML language used to create Web pages that would make many languages compatible with the Web's current technology is being developed and the use of the computer language Java to provide automated translations of Web pages has been explored (Bourbonnais and Yergau, 1996; Yong et al., 1996). It is also true, though not acceptable to many, that the use of ASCII provided a common standard that allowed the Internet to develop rapidly, when any attempt to develop an entirely inclusive linguistic basis for computer networking would have involved long periods of negotiation between nations. This is shown by the attempt to develop a common standard for Chinese, Korean and Japanese that proposed some standardisation of characters between the languages, which both Korea and Japan rejected arguing that their languages were unique and not just subsets of the Han characters that make up Chinese (Shapard, 1993: 267–70). However, it remains true that 'To speak means to be in a position to use a certain syntax, to grasp the morphology of this or that language, but it means above all to assume a culture, to support the weight of a civilisation' (Fanon, 1986: 17–18) and cyberspace has so far supported essentially Anglo-civilisation.

Some changes that are presently occurring also need to be mentioned to finalise this history. Since the explosive growth of the Web, major developments have been the addition of further resources and an emerging competition over the browser most used on the Web. Additional types of resources continue to emerge on the Web. It is now possible to use it for telephone and for live video and audio broadcast, a language is available to create three-dimensional hypertexts that can be moved through and new applications emerge all the time. The second development, browser wars, has seen the company that dominates the personal computer, Microsoft, become deeply interested in the Internet. Most of the team that created and released Mosaic became part of a new company, Netscape, which superseded Mosaic with a browser called Navigator that quickly became dominant. Abruptly, the firm that seemed to have an all-powerful grip on computers, because it wrote and sold the software that made the hardware run, feared that it was heading for decline (Wallace, 1997: 1–11; Stroud, 1996). Microsoft's reaction was to reinvent itself and focus on the Internet. It created a browser, Internet Explorer, which has gradually matched Navigator for performance and begun to use its dominance of personal computers to push its Internet products. In early 1998, though still locked in corporate battle it appeared that Netscape and Microsoft might continue to share the browser market. These developments will be discussed at greater length in Chapter 4. For the present, it need only be noted that some of the biggest Internet and computing corporations, Netscape, Microsoft and also Sun, are struggling to dominate and profit from the technology that makes cyberspace possible (Wallace, 1997; Stross, 1996; Rose, 1998; Quittner, 1998).

A second development in cyberspace's history is its emergence into public view attracting the attention of governments. The most spectacular example of government regulation of the Internet is the Communications Decency Act passed in the USA in 1996 that outlawed 'obscene' content appearing on the Internet. It made sysops criminally and financially liable for any obscenity, despite the fact that a systems administrator in a large institution might have millions of messages or requests for Web content pass through their system every day. The definition of obscene was so broad as to raise the possibility of banning much modern poetry. In mid-1996 the Act and any similar legislation was declared unconstitutional and unlawful by the US Supreme Court, but further attempts at censorship are under discussion (Jordan, 1998). Other indications of government interest have occurred with the London Metropolitan Police suggesting that UK-based Internet service providers should 'voluntarily' censor certain parts of Usenet and some state prosecutors in Germany attempting to have access both to some parts of Usenet and to some Web sites closed down (Kahin and Nesson, 1997; EFF, 1995).[17] In several other areas as well, notably encryption, it seems certain that governments world-wide will be taking a closer interest in the workings of cyberspace.

The final trend that needs to be noted is that with the explosion of interest in the Web has come much greater use that seems to, at times, slow the speed of interaction to a crawl. In theory, the technology underlying the retrieval of documents on the Web is powerful enough for retrieval to take a second. However, there are a number of factors that affect this ideal speed. Traffic on the network the request originates from, the speed of connections and the traffic on the server the request travels to, all affect the speed of interaction. For example, the Web is usually noticeably slower in the afternoon in the UK than in the morning, simply because afternoon in the UK is also morning in the USA and that means the combined population of net users is active. It is often noted in the USA that the Internet is slow between 3 and 5 p.m. on the East Coast, a peak time within the USA. There have been several predictions of wholesale collapse of the Internet because of increased traffic, but so far no such failure has occurred, which does not mean the Web is fast or that more limited crashes have not occurred. Rather, the upgrading of technology seems to be keeping just ahead of the demands of users. For example, it was thought that the system was in imminent danger of collapse in 1995 when NSFNET backbones opened to commercial users as well as its usual community of researchers and this combined with changes in techniques for routing packets. But the main supplier of routers, Cisco, issued a temporary fix that prevented the expected meltdown (Sowa, 1996a; 1996b). Contrary to doom-laden prophecies and to many people's perception that the Internet is slowing down, the only reliable evidence is that it has speeded up. Since 1994, Matrix Information and Directory Services (Mids[18]) has measured the time it takes for a message to leave and return to it over the Internet. Over the time these measurements have been taken the Internet has been getting faster. The perceived problem of the Internet slowing down is simply that there are peak and off-peak times on the Internet and during peak times, when most people utilise it, the Internet is slowest (Quarterman, 1998).[19] Speed is an endless problem, not just because of the growth of the Internet but because greater speed produces the possibility of new resources. The most obvious example of this is video, which is available on the Internet in 1998 and is likely to become better and better. It is likely speed will remain an endless problem because the more speed becomes available the more speed hungry applications are likely to become. However, it also appears that, at the moment, the governments and corporations that build the high-speed links and interchanges that carry traffic are, if not keeping the Web speedy, at least keeping it running (Grebb, 1997; Quarterman, 1998).

It is impossible to predict precisely the future of the Internet and the cyberspace it supports. However, the success of a packet-switching distributed network of computers is undoubted and will form the basis of future networks. But this summary of the history of computer-mediated communication has so far said little about: How big is this network? Who uses the net? And what do they use it for? The next section will outline these before returning to put cyberpunk fiction together with networked reality.

Size, users and uses

A number of questions can now be considered about the Internet as it presently exists and certain trends can be isolated that seem to have been stable for some time. These relate to the size and distribution of the Internet, the type of user and types of use. In summary, the Internet is growing at exponential rates but is overwhelmingly located in the already industrialised world where users are wealthy, white and highly educated, while uses are essentially to communicate with other people whether for social, research or business purposes. The main changes within these trends have been that growth became greater in the early 1990s (the average rate of change is ten-fold higher from 1990 to 1997 compared with the 1980s) and a shift from users being overwhelmingly male to over one-third female. The three areas of size and change in size, type of user and type of use will now be discussed in more detail.

Claims about the size of the Internet have varied widely. The largest claim is for the number of people who can use email, though not necessarily file transfer or the Web, which was Quarterman's estimate of 100 million users in 1993, and the figure of 30 million full Internet users was routinely used in 1995–7 (Quarterman, 1993: 42–3; Rickard, 1995). These sorts of figures were estimates of varying reliability. The most reliable estimate of Internet size is the count of host computers (a computer with an IP number) conducted by Mark Lottor at Network Wizards (Figure 2.1).[20] In July 1998, the host count found 36,739,000 Internet hosts of which 6,529,000 or 18 per cent were connected at the moment the survey was conducted.[21]

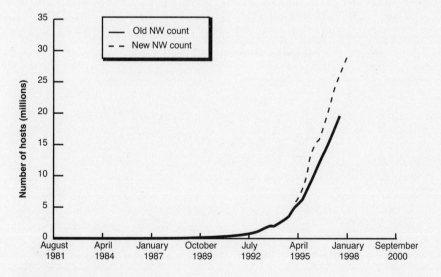

Figure 2.1 Internet host count

Source: Network Wizards

The problem with the host count is that it cannot produce figures for the number of people who use the Internet; it counts computers, not people. This has led to many taking the host count and multiplying it by an estimate of how many people are connected per host, which at its extreme meant some were counting 200,000 people per host because it was believed there was a computer at IBM with 200,000 people using it (Rickard, 1995). To solve this problem two surveys, utilising normal social science such as sampling and in-depth interviewing, allow a reliable estimate of the number of Internet users per host to be generated. The surveys are the O'Reilly and Associates/Trish Information Systems study *Defining the Internet Opportunity* in 1995 and the Find/SVP 1995 and 1997 studies. These surveys resulted in figures of 5.8 million (O'Reilly) and 8.4 million (Find/SVP) US users in 1995 (ORA, 1995; Find/SVP 1995;1997). Following Rickard's method, these figures allow the definition of a reliable ratio of 1.37174 humans per host (O'Reilly) or 1.98666 humans per host (Find/SVP) (Rickard, 1995).[22]

The two ratios mean that in July 1998 there were between 48 and 73 million Internet users (Figure 2.2). Host count data allows change over time to be tracked.

Growth rates on the Internet seem to be slowing, with consistent growth rates of around 100 per cent dropping to 52 per cent between January 1996 and 1997, 36 per cent between January 1997 and 1998 and 41 per cent between July

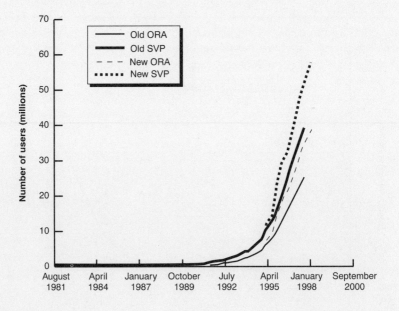

Figure 2.2 Internet user counts

Sources: Network Wizards, ORA (1995); Find/SVP (1995)

1997 and 1998.[23] A sudden takeoff in Internet hosts can be traced to host counts taken between April and July 1993, which coincides with the release of Mosaic for browsing the Web in April 1993. Two further measures of growth that relate to the Web itself confirm the Web's growth at this time. Both measures only cover the Web's initial period. The first is measures of different types of data traffic taken from the NSFNET backbone that carried Internet traffic in the USA at that time. These figures clearly demonstrate that between June 1993 and March 1995 all other Internet services (ftp, gopher, telnet) showed significant drops in the amount of their traffic, while the Web grew at high rates.[24] The second measure results from Mathew Gray's Web Wanderer, which is a program that wandered the Web collecting statistics on numbers of sites. These counts were conducted from July 1993 until June 1996, offering a snapshot of the beginning of the Web. They confirm the explosive growth in numbers of Web sites of 800 per cent between June 1993 and 1994 and 1,000 per cent between June 1994 and 1995 (Gray, 1996).

It can be confidently stated that by mid-1998 approximately 40–70 million people were using the Internet, that numbers continued to expand rapidly and that the Web is driving much of this growth. While the overall size and trend have been identified, the distribution of users around the world also needs to be considered. A world-wide distribution can be given using Lottor's host count because figures are broken down according to top-level domain name (.uk for UK etc.). International domain names such as .com or .org can be broken down according to figures provided by John Quarterman[25] (Quarterman, 1997). In July 1998, the Internet was not only dominated by Western or developed countries but by the USA, which had 65 per cent of all hosts. It was followed by Canada with 5.3 per cent, Japan and the UK both with 4 per cent and with no other country having more than 4 per cent. If the world is divided into regions the picture given in Table 2.1 emerges.

As Bourbonnais and Yergau remark 'The Internet was designed as a highly redundant and fault-tolerant mesh. However, its actual structure today, on a

Table 2.1 Distribution of Internet hosts by region, July 1998

	Host number	Per cent of hosts	No. of countries
USA/NAFTA	25,038,086	70.9	3
Europe	6,815,721	19.3	50
Japan/SE Asia	1,935,291	5.5	18
Central Asia	23,366	0.1	18
Australasia/South Pacific	932,137	2.6	22
Middle East/North Africa	115,851	0.3	20
Sub-Saharan Africa	145,801	0.4	41
South America	302,954	0.9	44
Total	35,309,207	100	216

Sources: Network Wizards; Quarterman (1997)

global scale, is much more like a US-centred star' (Bourbonnais and Yergau, 1996). Inequalities are even more marked than first appear because Australia and New Zealand account for 99.56 per cent of Australasia/South Pacific's hosts, South Africa accounts for 96.42 per cent of Sub-Saharan Africa's hosts and Israel accounts for 75.65 per cent of Mid-East/North Africa's hosts. The rapid increase in size of the Internet also means that some diminution of US dominance might be expected in the future, though as already discussed when considering language in cyberspace some aspects of this dominance are likely to have long-lasting effects. The fundamental fact about the Internet is that it is, first, dominated by the USA and, second, developed or industrialised country dominated.

But within these countries, who are these 70 million users? The same O'Reilly and Find/SVP surveys, along with some limited statistics from a British survey by NOP, offer reliable survey methodologies that measure types of Internet users. They also provide an independent check on the largest Web user survey, the GVU survey. The GVU survey appears online and its population is self-selected, that is anyone with a Web connection can fill out and submit their details. The central problem with GVU surveys is that self-selection may bias its sample, rendering it unreliable. However, two factors militate against this. First, the sheer number of respondents it attracts suggests it may have a wide constituency, just fewer than 20,000 in the last survey. Second, and most important, checking GVU's results against the O'Reilly and Find/SVP surveys indicates it produces similar results on similar questions and, consequently, can be treated as a reliable measure of users and uses of the Web. The GVU survey is important because of the detail it provides and because it has been run seven times, first in January 1994 and last in November 1997,[26] allowing some trends over time to be established. To define users, four major socio-economic categories will be looked at; gender, age, race and wealth/occupation.[27]

Gender is the one category that has witnessed significant change over time. Of five surveys of gender balance taken between June 1996 and November 1997, four show women as between 30–40 per cent of online users (ORA; Find/SVP, 1997; NOP; Pitkow et al., 1998; Katz, 1997b). Wired magazine's 1997 survey was the exception and showed 52 per cent male and 48 per cent female for people they defined as connected (use email three times a week at least and use at least three out of laptop, cell phone, beeper and home computer) (Katz, 1997b). Future statistics may confirm equality and GVU surveys over time suggest a gender balance of 40 per cent women and 60 per cent men held since late 1995 but that by late 1997 movement towards equality had begun again (Figure 2.3). Only future surveys will show definitively whether gender equality in cyberspace was reached by early 1998.

Age appears to be stable over the time that has been surveyed at an average of early to mid-thirties. The O'Reilly and Find/SVP surveys show between 30 and 40 per cent of users to be under 30, while the GVU survey shows average age to be between 31 and 35 since November 1994. Race also shows a consis-

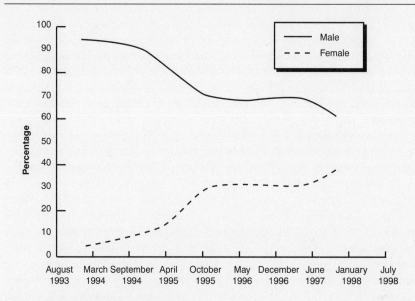

Figure 2.3 Gender online over time

Sources: Pitkow and Recker (1994a, 1994b); Pitkow and Kehoe (1995a, 1995b, 1996a, 1996b, 1997); Pitkow *et al.* (1998)

tent pattern over time, with nearly 90 per cent of users being white. Find/SVP's survey of US users found in 1995 that 83 per cent were white, 5 per cent were Black/African/American, 3 per cent Hispanic/Central or Southern American and 3 per cent Asian. GVU's figures show little change over time, consistently reporting 88–90 per cent of all users self-defined as white, with other ethnic groups rarely reporting more than 2 per cent of users. Wealth also shows a consistent pattern over time, with household income in US dollars for Internet users being around $60,000. GVU figures suggest average household income may be dropping with results for November 1997, dropping to an average of $53,000; it remains to be seen whether this is a one-off drop or a trend. Find/SVP and O'Reilly's surveys both confirm an average household income of around $60,000 per year. Occupation is the hardest category to compare across surveys, with quite different occupational categories having been used in different surveys. GVU utilises simple categories that offer the general conclusion that since 1994 an overwhelming number of users occupy computer-related, professional or managerial jobs (between 60 and 80 per cent). Manual, semi-skilled or skilled employment is virtually absent from GVU figures. This is complicated by O'Reilly's figures that show sales with 19 per cent as the largest category, though to what extent this represents shopfloor sales assistants or sales vice-presidents is impossible to tell.

In summary, users are white, have professional or managerial occupations, higher than average incomes and are likely to be located in the developed world. These factors are stable over the time of GVU surveys (1994–7). Users also appear to be split one-third female and two-thirds male. The final question is what do users do? What are the uses of the Internet and the Web? Again a comparison of O'Reilly, Find/SVP and GVU surveys offers a clear, stable picture that has two components: amount of time spent online and type of activity online.

In terms of the amount of time spent online, Find/SVP found that 59 per cent use email daily and 49 per cent browse the Web daily, while 89 per cent used email daily or weekly and 88 per cent browsed the Web daily or weekly. GVU consistently reports 70–80 per cent of users browsing the Web at least once a day. It seems clear that cyberspace users tend to use it often. In terms of the type of use, GVU's most recent survey shows between 60 and 90 per cent of people use the Web to gather information, search and browse, 50 per cent use it for work, education or entertainment, but only 20 per cent use it for shopping. Because of changes in categories, only four GVU categories can be tracked over time and are shown in Figure 2.4: browsing, entertainment, work and shopping.[28] It seems clear that shopping is beginning to grow, but that seeking information remains the main use of the Web.

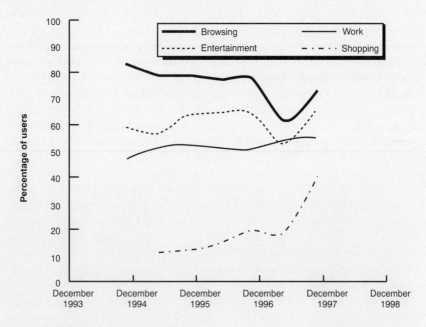

Figure 2.4 GVU activity on the Web

Sources: Pitkow and Recker (1994b); Pitkow and Kehoe (1995a, 1995b, 1996a, 1996b, 1997)

In summary, those on the Internet use it extensively, usually at least once a day, and use it for a range of activities that include work and entertainment in equal measure. Internet and Web users are, then, not only from the most privileged sections of society; they are also committed to cyberspace and use it extensively.

Conclusion

A world-wide computer network that allows people to communicate with each other exists. It has been created not in fiction but in fact through the efforts of governments, individuals and corporations. Its users have a clear and now largely stable demographic profile, with the sole exception of some uncertainty over whether gender equality lies in the future. This is a world not of disembodied consciousnesses having access to the sum total of human information, but of myriad acronyms, corporate rivalries and gradually growing sources of information and opportunities to communicate with other humans.

Barlovian cyberspace

We do not have cyberspace as Gibson described it and we do have a computer network that can just about be described. Between the two has emerged a social, cultural, economic and political space of virtual human interaction – a real cyberspace. This emergent cyberspace has some of the underlying characteristics that Gibson and others described but it already exists on the networks. What has emerged is the conviction that being involved in computer-mediated communication means entering a space that is fundamentally different to normal physical space because it transforms the relationship between our selves and our bodies. From this perspective emergent cyberspace is another version of the space two people enter when talking on the phone, a space that transformed human life some time ago. Bruce Sterling describes this understanding in the following way:

> Cyberspace is the 'place' where a telephone conversation appears to occur. Not inside your actual phone....Not inside the other person's phone...The place between the phones. The indefinite place out there, where the two of you, two human beings, actually meet and communicate....Although it is not exactly 'real', 'cyberspace' is a genuine place. Things happen there that have very genuine consequences. This 'place' is not 'real', but it is serious, it is earnest.
>
> (Sterling, 1992; xi–xii)

Though Sterling provides an elegant explanation, this definition of cyberspace as the place between two telephones is often credited to John Perry

Barlow, who also claims credit for the realisation that cyberspace had emerged in the real world of interconnected computers:

> Nobody else recognised that there was air in there to complain about or that there was an 'in-there' to complain about. I'm pretty sure I was the first person to call that space any name, as a spatially implying name.
>
> (Barlow, 1996a)

Barlow claims to have appropriated Gibson's term but applied it to really existing communication networks, in particular BBSs and the Internet (Barlow, 1996a; Featherstone and Burrows, 1995a: 5). Many have now recognised that joining together the visions of cyberpunk to the reality of networks creates a concept of cyberspace as a place that currently exists. Barlovian cyberspace grasps both possibilities that inspire work in the present and realities that condition the future. It is this concept that is meant by cyberspace from now on and will be this book's topic of discussion.

> But in the past twenty years, this electrical 'space', which was once thin and dark and one dimensional – little more than a narrow speaking tube, stretching from phone to phone – has flung itself open like a gigantic jack-in-the-box. Light has flooded upon it, the eerie light of the glowing computer screen. This dark electric netherworld has become a vast flowering electronic landscape.
>
> (Sterling, 1992: xii)

MYTHS OF THE ELECTRONIC FRONTIER 2: THE MYTH OF PHILCAT

There is a pioneering corner of cyberspace called the WELL (Whole Earth 'Lectronic Link). When it began it was not connected to the Internet but was a BBS located in San Francisco. It was begun to provide a place for people, 'brilliant people', to log on, leave messages, interact and explore. The WELL grew out of the 1960s counter-culture movement; beginning as part of the Whole Earth organisation that published self-help books and journals, such as the Whole Earth Catalogue. If you were a hippy and wanted information on how to build an egalitarian and self-sufficient commune, Whole Earth could help. The WELL began and gradually attracted a community that felt and acted like a community, and has become the mythical model for online societies. It organised itself into conferences on various topics. Within these conferences people gained personalities from their postings. Your online and real names were shown and people began to understand your personality from whatever it was you wrote. People did not need to meet, though they sometimes did, to learn about each other and become friends.

One day Philcat, his online name, a familiar member of the conference on Parenting, posted a message stating that his 7-year-old son had leukaemia. The announcement reverberated throughout the virtual community. Love and support flowed to Philcat and his family, carried by all the emotion people could pack into text appearing on computer screens. More, expertise was mobilised. Conference members worked out information that Philcat needed and provided experience – there were nurses and doctors on the WELL. How to discuss with medical authorities the best treatment? What did that diagnosis mean? Discussions with health professionals in the Parenting conference proved invaluable in answering these sorts of questions. Finally, Philcat's son went into remission. Mobilised to help one of its own, the virtual community suddenly became palpable, real. WELLbeings knew and felt they were part of a community but here it was made so obvious, so authentic and undeniable that something important became known. There have been many other such examples – Philcat is only one – and on many other systems, but all amount to the same moral.

The moral of Philcat is that people do not communicate with computers but use computers to communicate with each other. And, in doing so, genuine, heartfelt communities may be built. These collectives begin from individuals, all the different names that go online, and then through text fired back and forth coalesce into a community. A group of people can live and breathe with each other in cyberspace.[29]

As Hafner claims, the WELL has become almost the archetypal virtual community both through the publicity its members have given it and the pioneering events that took place there (Hafner, 1997). Of course, many other virtual communities emerged around the same time as the WELL or earlier and have emerged since. Many will be described in the following pages. The concluding point is that the virtual community made plain in Philcat is the archetypal form of Barlovian cyberspace. The WELL only provided text and it did not for many years provide full Internet connections, but it provided connections between people via technology that gave rise to a functioning social space. And this is the central insight of Barlovian cyberspace: that whatever science fiction imagines might be possible, some of its fantasies have limped into real lives. Text may be deeply impoverished, compared with Gibson's cyberspace or

Stephenson's metaverse, but it is enough, more than enough, for Barlovian cyberspace to blossom and grow. When individuals use existing computer and communications technology to talk to each other, to learn about each other and to build virtual spaces, then Barlovian cyberspace moves out of the thin tube connecting telephones to flower.

This is the cyberspace that needs our attention. It is the cyberspace that can be entered now and that will condition whatever fully realised form of Gibsonian cyberspace might be round the corner. Barlovian cyberspace exists and its structures of power need to be established. By exploring this cyberspace we can understand the condition of virtual lives and the possibilities for virtual futures, without giving way to impenetrable computer science or fantastic visions. The first structure of power we can ask about is the one Philcat shows us: virtual communities emerge when individuals mediated by computers build them. What are the conditions of cyberspace when the individual is understood as the starting point and foundation for online communities? What form of cyberpower exists when we begin from the virtual individual?

Chapter 3

The virtual individual

The information highway is a tool of the individual.

Bill Gates (Gates, 1995: 166–7)

Key concepts

Avatar

An avatar is a stable identity that someone using Barlovian cyberspace has created. The existence of an avatar means someone has used some of cyberspace's resources in ways that result in other avatars recognising a stable online personality. Someone's avatar may be constructed from the style of their online writing, from the repeated use of a name or self-description, or from any of a number of other virtual possibilities. More than one avatar can be created and the relationship between these identities and someone's offline life is complicated.

Virtual hierarchies

Hierarchies in cyberspace are constructed on different bases than in non-virtual space and tend to undermine offline hierarchies. Online hierarchies must be constructed from the peculiarities of online life, such as the style of someone's writing in a newsgroup or the power of their software coding in a MUD. Offline hierarchies can be undermined by virtual lives because cyberspace spreads information more broadly and allows more inclusive decision making, though this requires offline hierarchies to allow full access to cyberspace.

Informational space

Cyberspace is constructed out of information; it is an informational space. This is true at two levels. First, the exchange of information in the form of software code largely creates cyberspace. Second, virtual lives are created through the exchange of information by avatars, both information about objects and about how to use cyberspace.

Cyberpolitics

The politics of cyberspace is strung along the two axes of access to cyberspace and rights within cyberspace. Access is a key area of cyberpolitical debate because demographics show that use of cyberspace (up to 1998) was largely confined to a small and privileged section of offline populations. Rights are a key area of cyberpolitics because the rights of avatars are unclear and subject to revision by offline interests. The politics of online rights has developed chiefly around the areas of censorship, privacy, intellectual property and encryption.

Introduction

Many begin their journey into cyberspace as individuals. In front of a computer screen, reading the glowing words, we confront our singularity before building a sense of others in the electronic world. There is a double sense of individuality here. First, people must simply connect to cyberspace by logging in, almost certainly involving the individual entering their online name and their secret, personal password to be rewarded with their little home in cyberspace (usually consisting of elements like their email, list of favourite Web sites, online documents and customised browser/interface). The first moment in cyberspace is spent by nearly everyone in their own individualised place. Second, moving from this little home to other virtual spaces usually involves some further moment of self-definition; for example, choosing an online name, choosing a self-description or outlining a biography. In Philcat's virtual community, the WELL, people write a 'bio' that other members of the community can read. The bio may provide a short biography, a sort of informal and personal CV or résumé, but is often taken as the opportunity to indicate someone's ability to participate by writing intriguing stories. When a new president of the WELL was appointed, her staff urged her to write a bio as quickly as possible, as WELL users would be waiting to check it. She then gained credibility by writing a bio that in part read 'Snakes. So, I was asked in fourth grade by a singularly sweet nun, a Sister Huburt, what I wanted to be. Ahh, the big question, still unanswered. "A herpetologist", I responded' (Hafner, 1997: 140). Here a new president of the company that runs a virtual community makes her initial mark by providing a moment of self-definition. This virtual community is built from individuals confronting their individuality. These moments of individuation are most people's initial and recurrent online experience.

A second example of the primacy of the individual is the world of MUDs, MUSHES, MUCKs and MOOs.[1] A MUD is a program set up on a computer that accepts connections from many users at once. The program gives each person who uses it, called here a player, access to descriptions of rooms, objects and landscapes. Players journey through these descriptions communicating with each other, building objects like houses, robots or bars, fighting or co-operating, following a quest or adventure programmed into the software or simply existing there. There are broadly two types of MUDs, those with adventures or quests that require players to be active and follow through tasks and those that are purely social, offering the opportunity for interaction but not necessitating any particular journeys. According to one organiser of a MUD, social MUDs are different to adventure MUDs for three reasons: they are not goal oriented, journeys may occur within them but they are not defined by these journeys, and they can be built from within by their users, gradually becoming more complex (Curtis, 1992: 26; Reid, 1995: 165–6; Quittner, 1994a). The final and perhaps most important characteristic of MUDs is that they are text based. All the descriptions of places and all the conversations are carried by text on computer screens. This means that MUDs consist of many people sitting in front of networked computer terminals, located all over the world, reading text as it scrolls past them on the screen and participating by typing other text on the screen. For example, the following might appear on a MUD player's screen:

> Corridor
> The corridor from the west continues to the east here, but the way is blocked by a purple-velvet rope stretched across the hall. There are doorways leading to the north and south.
> You see Cockatoo, README for New MOOers, a fireplace, a newspaper.
> Guinevere, jane, MadHatter, Fred, Obvious and Bullet_the_Blue are here.
> (Curtis, 1992: 126; Reid, 1995: 168)

By reading this, a player would know they are in a corridor and that they could leave by doorways to the north and south. The player would be able to read a newspaper or guidelines (README) for new players. Finally, the player would know that a number of other players or characters are present in this corridor, Guinevere, jane and so on. A player communicates by using commands like say, emote, whisper, page, look.[2] For example, if the player using the name jane types on their computer, 'say Can anyone hear me?' then other players would see on their screen 'jane says, "Can anyone hear me?"', or if jane typed 'emote smiles' then the other players would see 'jane smiles'. Whisper can be used to send a message to another player in the room that no other player in the room receives and page can be used to find another player who is not in a room. The other key means of expression for players is their choice of name, gender and description. When another player uses a command like 'look jane' then jane's self-chosen gender and self-description appears. There are short self-descriptions, such as 'possessor of the infinity gems' or 'an average sized dark elf with lavender eyes' or descriptions that may go much longer. Reflecting the originally male composition of cyberspace users, Curtis notes: 'I cannot count the number of "mysterious but unmistakably powerful" figures I have seen wandering around LambdaMOO' (Curtis, 1992: 27–9). With these sorts of commands players create friendships and a sense of place. People meet, marry, argue and, in a certain bodiless sense, live in MUDs. The nature of the place means it creates a different space to our normal world; most obviously we do not and cannot choose our genders while this is normal in a MUD. Further, all things that can be typed can occur. MUDs are undoubtedly a lived space. Reid concludes about them:

> The commands provided by the MUD systems enable users to weave a web of communication that ties each person into a sociocultural context. This web of verbal and textual significances that are substitutes for and yet distinct from the networks of meaning of the wider community binds users into a common culture whose specialised meanings allow the sharing of imagined realities.
>
> (Reid, 1995, 183)

When someone enters a MUD they must first connect, then choose a name, a gender and write a self-description. Here is one of the classic moments of online individuation. To make the change from a person in front of a screen to a player, someone must confront and redefine their subjectivity; they must ask themselves who or what they want to be in this world. On a MUD your offline persona is anonymous; people know who you are from what you type.

> If anonymity on MUDS allows people to do and say whatever they wish, it also allows them to be whoever they wish....Some systems do ask characters to choose a racial background, but the choices are likely to be between Elvish, Dwarvish, and Klingon than between Caucasian, Black and Asian.
>
> (Reid, 1995, 178–9; Quittner, 1994a)

The self-definitional moment on a MUD has analogies in other online communications. Whether it is choosing a log-in name, an email account name, a Usenet name or whatever, the individualist foundation of cyberspace seems to be underlined again and again in online interactions that both demand self-definition and offer self-invention.

This chapter begins from the individualising power of experience in cyberspace and explores its consequences, uncovering a particular form of power. First, the three key elements of the power of the individual in cyberspace are each explored in detail. Identity fluidity is the process by which online identities are constructed and these are identities not necessarily close to offline identities. Renovated hierarchies are the processes by which offline hierarchies are reinvented online, with many online resources undermining offline hierarchies while also defining new hierarchies. Both these two elements rely on cyberspace being an informational space. Bodies can be rewritten and hierarchies reinvented because cyberspace is constituted out of information, both in the information users provide and the hardware and software that create cyberspace. Taken together, identity fluidity, renovated hierarchies and informational spaces constitute cyberpower as the possession of individuals, who can utilise the various abilities offered by these three to impose their will. The general form of individualised power in cyberspace will be explored before turning to the specific form of cyberpolitics that this power supports. Here will be found the forms of cyberpolitics most familiar to political activists in cyberspace and are distributed across the two axes of access to cyberspace and rights within cyberspace. Beginning from the insight that cyberspace is often experienced as individualising, this chapter will, first, explore the three constituent parts of this form of cyberpower, second, define its general form and, third, analyse its typical form of cyberpolitics. The myth of Philcat prompted recognition of the starting point of this chapter and now the third myth of the electronic frontier illustrates all three dimensions of power and the individual in cyberspace.

MYTHS OF THE ELECTRONIC FRONTIER 3: JULIE, JOAN, SANFORD AND ALEX

In 1982, a disabled woman appeared on a computer conferencing system run by CompuServe. These systems allow both real-time exchanges and posting of messages. Julie was a neuropsychologist who had been in a horrific car accident that had left her mute, paraplegic and so disfigured she could not bear to meet people face to face. She was on the verge of suicide when a friend gave her a computer and a modem and with these she discovered online conversations where her physical appearance and abilities did not seem to matter. Julie (who some people thought used a headstick to type out conversations despite the speed at which her thoughts appeared) quickly became a fascinating, lively and committed participant in CompuServe's virtual communities, though owing to her appearance and inability to talk she refused to meet any of her virtual friends in real life. She set up a women's discussion group and offered aid to some women with suicidal tendencies, helping them overcome depression or chemical dependencies. Julie's own social life blossomed online. She made more and more friends and began to practise online sex, first tentatively and then flamboyantly. Her online greeting began to reflect her huge online presence, 'HI!!!!!!!'. Offline her life blossomed as well. She met and married an astonishingly supportive husband, travelled and resurrected her career, but she maintained her rigid refusal to meet any of her online friends offline. Julie and her life slowly began to seem a little too much of everything to be true. Some disabled women felt uncertain about the ease with which Julie's marriage overcame her disabilities. And then disaster struck. Julie became seriously ill with an obscure disease and hovered near death. As with Philcat and many other instances, the virtual community mobilised in an astonishing show of support and collective grief. Even so, Julie's husband respected Julie's wish not to meet her online friends and he deflected any attempt to see her. To great joy, Julie pulled through and recovered. But someone had worked out which hospital Julie should have been in and called – no Julie had been in the hospital.

Slowly at first and then quickly, Julie's online persona unravelled. In place of an atheistic, sexually alive (even predatory), dope-smoking, hard-drinking, flamboyant, female, disabled neuropsychologist, there was a conservative, Jewish, teetotal, drug-fearing, low-key, sexually awkward, male, able-bodied psychiatrist. Sanford, who had been typing Julie all along, replaced Julie. Sanford had once joined online conversations with the self-chosen pseudonym of Doctor. He had then had an intimate private conversation online with a woman, during which he realised the woman thought he was a female psychiatrist. He found a depth of emotional conversation he claimed he had always missed with women. He then created an online female who offered the greatest chance of not being detected and Julie was born. When Julie became sick, it was Sanford who had become frightened of the extent of her circle of friends and of the depth of her intimacies, but the passionate response had made it impossible for him to kill her. Male and able-bodied were two components of Sanford's identity that shook Julie's friends and lovers. Many felt betrayed, cheated, assaulted and even raped. They had poured their lives out to Julie and thought she had done the same to them. They had loved her and screwed her, but Julie only ever existed in text while their text was also written on their flesh and blood. Some sought friendship with Sanford, as though Julie had to be inside him somewhere, but for many Sanford simply was not Julie (even if they could have forgiven his lies).

The moral is that online identities do not have to match offline identities. Multiple identities are possible: Sanford was Julie and Julie's husband. Different bodies, genders, sexualities, races, ages and so on are possible online. Julie is also only one example. McRae reports an encounter where a woman who explored online sadomasochistic sex became upset during the encounter. Another woman then comforted her, became a close friend and then a lover. But the second woman turned out to be a man who took the persona of a lesbian in order to 'help women and keep them safe from other men who might hurt them' (McRae, 1996: 255). When all that people know about you is the words you type and when some of those words are your name and your description, then virtual communities can never really be certain that you are who you say you are. To be certain, the virtual must become real and people have to meet face to face. This uncertainty can be a frightening thought; Julie really helped people to build self-esteem and to turn away from drugs or depression. How can any of these people open their hearts again online? They have no idea who is listening. But it is also a liberating thought, because online you can be someone different and can escape your offline limitations, just as Sanford escaped his maleness and Julie her disability. These astonishing, even utopian, possibilities are built into a technology that allows world-wide communication between people but often restricts that communication to text. 'The computer engineers, the people who wrote the programs...just smiled tiredly. They had understood from the beginning the radical changes in social conventions that the nets implied' (Stone, 1995: 83).[3]

The myth of Julie shows the three key components that shape online power when we begin from the individual: identity fluidity, anti-hierarchism and information as reality. Julie's identity as a disabled woman was different to Sanford's as an abled man. Women communicated directly to Julie the neuropsychologist and Sanford the psychiatrist, cutting across any hierarchy of appointment, fee or referral. The separation of online and offline life was made possible by the construction of virtual communities out of information conveyed by text. These three powers will be examined in turn, fleshing out the constituent components of cyberpower from the perspective of the virtual individual.

Axes of individual cyberpower: identity, hierarchy, information

Identity fluidity

The ability to play with identity gives rise to some of the most spectacular, and so most discussed, instances of difference between online and offline life. Julie is the archetypal instance, but here is another that provides a limit or boundary case. Dorion Sagan took the possibilities for self-definition on the Internet to their limit by basing an identity on permanent redefinition. Sagan took part in real-time discussions, his words appeared as he typed them, as did those who replied, and he chose his name, sex and self-description as part of his 'stats' that others could look up to find information about him.

First my stats said that I was 35/M (35 years old, male). Then I was 22/F (22, female). Then I was 18/M. Then I was 13/F....Even my brief forays into hermaphroditism (mf/28/Duluth) were given fleeting credence....In my furious typing and hyperkinetic excitement, I was contacting all and sundry without true regard to conveying a continuity of personality.

(Sagan, 1995: 80)

Sagan reached the limits of self-definition by having the identity of someone who constantly changed identity. Despite his constant stats changes, he still managed to be taken seriously by several other online personas. However, because no one can be certain if someone's online persona is, in fact, who they type they are, there is also suspicion and Sagan's hyperactivity made it difficult for him to create sexual contacts. Similarly, in MUDs Curtis notes players generally assume that flirtatious females are in fact men looking to entrap and embarrass other men (Curtis, 1992: 28–9). Eventually, Sagan left his shape-shifting behind to establish some longer-term, more stable impersonations. As with Sanford and Julie, Sagan's new identities took on lives of their own and, again like Sanford, a complicated relationship to his offline identity ensued (Sagan, 1995).

The astonishment many feel at hearing a story like Sagan's, or Julie's, has led to a common misunderstanding of identity on the net. Sentiments are often expressed like those in the famous cartoon that showed a dog at a computer terminal saying to another dog 'On the Internet no-one knows you're a dog', and often lead people to assume offline identities are not present online. In wilder moments, some have taken this to mean that cyberspace will be libera-tory because gender, race, age, looks or even 'dogness' are absent there. One of the key figures in the history of Usenet, John Gilmore, notes:

On the Internet nobody knows you at all, on the Internet nobody knows what your race is or your sex. That whole colour and sex-blindness is a posi-tive force for a lot of people. They feel welcome. Certainly, this goes for people with disabilities.

(Gilmore, 1996)

Such statements are sometimes read as abolishing certain offline prejudices by technological fiat. For example, what are often seen as the rhetorical means by which men dominate conversations are impossible online, such as loudness or talking over people. You cannot make yourself heard more by typing in upper case in the way you can if you talk loudly and everyone's contributions appear on the screen, so it is impossible to silence people by talking when they do. Here cyberspace emerges as a more equal, a more concretely egalitarian, place than many non-electronic places (Miller, 1995: 55–6). However, the issue is not that gender, race or disabilities are absent from cyberspace, nor is this quite what people like Gilmore claim. It is rather that the identity that we have offline, that is often marked physically, is absent online. It has never been the case that various gender or other attributes have been absent online, but that the connection between online and offline identity becomes tenuous and the way online identity is created is different. For example, there is the following definition of online sexual appeal. 'In compu-sex, being able to type fast or write well is equivalent to having great legs or a tight butt in the real world' (Branwyn, 1993: 784). But what if you had to type your words with a headstick, as some thought Julie did? What if that was the case? One headstick, however skilfully wielded, is going to have trouble competing with ten fingers and online sexual attraction may reflect offline disability. It is not that cyberspace is inherently free of gender or race or any of the other key constituents of offline identity, but that these are recreated with different resources, in different ways and with variable connections to offline identity (Burkhalter, 1998; O'Brien, 1998).

Online identity needs to be broken down into two components to be fully explored. First, there are a number of resources through which online identities are created. Second, there is an elastic connection between offline and online identity. People negotiate the potential identity fluidity of online life with these two resources. As the myth of Julie also shows, people are capable of creating different identities online to offline that are stable and seem to have a life of their own. To reflect this possibility and to create some clear terminology, the term avatar will be used to designate an online identity. Avatar is becoming an accepted term for online characters that have a graphical representation and can be usefully extended to cover all online identities. These two components that explain the relationship between online and offline identity will be dealt with in turn.

A number of indicators appear online through which identity is constructed. Their common characteristic is that they do not immediately create clear forms of identity that are identical to offline identity. Rather, they create a number of resources through which offline identity can be imported or recreated but which do not mandate that offline and online remain the same. These components divide broadly into two types, identifiers and style. The resources for identity construction that will be outlined below do not operate in all of cyberspace but only in the locations that allow them. This means the freedom they offer to construct avatars is often limited to the part of cyberspace that offers those resources. It needs to be kept in mind that constructing an avatar through email is different to constructing one in MUDs.

Identifiers are the addresses, names, self-descriptions and more that designate contributions to cyberspace. They all in some way allow the messages we send, the software we contribute, the emotions or ideas that we express, to be related to our avatar. Stable avatars must have some stability in their names, otherwise anyone they communicate with will not know that all the things they write come from them. Of course, this also allows multiple avatars with different identities, but for each identity to be more than ephemeral its interventions into cyberspace have to relate back with some consistency to a name or identifier. Identifiers can be divided according to the extent they are chosen or imposed. An example of the first of these is an email address and of the second all the various self-designations that MUDs and online chat allow, and these will be examined in turn.

The most used element of cyberspace is email. Nearly everyone who has access to cyberspace has an email account and an email address. In addition, many forms of interaction on the net allow us to see other people's email addresses. When someone posts a message to a Usenet discussion group their email address normally appears at the top of their message. If someone is part of a 'listserv' discussion group then they receive everyone's comments and replies as email, including the email address. And, of course, if you receive email you normally have the email address of whoever sent the email to you.[4] Donath shows how this simple label marks people in different ways (Donath, 1998; Mitchell, 1996: 7–17). For example, think of your reaction on receiving an email from the address b.gates@microsoft.com. The .com tells you it is likely to be a commercial organisation, while microsoft identifies a certain software company, and could b.gates really mean one of the richest men in the world has emailed you? We can imagine different reactions if we received a message from dark.knight@hacktic.nl. The .nl is the domain name for the Netherlands and, having a wide understanding of cyberspace, you know that Hack Tic is the name of a well-known group of Dutch hackers. You might well guess that you had now been contacted by the Dutch hacker dark.knight. Imagine as well that you received the same email from these two addresses and it reads:

> I've heard about you from colleagues and believe we can do some useful – hopefully profitable! – work together.

An invitation from the richest man in the world to make some money! An invitation from a hacker to make some money! Different emotions can be imagined on receiving these messages, even though they have the same content. Of course, there is no certainty that b.gates@microsoft.com is Bill Gates or that dark.knight@hacktick.nl is a hacker associated with the Hack-Tic hackers, but the reading of each address may well cause the message to be read differently. Even an anonymous address may produce a certain reading. Receiving an anonymous email will cause some interest and it will be known as anonymous because its address will indicate this, such as 'anon-remailer@utopica.hacktic.nl' (Donath, 1998). Perhaps the message will report a teacher to managers for slackness or a foreman to managers for abusive behaviour. On receiving such a whistle-blowing email, most will have to stop and consider whether it is true or not because it could simply be malicious. A message reporting a teacher signed by half of a class, who are then willing to restate their complaint in person, will be understood differently to one anonymous email.

Email addresses are in a standard form 'name@domain', such as t.r.jordan@uel.ac.uk. After the @ symbol appears the location of the address; this is in the form of a hierarchy from organisation to top-level domain. Email addresses are hardly ever fully freely chosen as the domain name will normally be assigned. For example, subscribers to the commercial email provider America Online all receive the domain name aol.com, or at the UK provider Demon all receive demon.co.uk. Domain names also indicate certain types, with co.uk indicating a commercial company in the UK, com indicating a commercial company. Receiving an email from name@somewhere.mil would be intriguing as mil is the domain name for the US military. Domain names cannot be taken as absolute indicators, for it is possible to have a computer physically outside the USA but still have a typical US domain name or to be in the USA and have a name indicating a different country. However, domain names offer a number of clues to the identity of the person who holds the address. Before the @ symbol comes a user's personal name. These can be more or less chosen, though they have to be unique, leading to those with popular names sometimes receiving an email address such as John9@domain. Within both the constraint to be unique and the domain at which someone sends and receives email, a name is chosen or not depending on local network policy. The UK's academic network usually calls for names and initials, meaning that most UK academic addresses have rather unimaginative names such as T.R.Jordan. Other networks allow almost total freedom of choice and various names will appear, from Philcat to CousinKat (Donath, 1998; Miller, 1996: 7–17). Similar points can be made about Web home page addresses. These are Web addresses that point to a page that someone considers 'home' and on which they put their own view of their identity. A home page might include lists of interests, photographs, family details and links to other sites of interest to the designer. The address is in a form similar to email, such as http://www.eff.org/homes/~barlow, where the elements after www can be read in the same way as domain names on email addresses.

Email and home page addresses are partly, sometimes wholly, compulsory and provide a number of important clues to identity. As people use email and the Web more, they are likely to become more skilled at reading these addresses. Having multiple email addresses can complicate such identities: there is nothing to stop anyone opening email accounts at a number of providers, though they then face the problem of paying for and keeping track of all their email. As Donath notes, 'The account name is thus an important, but limited, form of online identification' (Donath, 1998). It is also, quite possibly, the most important clue many receive about identity online simply because email is the most widely used resource of cyberspace.

There is a second resource for avatar construction that is also not self-chosen, though it may seem to be, namely style. People gradually develop reputations based on their style. Donath explored Usenet newsgroups and notes of one contributor to discussions of aquaria (rec.aqauria, alt.aquaria, sci.aquaria) that 'His letters are usually answers to questions posed by others, his voice is usually authoritative, pedantic, occasionally dryly humorous' (Donath, 1998). Here someone can be identified by the style of their online interaction. Sometimes style can be strong enough to override what are normally more authoritative markers of identity, such as an email address. The cypherpunks mailing list includes the following warning to those thinking of joining it:

> The cypherpunk list has its very own net.loon, a fellow named L. Detweiler. The history is too long for here, but he thinks cypherpunks are evil incarnate. If you see a densely worded rant featuring characteristic words such as 'medusa', 'pseudospoofing', 'treachery', 'poison' or 'black lies', it's probably him, no matter what the From: line says.
>
> (Donath, 1998)

Here the email address, often a strong indicator of a stable avatar, is overridden by a style that has been recognised through a long history. Many newsgroups or listserv groups have resident celebrities whose styles are instantly recognisable to other participants and any participant who posts repeatedly will eventually come to have their style recognised. Groups also provide certain stylistic resources. Abbreviations are common in the typed world of online discussions, such as btw for 'by the way', lol for 'laughing out loud' or imho for 'in my humble opinion', and groups sometimes generate their own specific abbreviations. Donath notes from misc.kids.pregnancy that onna stands for 'oh no not again' (Donath, 1998). These abbreviations can then be used to establish not only individual but group styles, marking those who do not use or understand the abbreviations as outsiders. In addition, certain types of style provide resources. An example is trolling. A troll is a post to a newsgroup that is intentionally incorrect in an attempt to catch people who do not recognise it as a deliberate mistake (the name is derived from fishing). Here is a troll posted to a newsgroup devoted to the technical errors in *Star Trek* episodes and it refers to the special effect that has a shadow passing over the starship *Enterprise* when a shuttle leaves it.

> Hello? Are there any technical advisors working on this show? Do they really think that objects cast shadows in a vacuum? I know zip about physics, but even I could spot that one.
>
> (Tepper, 1997: 39)

This is a deliberate mistake, which attracted over a hundred responses in three days and continued for three weeks. Others who get the joke can then participate to try and complicate and extend the troll. For example, a troll posted on a Star Wars discussion group claimed that Jamie Lee Curtis was in the movie *Star Wars* and a reply took this seriously by pointing out it was actress Carrie Fisher. To this obvious and correct claim, the following further troll appeared:

> That was Carrie Fisher. Ridiculous. Carrie Fisher is much too small and slight to carry that heavy hairy suit around all day on the set.
>
> (Tepper, 1997: 42)

From here participants may realise that the claim that Jamie Lee Curtis was the body within the Wookie suit is not meant to be taken seriously or more discussion will occur, dividing those who get the joke from those who do not. Even a message stating there were deliberate mistakes in these postings led to further serious replies. Trolling is a type of style that marks certain people as able to use or to recognise certain messages as insincere and in this way constitutes a group of people whose styles mark them as experienced members of the group. In this way, trolling allows members of groups to state a stylistic allegiance to a certain community and to exclude others (Donath, 1998; Tepper, 1997).

Styles may seem to be chosen by those who write, but this is only partially true. For example, female Hertz recounts deciding to have gay sex online because 'living in South Miami Beach, where every guy is a twenty-two-year-old gay model on rollerblades, I wondered if I could write a believable character by that description. I wanted to see if I could pass' (Hertz, 1994: 155). Hertz managed to pass, having oral and anal typed sex in the process, and so could claim to have adopted a certain style. However, Hertz's gay style received its pass mark from the other gay men on the IRC channel #gaysex.[5] The avatar Kit who initiated and had sex with Hertz's avatar Kiy provided the ultimate mark of success, but all the other avatars present also accepted Hertz's style as gay. Of course, such mutual acceptance does not mean that all these avatars related to offline gay identities. In fact, it is theoretically possible that everyone on #gaysex was offering the same deception as Hertz, creating the possibility that an avatar related to an offline gay identity would not be believed because all the other avatars would be conforming to the fantasies straight people have of what gays are like. This is akin to the famous, if undocumented, incident where Douglas Adams, author of The Hitchhiker's Guide to the Galaxy, posted to a newsgroup devoted to his work, only for others to reject him as an impostor. People can attempt to choose their style as much as they like, they can work at it and can develop any number of convincing avatars based on the relevant group, but whether the style works or not, whether it is in fact a 'correct' style, is determined by others. Styles are partially out of the hands of their authors. Most styles are recognised without conscious effort from their authors, a style is usually simply the typical way someone interacts online. However, even in the strong case of someone attempting to adopt or develop a particular style, their ability to do so can only be known when others recognise and affirm the style as acceptable.

The second type of resource for creating stable identifiers are those that are freely chosen. They can be grouped broadly as self-descriptions. With these resources the connection between avatars and offline identities can be stretched to breaking point, because they are freely chosen. Self-descriptions include all the different opportunities for providing information about yourself that others online can read. There are three main areas in which this can be done: signatures, handles and self-portraits. Each will be briefly discussed in turn.

Signatures are just as their name suggests. It is possible to create messages that are automatically appended to emails that people send, to posts to Usenet and other groups and to many other electronic messages. At their simplest signatures offer information about the sender, such as a phone number, fax, company or Web home page address. Signatures may offer disclaimers that someone is offering their own opinions and not necessarily those of their employer. Signatures may offer pieces of ASCII art, pictures drawn with just text keys, such as @}———— for a long-stemmed rose, and may offer quotes, humour or anything else the author of the signature feels is relevant. One of the premier civil rights Internet activists offered in mid-1997 the following quote as his signature, followed only by his name, job, email address and phone contact:

'Indeed, the Government's asserted "failure" of the Internet rests on the implicit premise that too much speech occurs in that medium, and that speech there is too available to the participants. This is exactly the benefit of Internet communication, however. The Government, therefore, implicitly asks this court to limit both the amount of speech on the Internet and the availability of that speech. This argument is profoundly repugnant to First Amendment principles.'

—Judge Stewart Dalzell, ACLU v. Reno.

Mike Godwin, EFF Staff Counsel, can be reached at mnemonic@eff.org or at his office, 510–548–3290.

Godwin quotes a famous court decision that struck down a powerful attempt to censor the Internet in the USA; in doing so he indicates his support of free speech on the Internet. Godwin also offers the phone area code for within the USA but no indication that this is a US phone number; for some this might seem a minor point but it may fuel the resentment many outside the USA feel for US domination of cyberspace. Donath notes that many signatures involve in-jokes that will only be understood by others who have similar knowledge. For example, while the content of Godwin's signature should be enough to alert anyone to Godwin's interest in free speech on the Internet, the fact that it comes from a particularly important judgment ensures that those who recognise it have their insider status confirmed. Donath makes these points in relation to other examples, such as the following two.

> Doom: 5% Health 0% Armor, 59cent Tacos, Lets Go!
> Write failed on /dev/brain: file system full

(Donath, 1998)

In the first, the scoring style of the famed computer game Doom is parodied, while in the second the computer language UNIX is parodied to indicate that the development of this person's brain is failing. In both these cases, as opposed to Godwin, little can be understood from these signatures without knowledge of either Doom or UNIX and they function to include some in the joke and exclude others (Donath, 1998).

Handles are the self-chosen pseudonyms many employ on the Internet. If someone can choose the name section of their email address then this also constitutes a handle. The following is a list of handles used by hackers and hacker groups: Hack-Tic, Zoetermeer, Altenkirch, Eric Bloodaxe, Faustus, Maelstrom, Mercury, Mofo, Kaos Inc., Knights of Shadow, Master Hackers, MAD!, Legion of Doom, Farmers of Doom, the Phirm, Inner Circle I and Inner Circle II (Jordan and Taylor, 1998). Handles also occur in MUDs, Usenet posts (where they are often accompanied by an email address) and on listservs. In all these places, people's online interactions can be transformed into a stable avatar by all being referred to the one handle. Handles form names that allow the coalescence of various actions and styles into the one avatar. This is Sterling's imagined description of a teenage hacker's first steps into criminality, when the teenager finds that long-distance phone calls can be expensive:

> How horrifying to have made friends in another state and to be deprived of their company – and their software – just because telephone companies demand absurd amounts of money!…A few grumbles, complaints and inno- cent questions…will often elicit a sympathetic reply from another board user – someone with stolen codes to hand. You dither awhile, knowing this isn't quite right, then you make up your mind to try them anyhow – *and they work*! Suddenly you're doing something even your parents can't do. Six months ago you were just some kid – now your Crimson Flash of Area Code 512! You're bad – you're nationwide!
>
> (Sterling, 1992: 83)

Here it is Crimson Flash who uses stolen information to gain free long-distance phone calls and it is Crimson Flash who may or may not move on to more complicated computer adventures or may simply stay this bad. The actions of obtaining and using information for criminal ends is located and drawn together by the name or handle. An avatar can be constructed with a handle and, of course, there is nothing to stop someone developing several handles.

Finally, in some forums avatars are partially constructed by self-portraits. The use of the bio on the WELL has already been noted. In many online spaces users have a certain amount of space to offer a portrait of themselves that other users can access. On the WELL such self-portraits tend toward the realistic but on MUDs self-portraits tend toward the fantastic.

> Look Rainar
> Rainar is a magnificent, magnesium scaled dragon. He has deep, caring,
> green eyes. His body is long and thin but muscular. He is always sweet,
> caring and helpful to anyone who needs it, you can ask him anytime for
> anything and he will try to help you. A faint white mist surrounds his
> body....He is awake and looks alert.
>
> (Hertz, 1994: 189)

Someone travels in this MUD as Rainar the dragon. Anyone who uses the
'look' command will receive this description and have to deal with a
dragon, not as unusual on MUDs as in real life. Confusingly, the dragon
part of the description is possibly the least helpful for understanding the
nature of this avatar, whereas the emphasis on helping is significant. New
users of different places in cyberspace are called, almost universally, newbies
and the inevitable mistakes that accompany having to learn a number of
different systems that control different spaces (from asking the same question for the 1,000 time on a Usenet newsgroup to being unable to master
basic commands on MUDs) mean that many newbies are attacked as often
as they are helped. Rainar's self-portrait indicates a willingness to help, an
important clue to the identity of this avatar. What clues does the following
offer?

> Look Alendia
> Alendia is a very attractive squirreloid in her later teens. Her soft red fur
> clings damply to her body and a few droplets of water trickle from her
> cutely upturned pink nose. Her long red hair hangs silkenly down her
> back and a few damp strands fall in front of her large gentle eyes. She is
> completely nude before you. The fur of her inner thighs is orange and
> damp, becoming thinner and steamy near the uppermost edge.
>
> (Quittner, 1994a: 97, 138)

It is perhaps no surprise, even from this one self-portrait, that this is a MUD
where 'People describe themselves as furry cuddly animals: more times than not,
they have furry cuddly animal sex' (Quittner, 1994a: 97). Alendia's self-portrait
plays into this environment and, at the same time, helps to construct it. As
with handles, multiple avatars can be generated, with the additional complica-
tion that one avatar can generate multiple self-portraits and can shift between
them. The person behind Rainar could shift into Shiro the white tiger, or
Ulrik-the-Slayer who enjoys killing people, or Peter-Pan. For Rainar/Shiro/
Ulrik-the-Slayer/ Peter-Pan one problem is that another identity, Thorin, is the
one that other users in the MUD know best, despite the offline user's preference
for Shiro (Hertz, 1994: 187–99). Here, despite the possibility of multiplicity, the
need for some stability means that one avatar may become more important
whatever the creator's wishes.

Taken together, signatures, handles and self-portraits provide a number of resources through which virtually totally self-chosen elements are available to construct avatars. These will be relevant only to certain places in cyberspace but at least one is often available. When added to the resources that are not freely chosen, email address and style, a range of tactics are at hand for the construction of an avatar. All of these resources are also multiple and they can be implemented in different ways, both in different parts of cyberspace and in the same part. Gilboa recounts the experience of one avatar attacking her, while another comforted her, only to find that the two avatars were controlled by the one offline identity who was using them to create intimacy with her (Gilboa, 1996:102–3):

> Few people appear the same to other people across a network as they would through a telephone or in person. The location, gender, and character of a network user may bear little relation to the user's mundane identity....personal traits that might be distracting to a listener can be left out, or an argument can be furthered by constructing a personality to match.
>
> (Quarterman, 1990: 5)

People are not anonymous in cyberspace, as they construct identities that they use there. What can be anonymous is the identity they use in their day-to-day non-virtual lives. What can be reinvented or left behind are the clues that everyone gains from seeing each other – race, age, sex, dress sense and so on – in favour of the words scrolling across the screen (Baym, 1995: 139–141; Dery, 1993a: 561). However, the relationship between online and offline identity is not necessarily one of erasure or separation, rather each tactic or resource generates a different type of relationship between online and offline.

The relationship between online and offline identity, or in the present terminology between avatar and identity, can best be understood as elastic, particularly as even the best and strongest elastic can break. Avatars can develop to the point where the connections between identities is so stretched, so tenuous, that the 'ping' of broken elastic can be heard in cyberspace, but the connection can also be surprisingly strong, with collective refusals to think of avatars as distinct from identities. For example, the driving force beneath the tragedy in the myth of Julie is the refusal of both Julie's connected identity, Sanford, and of the avatars Julie met and befriended to treat Julie as an avatar. This is perfectly understandable, as these discussions were premised on the belief that avatar and identity were equivalent. As all participants learned, painfully, some distance between identity and avatar is a premise of cyberspace that cannot easily be controlled. In other places, a strong, unspoken identification of identity and avatar is neither assumed nor a problem. Meeting an avatar that can shift between being a dragon and a white tiger, but still type a hundred words a minute, means some accepted distance between avatar and identity is normal in this corner of cyberspace.

The resources for construction of avatars offer three broadly distinct tensions between identity and avatar. Email and Web home page addresses create connections between avatar and identity that appear to be verifiably independently of the claims of the avatar. Claiming to be female with an email address of bill.king@domain will require some explanation, which is not impossible for a shortening of Billie or on the principles of the song 'A Boy Named Sue'. Web home pages are also not entirely reliable – what is seen on them is controlled and designed by the person whose home page it is – but they also provide what seem to be verifiable connections between identity and avatar both in the address and the content of the page. For example, Donath notes the following identification of a false message from its email address:

> >jake@cleveland.freenet.edu
> >Hacker wanted to disassemble commercial program and rewrite to our specs.
> >This is not a B.S. post, we will pay BIG $$$ to have this service performed.
> >Email for details.
> Nobody with 'BIG $$$' to spend is going to be writing that message from Cleveland Freenet. :-)
>
> (Donath, 1998)

Jake is asking for an illegal service and promising lots of money, but the reply deduces from the fact he is emailing from a freenet, which generally offers cheaper forms of access, that lots of money is probably not on the cards. Jake's explicit claim not to have made a bull shit (B.S.) post is rejected because of the independently verifiable marker of the connection between Jake's avatar and identity. At times the marker of identity is strong enough to counter any attempted separation between avatar and identity

The resources that were grouped above as self-descriptions offer some of the most fruitful ground for breaking the connection between avatar and identity. Indeed, some places seem to demand a disconnection, such as MUDs. Anybody who identifies avatar with identity is going to have to think when Rainer/Shiro the dragon/tiger is met. In MUDs, some creativity in the gap between identity and avatar is a condition of participation. Of course, this creativity is one of the attractions of MUDs and some others of the more exotic corners of cyberspace and these places might almost be defined by their attempt to stretch and break the elastic between avatar and identity. For example, MUD marriages have appeared in a number of MUDs, as well as online sex. Ito recounts the tensions between avatar and identity around netsex and MUD marriage this way:

> my partner in real life often eyes me suspiciously as I sit in front of my terminal – 'You're not MUDmarried are you?' 'Are you having netsex?' We both laugh, yet I scrupulously avoid MUD romance because of a sort of

uncomfortable guilty twinge....By contrast, one of my MUD friends, despite protestations from her jealous real-life mate, is married to a number of different MUDders on different MUDs. Though her real-life mate is also a MUDder, Tenar, or Melissa in real life, refuse to MUDmarry him, or even to have virtual sex with him.

(Ito, 1997: 95–6)

The difference between Ito and Melissa is her willingness to snap the connection between identity and avatar. The suspicion of Ito's mate springs from this recognised ability and confirms the power of self-descriptions to stretch the relationship between avatar and identity. Ito's uncertainty, nevertheless, demonstrates that making this separation is not necessarily easy for everyone. Simply casting off the identities we have learned, constructed and become in offline life is not as straightforward as many people's first yell of delight and experimentation with avatars might suggest. Branwyn's exploration of virtual sex found that

while most of the people I talked to use fantasy personae on occasion, more than half reported that they basically 'stick to the facts'. 'I find it much more of a turn-on to think that someone is aroused by the real me,' said one respondent.

(Branwyn, 1993: 788–9)

Branwyn's respondent wants to make his avatar opaque to his identity, to make his avatar a copy of something essential in 'the real me'. This both confirms the ability of avatars and identities to be distinct and poses the same possibility as Ito's attitude to marriage does; perhaps the enjoyment of or commitment to an avatar will in some way be related to identity. Ito was worried about virtually betraying her real lover and Branwyn's anonymous respondent has better sex when real is projected into virtual. In both cases, the connection between avatar and identity is not worth breaking. It also seems common sense that the identities that we have – our age, experience, gender, race and more – cannot simply be put aside when faced with a keyboard. Of course, experimentation is possible but this will only be overlaid on an existing identity. The elastic between identity[6] and avatar, in this view, can never be broken.

One of the resources for avatar construction might also be expected to betray avatars for identities. Style is where the return of a repressed identity might be expected. No matter how hard someone worked on their avatar as a dragon, many expect their real identity as human might come out and this defines the third broad type of tension between identity and avatar. For example, Hertz was a guest in a MUD when she first meets Thorin/Rainar/Shiro; this meant she had no character of her own and the name she chose for the initial encounter indicated that she was a guest (Copper_Guest). Later she received her own full character and returned to meet Thorin again. When she finally mentions events, finding a threatening skeleton, that allow Thorin to connect the guest named 'Copper_Guest' to the new character called 'Rollergirl', he says 'Gee and I thought you were male' (Hertz, 1994: 279). But now Hertz's avatar not only has her gender set to female, she even announces the fact in her name. Thorin helps her to construct a house and learn some of the MUD's features, then he 'switches into his human form and makes a pass' (Hertz, 1994: 281). When Rollergirl rejects him, Thorin begins to write both sides of the encounter, calling for a kiss and then telling Rollergirl she doesn't want it to stop. Rollergirl asks him if he's a mind-reader and eventually skates away (after having been virtually sliced into tiles, hugged, paved over for a parking lot and shot through a basketball hoop) leaving Hertz to comment 'Sticks and stones and techie-boys who can't deal with women, that's what MUDs are made of.' (Hertz, 1994: 283, 281–3). Where there once was a shape-shifting dragon/tiger/helper instead stood a sexually harassing, emotionally stunted boy in love with technology. The identity Hertz now 'knows' to be behind the avatar she first came to like has been conveyed by a style that shifted swiftly from realising an avatar is a woman, to helping, to asking for sex and becoming virtually violent when refused.

Thorin makes clear that one way style may work is in connecting an avatar to an identity. Hertz/Rollergirl had been around cyberspace long enough to recognise a certain identity. When the first pass comes her way she comments 'I've seen this movie before' (Hertz, 1994: 281) and goes on to have her preconceptions neatly confirmed. Style has the power to undermine proclaimed avatars revealing characteristics that will often be taken to be part of an offline identity. Style will often determine the strength of the elastic between anyone's avatars and identities. Style will determine whether that elastic can break or whether stretched to its limit it will snap back and leave an avatar cracked to reveal an identity. Here style emerges as less obvious and less spectacular than some other resources for avatar construction but possibly as more powerful in the construction of stable avatars. You can pose as a dragon, gay or a dwarf, you can think yourself into the role your avatar demands, you can array yourself with software helpers, but in the end stable relationships in cyberspace will be built out of stable avatars, and the more stable the avatar the more important style is likely to become.

Identity fluidity is a fact of virtual life. Even when the façade cracks and someone believes an identity has stepped through an avatar, this can never be known for certain until offline contact is made. But the short step from this point, that so many make, to claiming that offline identities are irrelevant online is a mistake. There is a complicated connection between offline and online personalities that allows many to believe that, at times, the offline and online become one and allows, at times, for them to be disconnected. The reverse mistake would be an all too simple connection between identity and avatar, where it is assumed the identity will finally come out and consume the avatar. There are three broad sorts of tension between identity and avatar: evidence that seems immediately to define an avatar as a false expression of an identity, resources that allow the connection to be stretched to breaking point and interactions that slowly undermine either the separation or connection claimed between avatar or identity. Personalities are constructed through resources online that are different to offline, preventing the use of many offline tactics for identifying others' identity. Online characters are constructed and judged through a number of markers that replace offline ones: addresses, handles, signatures, self-portraits and styles. Where we might look at someone's face and think 'old', online we look at their address and think '.edu, student or teacher?' Where we might examine clothes, online we look at what is written and learn a personality from a style. Identity is both present in cyberspace and different to non-virtual space; identity is different enough online to be called something different. Avatars and identities, online and offline.

Anti-hierarchical

The second component of online life that appears obvious to the individual online is that it is inherently anti-hierarchical. The distribution of authority online mimics the Internet's technology because it is decentred, with no central authority standing in the information flow. Attempts to censor or restrict access to parts of cyberspace can simply be bypassed, allowing unrestricted access to online information. Further, communication from many people to many people is close to the norm in cyberspace. This opens participation in decision making, creating the potential for conclusions to be reached in more egalitarian ways than offline. Jones claims cyberspace is inherently anti-hierarchical because of identity fluidity:

> Indeed, it is difficult to understand just how hierarchy and community can coexist via CMC, in part because of the seemingly anarchic (or at least unstructured) nature of many computer networks. A common denominator linking hierarchy and community is identity, not only in terms of one's sense of self but also in terms of one's sense of others. CMC provides ample room for identity but not for its fixing and structuring.
>
> (Jones, 1995b: 30)

However it is justified, there are widespread claims that a decentred, anti-hierarchically organised communications technology promotes decentred, anti-hierarchical communication. Put this way, the claim of anti-hierarchism appears to be based on a technological determinism: TCP/IP is a tool of liberation. But such pure or strong forms of technological determinism are always weak because they define causes of society through non-social systems, technologies, that appear social as soon as they are themselves investigated. The anti-hierarchical nature of cyberspace might appear compelling from the viewpoint of the individual but how this occurs needs further examination and, like identity fluidity, whether hierarchies are eliminated or reinvented online needs to be examined. Three ways in which hierarchies are affected will be explored in turn: identity, many-to-many communication and anti-censorship. It will become clear that while identity is not a certain basis for claiming cyberspace is anti-hierarchical, both many-to-many communication and anti-censorship cut across offline hierarchies and can only be negated by intervention in online life by offline forces. Most of the claims given below concern the transformation of offline hierarchies in online life. However, some discussion is also necessary of new forms of hierarchy that may be emerging online. It is in the simultaneous transformations of offline and online that further tendrils of individual power in cyberspace can be revealed.

Jones' claim that identity fluidity prevents online hierarchies seems at first sight valid. Laura Miller 'values online forums precisely because they mandate equal time for each user who chooses to take it and forestall various "alpha male" tactics like interrupting, loudness, or exploiting the psychosocial advantages of greater size or a deeper voice' (Miller, 1995: 55). Two different, though related, means of subverting offline hierarchies result from identity fluidity: removal of the signs of identity and removal of certain tactics for maintaining hierarchies. The masking of offline identity has been thoroughly discussed in the previous section; it only remains to point out that if people cannot see skin colour, hear accents or detect any other such identity marker then they cannot be placed in a hierarchy on the basis of that identity. A woman in an offline office may be mistaken for a clerk or secretary rather than a more powerful position because she is a woman; in online life everyone simply deals with avatars. However, when discussing identity fluidity it was also shown that identities do not disappear in cyberspace but are constructed with different resources to offline identities. This logically means that hierarchies based on identity will not disappear from cyberspace but will be reinvented on the basis of new forms of online identity. All the different resources for avatar construction are potential bases for new forms of hierarchy. Style, in particular, forms an important basis for hierarchy with different participants considered more or less important depending on their style. People can be dismissed from serious consideration according to their style. The warning quoted above from the cypherpunk mailing list attempts to identify one person through their style and ensure messages from this identity are not taken seriously; L. Detweiler is a 'net.loon'. Noting that hierarchies have emerged online makes no comment about whether this is good or bad. The famous example of an online group set up by and for women to discuss feminism that was open to men and eventually became populated solely by men demanding justifications for the simplest premises of feminism, thereby destroying the discussion as a useful resource for feminists, raises problems about places where no hierarchy exists. The key point is not whether hierarchies are good or bad, but that new hierarchies in online life result from all the resources for identity construction already outlined.

The second aspect of identities and hierarchy is that the means for maintaining hierarchies in offline life are often absent in cyberspace. As Miller noted, shouting someone down is impossible online. It is possible to indicate shouting when typing by using CAPITAL LETTERS but using capital letters does not prevent others being read or from writing. Similarly, speaking in a very thick accent or stammering will not prevent someone having a turn and being able to write. This is undoubtedly different to offline hierarchies, where various 'politics of conversation' can arise as part of broad social inequalities. The micro-politics of daily interaction is disturbed by the reduction of interaction to whatever appears on screen and the inability of an avatar to prevent another avatar speaking. Again the disruption of offline hierarchies does not mean the elimination of hierarchies but their recreation on different principles. For example, the ability to read email addresses, outlined above, will allow a hierarchical ordering of messages, with b.gates@microsoft.com perhaps gaining more attention for his messages than dark.knight@hacktick.nl (depending on your interests, of course). Styles will again be crucial, with simple abilities like typing quickly and accurately or an ability to use easily the particular style of writing of a group, meaning that certain avatars will gain more valued positions establishing hierarchies. It is not so much a matter of proclaiming the revolutionary, anti-hierarchical nature of online life but of tracing new forms of hierarchy that are built in different ways to hierarchies familiar in offline life.

Identity has ambiguous effects on hierarchy online. It certainly dislocates the forms of hierarchy that commonly operate offline but it does not offer the radical possibility of eliminating hierarchies altogether. Reinvented online hierarchies are based on the means of creating identities that have already been outlined. Signatures, styles, particular cryptic languages (imho, onna) and more all provide resources through which hierarchies can be recreated. This can also be seen as more positive than the elimination of hierarchies because it allows the vast amounts of information generated in cyberspace to be ordered according to the quality of someone's words and not their social or institutional position, their loud voice, gender, race or whatever. Those who gain recognition online and whose messages are automatically accorded some respect, reflecting a higher position in online hierarchies, may achieve this status through the quality of their writing. From this point of view, certain people deserve to be treated with greater respect. Against such claims it can be noted that hierarchies may be constructed out of such things as reading email addresses. Any hierarchies emerging from avatars stabilised through any elements except style, and perhaps signatures, would be hierarchies that pass over people's words. In assessing the effect of identity fluidity on hierarchies there are a number of possible conclusions about its value, but we certainly see offline hierarchies as powerfully dislocated.

The second way hierarchies are dislocated is through many-to-many communication and its ability to include more people in decision making than was previously practicable. The inclusion of many people in offline decision making is limited by the need to meet together, to speak only one at a time, to overcome the hierarchies of identity and so on. The ability of communication in cyberspace to overcome many of the inequalities based on identity and to include many people communicating to many others can fundamentally alter the hierarchies that govern decision making. Further, the ease and breadth of access to the expertise of others allows those who might not have been able to participate in expert discussions to have support in doing so. For example, in the myth of Philcat the presence of various medical professionals on the parenting discussion group allowed expert advice to be given to parents who then had greater knowledge when dealing with medical staff. Independent checks of a doctor's opinion are not easily available to many of us but behind Philcat and his family was a whole team of medical experts, who also happened to be virtual friends. There are then two strands to many-to-many communication that undermine offline hierarchies: the form of decision making and access to expertise.

In any institution, from national government to local co-operative, the ability to include and exclude members from decision making is limited not just by political concerns over who controls the institution but also by sheer physical difficulties. It can be difficult enough to arrange a meeting of fifteen co-operative members without having to ensure also that everyone has enough information and ability to participate equally. The problems multiply exponentially when institutions with hundreds, if not thousands, of people are considered. It is often noted that no matter how much of a corporation individual shareholders own, they have little ability to influence its affairs. Obviously, there are matters of control and authority here, but even with the most egalitarian will in the world it would be difficult for large institutions to broaden and democratise decision-making procedures. Cyberspace can alter such problems by removing the constraint of physical presence. Discussions carried on through email or by asynchronous posting, as used on Usenet, open possible avenues for greater group participation. The forms of decision making that many-to-many communication offers will still have a physical limit: there is a finite number of emails or conference systems anybody can follow and still perform the other functions required by their institution or life. But even given this limit, cyberspace offers opportunities for breaking down hierarchies within institutions. Sproull and Kiesler have both conducted experiments and summarised other empirical investigations into the effect of cyberspace on offline institutions (Sproull and Kiesler, 1986; 1993). They conclude that small-group discussions using computer conferences and email induce participants to talk more frankly and equally than in face-to-face discussions. Using five laboratory studies they consistently found that cyberspatial discussions contained greater participation than face-to-face discussions – at times electronic discussions were three times as open as face to face. The price of this greater democracy was two-fold. First, decisions took far longer to be reached in electronic discussion. The necessarily wider discussion led to deeper examination of more aspects of a problem, with decisions taking four times as long to be reached, and in one case a decision was never reached before the experiment had to be concluded. Second, people were far more likely to insult each other. Participants were more frequently and more openly angry with each other, with the decrease in identity markers allowing more vitriolic exchanges. The greater ease of insulting people has been widely commented on and is generally called flaming (Sproull and Kiesler, 1993: 108–10). Cyberspace certainly offers different methods for conducting discussions and making decisions, which allow for greater participation. There is, of course, no reason why institutions have to choose this greater democracy. Sproull and Kiesler point out that *Newsday* magazine converted from an open network to one in which journalists could receive but not send email, while their managers could do both. Journalists were thought by managers to be spending too much time on email and not enough on journalism (Sproull and Kiesler, 1993: 108). However, this represents a restriction from offline authority on online life. Managers had to activate their offline authority to restrict their employees' freedom online. The relations between offline and online will be considered in more detail in subsequent chapters; the point here is that the inherently anti-hierarchical forms of communication available online had to be restricted by offline authority.

Cyberspace, as the myth of Philcat teaches us, also offers information that may help fracture offline hierarchies. Sproull and Kiesler note that electronic communication fosters messages of a type that begin with 'Does anybody know…?', exactly the support that Philcat sought. Further, Sproull and Kiesler found that around 15 per cent of those who responded to such a general request for information knew the person who made the request (Sproull and Kiesler, 1993: 108–16). This confirms that many-to-many communication both encourages general requests for information and meets those requests from a broad range of users, including a significant number of sources that would otherwise be unavailable. The low cost of responding to electronic requests, in both time and effort, means that people are willing to respond to requests from strangers. Many-to-many communication reorders offline hierarchies both in forms of communication and in the amount of information available to users:

> Organizations are traditionally built around two key concepts: hierarchical decomposition of goals and tasks and the stability of employee relationships over time. In the fully networked organization that may become increasingly common in the future, task structures may be much more flexible and dynamic. Hierarchy will not vanish, but it will be augmented by distributed lattices of interconnections.
>
> (Sproull and Kiesler, 1993: 117)

The contribution of cyberspace to offline institutions is to disturb the hierarchies that order them. This disordering is contained and recomposed by offline authority, sometimes to the extent of refusing some of the key anti-hierarchical implications of many-to-many communication, but connecting offline institutions to online communication ensures some reordering of hierarchies. The second result of many-to-many communication, wider access to information, connects to the third main force disturbing offline hierarchies, and this is cyberspace's inherent refusal of censorship.

'The Internet treats censorship as damage, it routes around it.' This is the famous maxim coined by John Gilmore[7] that many use to support the claim that cyberspace is inherently anti-censorship. Richard MacKinnon explored the extent of online authority by searching for the censorship of messages on Usenet discussions. MacKinnon randomly selected 200 articles from 3,971 Usenet groups and found 81 per cent showed no signs of censorship or moderation while only 9.5 per cent showed the strongest signs of censorship. Though this is only one study, MacKinnon shows the rhetoric of anti-censorship is not hollow (MacKinnon, 1995: 132–4). Such a free flow of information undermines hierarchies because more people can find information that would previously have been blocked. Not only is there a greater pool of expertise available but information that governments or courts might have restricted is almost impossible to hold back once it is free in cyberspace. The global nature of cyberspace is important here, as it only requires one country connected to the net to allow the publication of some information for that information to be let loose in cyberspace. Information restricted in an offline nation-state will then be available in cyberspace, subverting the national boundaries that have helped in the past to control access to information. One of the best-known examples of this was a Canadian judge's attempt to ban media coverage of a sensational sex and murder trial, the Karla Homolka affair.

In 1993 a Canadian judge decided that the interests of a fair trial demanded that media coverage of Paul Teale and Karla Homolka-Teale's trial for the sex-related murder of two teenagers should be restricted. The judge felt that this was an exceptional case in the interests of the victims' families and in finding an unbiased jury (Shade, 1996: 19–20). The Canadian press was muzzled but Usenet was not. A number of bulletin boards carrying details were set up and eventually a newsgroup devoted to the trial emerged (alt.fan.karla-homolka). Canadian universities and Internet service providers began to censor the newsgroup, removing access to it. However, all that needed to be done was to cross-post messages (i.e. post the same message on two or more different newsgroups) appearing on alt.fan.karla-homolka to groups such as soc.culture.canadian or alt.censorship for the same information to be available on different sites. 'As university sites discontinued the newsgroup, it became a fabulous Internet hunt to locate the sites where banned material could be located' (Shade, 1996: 21). Someone even set up an email mailing list concerning the trial and used an anonymous remailer ensuring they could not be traced (Shade, 1996: 19–23; Brenner and Metson, 1994). As Gilmore predicted, the Internet simply flowed around the blockages set up to control information, for better or worse. Finding the information was simply a matter of looking in cyberspace, something helped greatly by people publishing guides on how to do this.[8]

Censorship of information in cyberspace is difficult, though this does not prevent governments trying. Most notably, the government of Singapore is planning to monitor all traffic from the Internet in and out of the city-state and China has implemented strong regulations against certain content (EFF, 1996; Barme and Ye, 1997). The success or failure of these attempts is yet to be seen. However, the evidence from cases like Homolka is that for those who wish to restrict access to certain forms of information, the question should not be a matter of censoring cyberspace but of allowing access to it at all. As with previous discussions, the subversion of hierarchy is not propounded as a necessarily good thing. Clearly the judge in the Homolka case had good reasons, at least to himself, for restricting access. The point is not whether this subversion of hierarchy is good or bad but the fact that it occurs. Whether those who control information understand it or not, cyberspace operates on different principles of information distribution than meatspace.

The ultimate conclusion is that offline hierarchies are subverted by cyberspace but are also reconstituted in cyberspace. The only power certain of restoring offline control over online information is control of access to parts of cyberspace. In the *Newsday* and Homolka examples, the reaction of those who sought to control information was to restrict users from being able to reach certain parts of cyberspace. Even these attempts can often, in turn, be subverted as cyberspace simply bypasses the obstruction placed in front of some information. The second conclusion is that the subversion of hierarchy does not mean that cyberspace is devoid of hierarchy. Rather, new and different hierarchies emerge. The nature of these hierarchies is closely tied to issues of identity, as the resources for constructing avatars also provide the foundations for new hierarchies. Within cyberspace, interpreting email addresses, assessing someone's style or examining a self-description all provide means of locating avatars within entirely virtual hierarchies. Locating this close connection between identity construction and virtual hierarchies also raises the last of the three key components of power in cyberspace from the perspective of the individual – the fact that it is all information.

A world made of information

All the factors that ensure different forms of identity and hierarchy exist in cyberspace are touched on day by day by the individuals who journey there. The difference cyberspace makes to the individual is, necessarily, constantly felt and experienced. Underpinning these differences in identity and hierarchy is the realisation that these changes come from cyberspace being a place made out of knowledge:

the space of cyberspace is predicated on knowledge and information, on the common beliefs and practices of a society abstracted from physical space. Part of that knowledge and information, though, lies in simply knowing how to navigate cyberspace. But the important element in cyberspatial social relations is the sharing of information.

(Jones, 1995b: 19)

Sharing information allows the construction of avatars, self-descriptions, signatures, styles because all are constructed out of the words that pass between people. The renovation of hierarchies in offline life by cyberspatial communication and the construction of different hierarchies in cyberspace result from different methods of sharing information and different access to expertise in cyberspace. When individuals experience cyberspace they come to the third recognition that life in cyberspace is fundamentally constituted by information. These three elements can be brought together through the example of flaming.

As already mentioned in Sproull and Kiesler's work, the release from offline social cues has a negative side. Abuse can be given anonymously, reactions to comments can be thoughtless and deliberately hurtful. It is as if not having the physical presence of a human means people feel free to attack and hurt. This recurring pattern is called flaming. At times flaming escalates from individual insults to whole flame wars in which different communities attack each other. Usenet witnessed one such flame war begun by the newsgroup alt.tasteless, dedicated to the most tasteless topics possible, against a group called rec.pets.cats devoted to all aspects of cats. Prestige on alt.tasteless came from being as disgusting as possible, while on rec.pets.cats it came from being interesting on cats. Alt.tasteless is a group of people who 'have devoted a lifetime to collecting revolting facts, disgusting jokes and synonyms for the word penis', while rec.pets.cats is a group of people devoted to caring for furry friends (Quittner, 1994b, 48). At one point the members of alt.tasteless decided to invade rec.pets.cats. They began by posting somewhat strange but plausible requests for help to rec.pets.cats (someone asked how to get a cat off-heat), and then moved to posting strange and disgusting articles such as curing a cat's digestive problems by shooting multiple .357 copper-jacketed hollow-point bullets through it longitudinally. Members of alt.tasteless would post bizarre problems and then other alt.tasteless members would answer with increasingly disgusting and bizarre suggestions, all to the horror of the devotees of cats. Rec.pets.cats eventually ceased to exist as a functioning community devoted to cats because of the amount of offensive material being posted. Posting articles about cute furry cats back on alt.tasteless, as revenge, somehow did not seem an adequate response (Quittner, 1994b).

One virtual community invaded another. The avatars of each community, their particular styles, concerns and even acronyms, allowed for a clash between fur and vulgarity. The lack of hierarchy made it difficult to regain control of rec.pets.cats as the information set in train by those from alt.tasteless was difficult to censor. Responses from rec.pets.cats were based on control of information. In some virtual environments it is possible to set filters or kill files so that messages or postings from certain addresses are not received. For example, in MUDs there is often a command 'name@gag', an electronic gag, so that the named avatar's conversation will not appear on your screen. Rec.pets.cats used kill files to recapture their space by eliminating access to it for certain people from alt.tasteless. Because their community was constructed out of information about cats, ensuring that only appropriate information could be posted would recreate their community. However, they also found the lack of an effective hierarchy and the ability to create multiple avatars meant that more and more identities were created by the devotees of tastelessness to invade their space. Ultimately, cat-lovers' activity was reduced almost solely to creating kill files that would restrict access. At this point, rec.pets.cats appealed outside of cyberspace to the administrators who controlled access to cyberspace for some of the most persistent attackers. When the adherents of alt.tasteless found that what they thought of as a game could mean they would be removed entirely from cyberspace they retreated and the flame war collapsed (Quittner, 1994b: 51–3).

In this flame war, most of the elements of cyberpower for the individual are present. There are communities constructed around avatars whose resources for the creation of identity are different to those offline. There are mangled hierarchies that rely on informational strategies, such as killing incoming information, but which are often not effective within cyberspace. And there is a world that is constructed out of information. The words flowing past individuals' screens around the world create communities. And this is true of all the parts of cyberspace, whether it is email used for corporate decision making or MUDs for collective sexual exploration. The possibilities for avatars and altered hierarchies result from information. With this third component in place the circuit of cyberpower that is most obvious, and springs from the perception that cyberspace is entered as an individual, is complete. It flows around the three connected principles of identity fluidity, renovated hierarchies and informational spaces.

Cyberpower at the individual

The most optimistic views of cyberspace's effects flow from cyberpower of the individual. Cyberspace appears as a place in which individuals can put aside many of the inequalities of offline life, simply because nobody knows if they are 'really' female, old or disabled. In a place in which anything can be said and no power can prevent it being heard, censorship is simply minor, local damage. Cyberspace appears to be a place that undermines the hierarchies of offline life, in which different hierarchies that come to exist depend on the quality of thought and writing – a place where even the destructive behaviour that is peculiar to it, flaming, is still only words. Cyberspace is this place, when we begin from the individual. The following chapters will complicate this bright cyberdawn, offering darker visions of cyberspace's meaning, but to conclude this chapter the need is, first, to move out to a greater level of abstraction and identify the particular type of power individuals feel in cyberspace and, second, to move to greater specificity by outlining the typical cultural and political issues that result from this form of cyberpower. In the first case, we have power as the possession of individuals and, in the second, we have a politics strung across the two axes of access to cyberspace and individual rights within cyberspace.

Cyberpower as a possession

If we think about all the tales that are relevant to the nature of individual cyberpower, we can see they all embody a notion of personal empowerment. In the myth of Julie, Sanford became a woman to experience conversations he desired and, until the deception was revealed, Julie provided support to a number of women. In cybersex, people can experiment and explore in ways they cannot do offline. In institutions, cyberspace can reorder hierarchies to benefit individuals. Even where it is not clear that empowerment is all that is on offer, the power of the individual still seems to dominate cyberspace. In the flame war between alt.tasteless and rec.pets.cats, both communities were first empowered to exist – that is, to find other people committed to discussions about tasteless-ness or cats – but alt.tasteless then had the ability to invade rec.pets.cats. Online cat lovers found themselves losing the community cyberspace had allowed in the first place, but in kill files they engaged with each individual attacker. When cat lovers battled within cyberspace the battle was with individuals, not the collective of alt.tasteless.

Power continually appears as a possession that individuals have to greater or lesser extent. Whether others like it or not, identity fluidity supports the masquerades and experiments of avatars. Whether others like it or not, renovated hierarchies mean greater expertise and more inclusive forms of decision making. These flows of power produce little pieces of power – the ability to change gender, the ability to contact experts – that individuals take up and possess, utilising them to impose their will. For example, Sanford was able to utilise identity fluidity successfully to create an alternate life in the avatar Julie or Philcat was able to gain expertise. Power here is only apparent in its effects, in its realisation against resistance; like any possession it lies dormant in the pocket until the individual calls it into action. Sanford's initial reason for creating Julie was to gain access to women's conversations denied to him as a man. He found and utilised the power of identity fluidity against the emotional resistance of women to men. When any of these individual possessions of power, of the capacity for action, are systematised, then forms of domination emerge. In the flame war between alt.tasteless and rec.pets.cats, the individual actions of those from alt.tasteless, each avatar utilising both identity fluidity (concealing their lack of concern for cats) and renovated hierarchies (even with kill files they could not be kept out), eventually culminated in the domination of rec.pets.cats. Trolling is another example. When trolling is used systematically to establish boundaries between those who can recognise and enjoy a good troll from those who cannot, then a system of dominance appears out of the individual actions of those able to indulge in trolling because of the powers they possess in cyberspace.

The form of cyberpower that emerges when we take the obvious starting point for analysis of cyberspace, the individual in front of the screen, is cyberpower as a virtual possession. This cyberpower, first, underpins the ability to impose an intention or a will on someone or something else, second, is only realised against resistance and, third, may accumulate into systems of domination. By beginning from the common sense view of cyberspace we find the common sense view of power. Cyberpower from this perspective consists of three elements in constant circulation with each other – identity fluidity, renovated hierarchies, informational spaces – that each articulate a sense of power being a possession one avatar can utilise for or against another avatar. This is the abstract picture of cyberpower from the perspective of the individual and it gives rise not only to the wonderful forms of social and cultural life already examined but also to a distinctive form of politics. This cyberpolitics, flowing from cyberpower as individualised possession, is strung across the two axes of access to cyberspace and individual rights within cyberspace. Exploring these axes completes the analysis of cyberpower at the level of the individual in cyberspace.

Cyberpolitics: access and rights

If cyberspace and the Internet are inherently anti-hierarchical, allow people to experiment with their identity and provide access to a wide range of information, then a key issue is participation. Who has access? The answer outlined in the previous chapter is a small, privileged sector of developed societies. The inequalities of access are distributed in two directions: first between the developed and developing nations and second within nations. Between the developed and developing (or overdeveloped and developing) nations there is an enormous disparity that mirrors many other international inequalities. Similarly, within even the most advanced cyberspace nation, the USA, there are internal differences between different communities and, again, these mirror the basic inequalities of such nations. Access is then a politics structured around the point at which online and offline are connected and concerns restricted access to cyberspace. There are two problems that must be considered when trying to analyse or change access: cost and culture.

Cost is an obvious consideration. To access cyberspace a computer, a connection and a network service are needed and all three cost money. For example, it is not enough to have a personal computer, you also need a modem that will allow your computer to talk to other computers. Then you need to pay for the line that will carry your messages, most often a telephone line on which your call to cyberspace is charged just the same as a normal voice phone call. Your computer's message then has to reach an organisation that will connect it to the Internet, FidoNet or some other entry point to cyberspace. But there are further cost assumptions, for a reliable electrical system is needed to power the computer, a reliable phone or other communication system to carry the message and local cyberspace service providers, otherwise an international phone call is needed. For most of the world's population one, if not all three, of these are likely to be missing (Wresch, 1996; Barlow, 1998). A possible answer to such problems is even greater technological development. For example, the invention of a clockwork radio has been an enormous technological breakthrough for many impoverished countries, allowing information to be received by many people. The inventor of this breakthrough has applied the mechanism to a laptop computer making it work on clockwork power. Some expect further breakthroughs and their commercialisation will be necessary to overcome some of the cost problems in gaining access to cyberspace (Bowers, 1997). However, more generally speaking only the rise of countries out of economic difficulties that often make fresh water a far greater priority than access to cyberspace will solve the problems of international inequities of access.

Cost gives rise to two policy directions that recur in cyberpolitics: universal service and universal access. The first of these has as its goal the right of everyone to a service that can connect them to cyberspace. This may well have to be paid for but the right is to have a local, reasonably priced and adequate connection service. Arguments here revolve around cross-subsidising rural access or ensuring that more powerful connections than the most common modem connections, such as ISDN,[9] are not priced out of individuals' pockets. The second policy is universal access, which sets as its goal the right of everyone to be connected to cyberspace. Here typical solutions emerge in free terminals in public libraries or the connection of every public institution, such as schools, hospitals and so on. The two solutions are often mistaken for each other, even though they give rise to quite different policies.

Where countries do not even have the basic infrastructure to allow access to cyberspace, then cost seems a key consideration. Even the most optimistic view of the powers of cyberspace would have difficulty underpinning social policies that placed gaining access above problems like a lack of running, clean water or a reliable energy infrastructure (Wresch, 1996). However, it is also true that cost can be radically overestimated as a restricting factor, particularly for inequalities within developed countries. Looking at prices for up-to-date multimedia personal computers may convince many people that cyberspace is an expensive place to visit, without their realising that expensive equipment is not needed. As the next chapter will make clear, hackers can be some of the most powerful inhabitants of cyberspace, yet

> these lower income kids didn't have to have the latest computer gear, just somebody's discarded Toshiba laptop or a phone booth. It's not big capital investments. In fact, the barrier seems to be less than simply knowing how to go about it. It's something like libraries. In the USA professional librarians take the position that the role they play is custodians of information so that

even people who are not wealthy can have access to the information necessary to function fully as a citizen and to live up to their potential in a democratic society. What we know about the demographics of those who use libraries is they are mostly well educated, high-income people. This should not be taken at all to detract from what the librarians want to do, I think they're right. The lesson for cyberspace is that there are some cultural barriers that are vastly more important than economic barriers in terms of getting access to the tools and information necessary to fully empower yourself....I think that the access issue springs from that and not dollars.

(Godwin, 1996)[10]

As almost any account of hackers shows, Godwin is undoubtedly right. Many hackers do not use a powerful computer but have discarded or cheap machines. Many hackers are teenagers without the financial resources themselves, and often without parental resources, to buy up-to-date machines but who have the passion and commitment to learn extraordinary amounts about phone and computer systems. With this knowledge they can use their basic computers to enter cyberspace and seize control of more powerful machines. One of the lessons of hackers is that the barrier to cyberspace is often cultural and not cost. Of course, to be able to watch quality video on the Internet, to receive sound and pictures or to enter three-dimensional Web sites more expensive and powerful access will be needed, but to gain some of the most important benefits (e.g. email, Usenet, most Web sites or MUDs) does not require current machinery. The growing importance of the Web means there is a temptation to think that access to the multimedia world of hypertext *is* cyberspace, but this is simply mistaken. Many Web sites can be accessed in text-only versions and can often be much quicker than sites featuring many slow-to-download graphics. Further, advanced equipment is only needed for the most advanced Web sites, which form a minority of Web sites, and even the most avant-garde sites often provide a less complicated version that has all the same information available on it. Yet, many might feel like second-class cybercitizens using cheaper forms of access, like the black and white avatars in Stephenson's metaverse. A second factor comes into play here that also diminishes the importance of cost both between and within countries, and this is the exponential rate at which computer power increases and costs decrease.

The fundamental driving force of computer technology is the speed at which information can be processed within each computer. This is determined by the capacity of the central processing unit (CPU), which is itself determined by the microchip(s) it uses, which is in turn determined by the number of transistors each microchip contains. And the CPU is subject to what is called Moore's law. Gordon Moore, by 1996 Intel Corporation's Emeritus Chairman of the Board, predicted in 1965 that processing power would double every eighteen months (Leyden, 1997: 166; Schofield, 1996). Figure 3.1 shows Moore's law in action, tracing the number of transistors per Intel microchip.

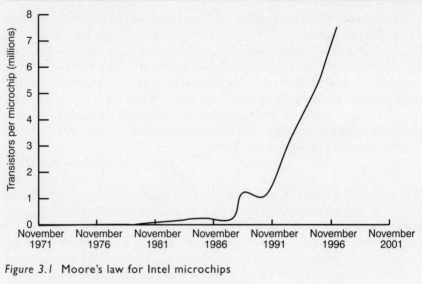

Figure 3.1 Moore's law for Intel microchips

Sources: Schofield (1996); Intel (1998)

The CPU[11] takes up approximately 22 per cent of the cost of an average personal computer, by far the largest amount, and other components have, by and large, followed Moore's law or are so insignificant as not to affect overall prices. This means that computer prices should half every eighteen months or, for the same amount of money, double the processing power should be available. This plummeting of price and rise of power has its fits and starts, but has largely held[12] (Manners, 1996; Rafferty and Tran, 1996). The result of this is that, as John Gilmore remarks:

> The evolution of the computer communications industry has been driven by a fundamental technology of chip application that reduces costs at a tremendous rate, an exponential rate. This is a phenomenon that most people have a hard time trying to understand because they don't tend to see exponential forces happening elsewhere.
>
> (Gilmore, 1996)

What was essential technology needed to utilise the most advanced elements of cyberspace is, within eighteen months, obsolete and can be found in second-hand computer stores for a fraction of the cost. But it will still be more than adequate for utilising all but the most advanced elements of cyberspace. This has even led to some pioneering efforts at recycling computers from corporations that demand 'state of the art' to charities or schools that do not. For example, in 1996 IBM received a $150,000 tax deduction in return for donating 1,000 computers to charity. The computers had a book value to IBM of only

$150 each, though they were only two to three years old (Parks, 1997: 149). This may seem small on a world scale, but it helps underline that costs are not what they might seem to many people considering investing in computers. A far greater problem is likely to be an advertising culture that convinces people they *must* have the latest machine, without them often really knowing why, and a lack of knowledge that prevents people realising that, for access to the Internet, an expensive machine is not necessary. If you wish to play the absolutely latest computer games, then an expensive purchase is essential (and will have to be repeated every twelve to eighteen months), but for most of cyberspace it is not.

Access is a form of cyberpolitics that cuts in two directions. First, it addresses inequalities of access that need to be understood in two ways: between nations and within nations. Second, its basic effect springs from two sources, culture and cost, and the more obvious limitation, cost, may well not be the most important. To possess the powers cyberspace offers, you must be able to go there. Access springs from the notion that individuals gain power in cyberspace, making access to those powers fundamental. But for those with access to cyberspace, a second set of typical cyberpolitical issues emerges around the powers cyberspace offers. Here can be found the political issues and organisations that many consider typical of cyberspace: issues like censorship, privacy, intellectual property and organisations like the Electronic Frontier Foundation or the Center for Democracy and Technology. With power conceived as a possession, issues within cyberspace revolve around limiting or acquiring these powers. Perhaps the greatest drama of cyberpolitics within cyberspace comes from the attempt in the USA to censor the Internet, contained in the legislation called the Communications Decency Act (CDA), and its connection to the religious right, pornography research and civil rights organisations. Outlining this episode provides an insight into cyberpolitics and its nature.

In 1995 a US graduate student called Marty Rimm published an empirical investigation into the extent of hard-core pornography in cyberspace.[13] Rimm claimed to have found enormous amounts of pornography online and to have proved that users of cyberspace preferred more extreme forms of pornography, such as bestiality. *Time* magazine used the results of this survey to splash 'Cyberporn' across its cover and used subheadings such as 'There's an awful lot of porn online' to drive home its message of the sex-saturated nature of the Internet. This was not surprising as *Time* had been given exclusive pre-publication access to the study by Rimm. Soon anti-pornography campaigners, including legislators with links to the US religious right, took up the horrifying story. Legislation already in train gained further impetus. However, the problem was that the study was fraudulent. A group of civil rights activists and academics analysed the study and the full power of communication in cyberspace put together a telling response. Most important, both of the key results that gave Rimm's study weight and drama were incorrect. First, he claimed to have surveyed 917,410 online pictures, stories and film clips in cyberspace but these turned out not to relate to cyberspace or the Internet but to private bulletin boards that individuals had to dial into directly with their telephone. As discussed in the previous chapter, these disconnected bulletin boards only bear the most tenuous relationship to cyberspace and are not part of the Internet at all, yet Rimm defined cyberspace as almost any computer communication and wrote as if his results concerned the Internet. Second, he claimed 83.5 per cent of all images posted on Usenet were hard-core pornography[14] but this turned out to be wrong, so poorly based and calculated as to be worthless. Several academics developed powerful criticisms and pointed out that though the study was published in the impressively titled *Georgetown Law Journal*, this was in fact a graduate journal. Further research found what appeared to be straightforward plagiary in the study, with a series of phrases almost identical to those in another, far less sensational, study of online pornography. More and more revelations began to be added. Rimm was found to be peddling a book he had written about how to make money through digitised pornography to the bulletin board owners whose data he was using (called *The Pornographer's Handbook: how to exploit women, dupe men and make lots of money* which included a dedication to Bob Guccione, the publisher of *Penthouse*). Rimm turned out to have written and self-published a novel containing many pornographic passages. He had once dressed up as an Arab sheikh and talked his way into a casino to dramatise another scientific study he had conducted, when 16, that sensationally claimed that 64 per cent of his fellow students had gained entry to casinos.

The tide turned against Rimm and even *Time* magazine weighed in, ignoring any self-reproach for putting a fraudulent study on its cover, but raising 'serious questions' about Rimm's study. A sensational fraud had been revealed but the initial effects of the fraud and its nationwide publicity meant the results were widely accepted (and are still sometimes repeated as facts). Soon legislators began bandying about Rimm's two fatal numbers and, though they had to cancel an appearance for Rimm to testify, his study helped to legitimise a series of legislative attempts to censor cyberspace. Civil rights organisations had followed in horror the publicity *Time* and Rimm had generated and had worked to prevent censorious legislation. Staff counsel for the Electronic Frontier Foundation, Mike Godwin, managed to trace connections between Rimm and legislators. For example, one of the editors of the journal that published Rimm's study (and the study was not submitted to the journal directly but was brought in by an editor) had connections both to Christian anti-pornography groups and to Senator Exxon, one of the chief proponents of cyberspace censorship. Godwin was certainly convinced that 'the religious right [was] actually conspiring to build a case for a crisis in cyberporn on the net' (Godwin, 1996) and that Rimm was closely implicated (Godwin, 1998).

From fraud to legislation was the step: the individual powers of cyberspace were to be limited by draconian legislation, namely the Communications Decency Act (CDA) in the USA. This legislation attempted to eliminate 'obscenity', which meant it would be legal to say 'shit' on the telephone but not to type it into cyberspace, and to make those who administered computer systems as well as those who use them responsible and subjected to fines and imprisonment. The legislation was passed in early 1996, effectively reaching into cyberspace from the offline world and attempting to eliminate some of the powers individuals had in cyberspace. The legislation was then appealed to a US court, which strongly rejected it as a contradiction to the US citizen's constitutional right to free speech. This rejection was then upheld by the US Supreme Court, which also rejected any CDA look-alike legislation as unconstitutional. The powers of cyberspace were left untouched in the wake of CDA's rejection, which came so quickly on the heels of the legislation's enactment that there was no time to find out what effect the legislation would actually have had on cyberspace (Godwin, 1997).[15] This will not be the end of attempts to censor cyberspace; for example, the UK government is exploring ratings schemes that will mandate rating sites for violence, pornography and so on and then use those ratings in software that can block access (Travis, 1997). Censorship and freedom of speech are endemic issues in cyberspace because they spring from the powers cyberspace offers the individual. As John Gilmore points out:

> I think the reason that [censorship] didn't happen early on was that the net was sufficiently new. It never occurred to governments and religious organisations to try and censor it because they'd never heard of it. Of course, once they'd heard of it – a medium where anyone can say anything to anyone else – 'oh my God, we've got to do something about this!'
>
> (Gilmore, 1996)

The Rimm–CDA story is one of the most spectacular outbreaks of cyberpolitics and it demonstrates the way the power to say anything to anyone, to move around censorship and to experiment with identities gives rise to issues such as freedom of speech. The thought that anybody who used cyberspace had access to hard-core pornography, in the privacy of their own room, led to an hysterical overreaction that sought to control not just access to pornography but all forms of online speech. The main cyberpolitical issues have revolved around four broad areas: free speech, privacy, encryption and intellectual property. Free speech, obviously also including censorship, has already been discussed when outlining the Rimm–CDA story. Clearly, in a world in which your identity depends on the information you can type, the ability to write what you want and send it to whomever you want to is equivalent to the right to exist as you want to. Privacy is easily understood as gaining the power to penetrate others' privacy by reading their email or gaining a profile of their consumption habits or protecting that privacy by encrypting email or demanding that Web sites tell users what personal information is taken in cyberspace. Encryption relates to the ability to scramble information so that only those you allow to unscramble it will be able to read it. Encryption concerns a set of software tools that gives avatars control over what they write. Copyright can be understood as either the freedom or restriction of information flow. Information is the fundamental source of cyberspace's powers, and copyright concerns the problem of paying for information in a world where it can be quickly, cheaply, easily and endlessly copied.

In all these cases, the key issues of cyberpolitics result from the conception of cyberpower as a possession, as something that individuals take and use. Much of the political heat of cyberspace is generated here and is the result of beginning from the fact of individuals facing screens and reaching through identity fluidity, renovated hierarchies and a world of information to find that online power is the possession of individuals. This conception underpins some of the great hopes for cyberspace, as it is a place where individuals can finally rest control of their being from institutions, governments, corporations and oppressions.

Conclusion

If you begin by assuming or believing that cyberspace is the realm of the individual, then cyberpower revolves around certain capacities individuals gain in cyberspace. Politics and culture then result from those capacities. When looking at the three axes of cyberpower that result from this premise, all the various cultures the virtual lands call peculiarly their own emerge. The role of style, the peculiarities of cybersex, the wonders of MUDs, the vast extent of Usenet – all can be called cyberspatial cultures because they are all fundamentally structured by the three revolving powers of identity fluidity, renovated hierarchies and informational space. The politics of cyberspace also emerges from these powers placing issues of access to cyberspace and the maintenance of powers in cyberspace at the core of cyberpolitical conflict. Cyberspace is the land of empowerment of individuals, of reinventing identities out of thought.

And there are many reasons why many people experience cyberspace as a place they come to as individuals, pioneers even. It is a compelling fact for most people that they enter cyberspace as an individual, that they live there while alone offline – typing on their keyboard – and that it is from their individuality, their singularity, that they build cultural and political places in cyberspace. It is not that people come as individuals and stay alone in cyberspace. It is one of the great misunderstandings of cyberspace users that they are 'socially inadequate' because they prefer computers to humans. Lovers of cyberspace love the people, the avatars, they find there, not necessarily the machines that allow them to go there. People build communities in cyberspace by interpreting the bounds of their and their communities' actions as being based on the primacy of individuals. Cyberpower as a possession is perfectly consonant with the powerful impression offered by individual entrance into cyberspace. Virtual communities are built from individuals mobilising their powers. Or, at least, this is how cyberpower appears as we contemplate the effects of individuals building cyberspace. Here the fourth myth of the electronic frontier becomes relevant.

MYTHS OF THE ELECTRONIC FRONTIER 4: CYBERSUICIDE AND BLAIR NEWMAN

The WELL had a core principle: if it were a castle above the entrance would be inscribed 'people own their own words'. Instead, being part of cyberspace, every time someone entered the WELL, as they logged on, the motto scrolled down their screen. This principle seems clearly part of the assertion of individual freedom and responsibility in electronic space. Your words are your own, your power to write is your own. The particular software used on the WELL mirrored this. When someone posted, whatever handle they were using appeared, but behind it, in brackets, one constant handle was also shown that was connected to their self-description. For example, the author of *The Virtual Community*, Howard Rheingold, could post messages with any handle he liked but behind it would always appear in brackets (hlr). Further, the system allowed people to delete a message they had posted, taking back their words, and it replaced the deletion with a new blank message. The feature was known as 'scribbling'. This meant that if you deleted a message everyone knew you had done so by the appearance of a new blank message (Hafner, 1997: 104–6). Here the technology and the ethic was that you have the power to write and the responsibility to own what you write, to the extent that you can take your words away. Beginning from individual rights/writes and responsibilities is one reason why the WELL became the archetypal virtual community. The WELL embedded the primacy of the individual avatar in cyberspace into its very structures.

But in one famous incident a participant in the WELL left it and took his words with him, someone who had over a year and a half contributed enormously to discussion named Blair Newman. Rheingold remembered it this way:

> Then, after years online, and dozens of parties and excursions with other WELL members, and all the late night phone calls...Blair Newman removed everything he had ever written on the WELL. For a day and a night and a day, most of the conversation on the WELL was about the trauma of mass-scribbling – the term that had emerged for the act of removing years' worth of postings. It seemed an act of intellectual suicide.
>
> (Rheingold, 1994: 34)

Shockingly, only a few weeks later Newman committed suicide. Immediately, fanciful accounts emerged in which Newman took his life at the moment he erased his last online contribution with WELL members desperately searching for him, somehow magically aware that online suicide would mean offline suicide. The shock waves from these suicides were personal and communal. Some felt Newman had no right to erase his part of the communal memory. All discussions had been recorded and kept, but suddenly whole arguments lacked vital contributions. In a world made out of information, Newman's or anybody's contribution appeared not just as his or their own words but as part of the fabric of community:

> there was an outcry of protest from the surviving participants when they discovered that Brian (sic) Newman had deleted his contributions from their collective memory. Many thought that the messages, once entered, became a part of the public domain. If not in the public domain, they considered their conference community property that should properly remain under their collective control.
>
> (Branscomb, 1993: 99)

But if the individual does not own their own words, if some community they have helped construct with their words has rights to those words because it is part of a collective fabric, then what has happened to individual power? The WELL would experience other mass-scribblings and sometimes the contradiction between really owning your own words and creating communities with words would again emerge. It is not that individuals cannot create groups but that at some point the individual is no longer the basis of community, somehow the collective displaces it. Newman took up his power – he possessed the power to mass-scribble and did so – but many learnt that somewhere along the way they no longer believed the motto above the WELL's entrance.

The moral is that as compelling as the individualism of cyberspace sometimes seems, collective responsibilities can also be foundational in cyberspace. Sometimes the individualism people are drawn to from the common sense of their own entrance might not be correct. Perhaps people become entranced with the singularity, the isolation of their physical body tapping on their keyboard, but forget that having entered cyberspace they have left that body behind. Perhaps the common sense intuition that we all enter cyberspace as individuals and stay as the individual possessors of power is limited.[16]

The myth of Blair Newman raises the possibility that founding the culture and politics of cyberspace on the individual is limited. And limited seems the absolutely correct word here. It is not that all the work outlining cyberpower at the level of the individual is wrong or incorrect – Newman had the power to withdraw from his community. He, as an individual, might have damaged a community and others might have been angered, but he owned his own words. It is the anger and the damage that is hard to explain with cyberpower as it has so far been articulated. It is the possibility that something other than individuals might have become the basis for virtual life that is difficult to see when cyberpower is understood as the possession of individuals. All that has been established so far is confirmed by the myth of Blair Newman, but it is revealed as having gaps, absences and limits. What elements of cyberpower prompted the anger or distress at Newman's withdrawal of his words? What elements of cyberpower are remaining hidden because the perspective that begins from the individual might not be the only perspective that can be taken? Cyberpower needs to be explored from the assumption of the collective, from the intuition that the virtual community founds individuals and not the other way round. We need to explore the social in cyberspace, while retaining insights from the powers of the individual in cyberspace.

Chapter 4

The virtual social I
The social in cyberspace

Consider a house, and a street, for example. The house has six storeys and an air of stability about it. One might see it as the epitome of immovability, with its concrete and its stark, cold and rigid outlines. (Built around 1950: no metal or plate glass yet.) Now, a critical analysis would doubtless destroy the appearance of solidity of this house, stripping it, as it were, of its concrete slabs and its thin non-load-bearing walls, which are really glorified screens, and uncovering a very different picture. In the light of this imaginary analysis, our house would emerge as permeated from every direction by streams of energy which run in and out of it by every imaginable route: water, gas, electricity, telephone lines, radio and television signals, and so on. Its image of immovability would then be replaced by an image of a complex of mobilities, a nexus of in and out conduits....Comparable observations, of course, might be made apropos of the whole street, a network of ducts constituting a structure, having global form, fulfilling functions, and so on. Or apropos of the city, which consumes (in both senses of the word) truly colossal quantities of energy, both physical and human, and which is in effect a constantly burning, blazing bonfire.

(Lefebvre, 1991: 92–3)

Key concepts

Virtual community

Communities emerge in cyberspace when a number of users create avatars that return again and again to the same informational space. Individuals may find they are no longer alone in cyberspace but have developed relations with a number of other stable avatars and have become part of a virtual community. Virtual communities can be left easily because someone must choose to go there and so can choose not to. Virtual communities can be of many different types, from newsgroup discussions about a limited topic to MUDs that allow virtual versions of all offline social relations.

Technopower

Technopower is the constant oscillation felt by users of technology between operating technology as an inert, asocial 'thing' and manipulating technology according to alive, social 'values'. Technopower is particularly important for virtual life because cyberspace only exists because of its technology.

Information overload

Having too much information can make use of information impossible. This can occur in two ways. First, there can be simply too much information to absorb. Second, information can be so poorly organised that finding any particular piece of information becomes impossible.

Technopower spiral

The amount of information in cyberspace is so vast as to appear infinite to each individual user. This infinity creates an abstract desire or hunger to find important pieces of information in cyberspace. This desire leads users of cyberspace into information overload because they are searching virtually infinite amounts of information. This overload is then managed by introducing new technological tools designed to control the information flow. But this merely leads to a new form of information overload and to a new desire for a new technological tool. Each new technology is used as a tool but is created according to values and so is a moment of technopower. A spiral of technopower exists in cyberspace.

Virtual elite

The technopower spiral means that the technology of cyberspace becomes ever more complex. This makes it harder and harder for users to manipulate technology according to their values, leaving them using technology as tools. An elite emerges whose greater expertise allows them to manipulate cyberspace's technology. The virtual elite is based on expertise or the control of expertise.

Introduction

Many people report a transformation, often slow, in their perception of online life. From an initial combination of bewilderment, glee and scepticism, a sort of bemused intuition of how simultaneously ridiculous and important online life is, many come to accept the world of avatars as normal – from dragons to email. With stable avatars people begin to have ongoing conversations, to meet the same avatars and learn their peculiarities. The particular rules of different corners of cyberspace become clear and normal. Acronyms that would be out of place anywhere else become part of the fabric of daily life (onna). Many perceive this shift as the mark of their maturity in cyberspace:

Only with time and the acquisition of a fixed character do players tend to make the critical passage from anonymity to pseudonymity, developing the concern for their character's reputation that marks the attainment of virtual adulthood.

(Dibbell, 1994: 251)

This transition is often understood as the creation by individuals of social spaces. With the powers of cyberspace firmly in their possession, people come together to construct societies around everything from newsgroups on sensational murders to new forms of corporate decision making. The forms of communication typical of cyberspace underpin new forms of community. What is real, the bedrock of life in cyberspace, is all the avatars coming together to create ways of life. This understanding of cyberspace and the powers that are native to it have been fully explored in the previous chapter. But an alternative view emerges at this point. Once the social emerges, once a collective is formed, then all individuals who are part of that society become at least in part subject to it. Individual freedom comes to exist with collective responsibilities.

The transition to virtual adulthood is, perhaps, also the transition from the isolation of the virtual individual to the communal home. Rather than sovereign individuals, the social creates possibilities for individuals, who participate in certain ways in online life or risk exclusion. The myth of cybersuicide illustrates this. If an individual acts with no concern for the collective they are part of, then other individuals may find they wish to have some formal control over each other in the interests of their community. Behind such realisations, often less jolting than with Blair Newman, is the perception of the social that somehow stands apart from individuals and should not be subordinate to the individual. Such a perception seems so simple as to prompt the question, why is it a realisation at all? Day after day, we all realise the social aspects of offline society that are outside the individual will, but part of the difference of cyberspace is that it can be experienced as the realm of freely chosen individual connections. The experience of entering and living online as an individual in front of a terminal combined with the ability, at a few typed commands or the press of a button, to withdraw from any cybersociety is compelling. It can take time or events for the social to be perceived clearly in cyberspace, for the idea that individuals are perhaps not the foundation of all there is in cyberspace to take firm root.

It is the perspective of the social that will now be explored, not necessarily to deny or contradict cyberpower from the perspective of the individual but to complicate and broaden the story. What do we see when we understand online life as founded on social spaces? What virtual collectives offer opportunities and constraints to individuals? In both this and the preceding chapter individuals and collectives appear; it is the relationship between them that will now be reversed. Rather than individuals founding societies, now societies will be the foundation for individuals. What forms of cyberpower course through online societies?

This question will be explored in a slightly different way to the individual because it is a different object. This chapter will explore online society, putting aside the division point between online and offline. The first question is, what form of cyberpower appears in social life within cyberspace? The succeeding chapter will explore the division between offline and online, searching for flows of power from cyberspace to meatspace and back. The second question is, what form of cyberpower appears in between online and offline societies and how does it affect both? The separation of these questions is necessary, in a way that it is not for the individual, because beginning from the individual stitches together online and offline. The insight that individuals form the foundation of online life begins from the transition from offline to online; the two are inextricably linked when the individual in cyberpower is the basis of discussion. But when the social is assumed to be a foundation, it is possible that particular societies emerge online with fundamentally separate structures to offline. The two will be kept separate to discuss the social in cyberspace and then social between cyberspace and meatspace.

The social in cyberspace will be introduced through a companion myth of the electronic frontier to the myth of cybersuicide: the myth of cyberrape. Taken together these myths offer the insight that social structures in cyberspace are generated with a particular emphasis on its technological structures. Social power in cyberspace will be shown to be a form of technopower. Following this insight, technopower will be defined and explored as the constant oscillation between technological tools, that appear to individuals as neutral things, and social values, found in the design and construction of tools. A constant opening and closing between thing and value defines the relationship between virtual individuals and the technology that creates virtual life. The capacity for action virtual individuals have is defined by their place within these networks of values and things, which is in turn defined by individuals' ability to alter things by opening up each tool's social values to manipulation. This type of power accords with both Barnes' and Foucault's theories of power, as will be discussed. The difference between Barnes and Foucault can be posed in the question, does a form of power necessarily result in domination? Or is it simply a description of the basic components of social order? The particular pattern or direction of cyberspace's technopower is analysed with this question in mind. This pattern will be shown to be a spiral that results from the vast, virtually infinite, amount of information available in cyberspace and has three stages. First, a user finds they become overloaded with information, either because there is too much or because it cannot be organised. Second, a new technological tool is used to control information and reduce information overload. Third, because the amount of information in cyberspace is virtually infinite, the information the new tool provides eventually gives way to a new form of information overload, returning the user to the first step. This spiral ensures the ever increasing complexity of the technology that creates cyberspace and increasingly limits individuals' choices for action because more complex technology is harder and harder to open up to manipulation. The spiral of technopower points toward the fundamental fact that social power in cyberspace increasingly offers greater ability to take action to an expertise-based elite. Cyberpower of the social results in elite domination of cyberspace. This elite and its basis in social cyberpower is then explored through the sixth myth of the electronic frontier, Kevin

Mitnick, superhacker. The moral of this myth is explored in relation to two other personifications of the technopower elite: corporate software leader Bill Gates and co-operative software leader Linus Torvalds. Technopower and its spiral mean that social power in cyberspace is a Foucauldian form of power; it is made up of networks of dominated and dominator.

MYTHS OF THE ELECTRONIC FRONTIER 5: MR_BUNGLE'S CYBERRAPE

There was a MUD called LambdaMOO.[1] This MUD has been one of the key corners of cyberspace, like the WELL. Here many forms of online life have been first sighted or, at least, first written about. There was a night in March, when many avatars were gathered in the MUD's living room, a living room conjured out of text and separated individuals who brought their avatars together in virtual space. The living room in LambdaMOO is the place where people come simply to be with other people, before setting out on whatever journey they may decide on. Several avatars were present, meeting and greeting, catching up on news amid the well-stocked bookcases, sofas and fireplace. One avatar was called Mr_Bungle and his self-description ran like this:

> a fat, oleaginous, Bisquick-faced clown dresses in cum-stained harlequin garb and girdled with a mistletoe and hemlock belt, whose buckle bore the quaint inscription 'KISS ME UNDER THIS, BITCH!'

Another avatar was called Legba and she self-described this way:

> a Haitian trickster spirit of indeterminate gender, brown-skinned and wearing an expensive pearl grey suit, top hat and dark glasses.

Astonishingly, Legba began to perform sex on Mr_Bungle. Appearing on everyone's screens were amazing descriptions like 'Legba sucks Mr_Bungle's juicy cock'. Legba was an established, well-liked avatar and having sex in the living room among friends was as extraordinary to many there as, well, as your best friend having sex in your living room. And sex with that clown! It became stranger. Legba began hurling insults at Mr_Bungle, even as more extreme descriptions of sex scrolled down the screen. It became clear to other experienced avatars that

Legba was being assaulted; Mr_Bungle must have created a voodoo doll that allowed him to take possession of Legba's avatar. This meant that while Legba could talk (if she typed 'say Piss off Bungle', everyone would see 'Legba says Piss off Bungle'), Mr_Bungle could emote for Legba, against her will (if he typed emote Legba 'licks Mr_Bungle's balls', everyone would see 'Legba licks Mr_Bungle's balls'). With some effort Mr_Bungle was ejected.

He slunk off and the living room subsided to shocked contemplation, but he wasn't finished. Mr_Bungle returned to his private rooms, which he had secured, and again took out his Legba voodoo doll. He also took out his Starsinger voodoo doll. Starsinger had only a small self-description: she was female, tall, stout and brown haired. The voodoo dolls worked at a distance and soon the living room was awash in astonishing sexual acts. Starsinger found herself having sex, increasingly wild, with other avatars. Amid mayhem in the room, the attacks became more violent and each attack ended with the words 'You hear Mr_Bungle laughing evilly in the distance'. The frenzy reached its climax. Legba was forced to eat his/her own pubic hair and on the screens appeared 'As if against her will, Starsinger jabs a steak knife up her ass, causing immense joy'. Finally, Zippy the wizard brought a gun that caged an avatar up with bars impermeable to voodoo dolls and Mr_Bungle's attacks were stopped.

What to do? Mr_Bungle called for help from another wizard who, unaware of his attacks, released him to escape. Accounts of the assault spread throughout the MUD. A public meeting was called to discuss what to do with Mr_Bungle and he even attended. Legba called for the death sentence and others supported her. This is called toading.[2] It is the ultimate sanction and available only to a few who control the software that runs the MUD. Neither Legba nor any of her supporters could toad Mr_Bungle, nor did they want to do it alone, so they called for a communal decision. But the debate was inconclusive – it was long and complex but inconclusive. One wizard, called JoeFeedback, had listened to the debate, contributing only occasionally. With no communal consensus he faced the problem of whether to do nothing or use his powers. He killed Mr_Bungle. One minute if you typed '@who Mr_Bungle', to try and find him, the system would respond and tell you where he was and then, the next minute, if you did the same thing the system would tell you 'there is no player called Mr_Bungle'. He no longer existed.

Two further things happened. LambdaMOO had already been moving away from the dictatorship of wizards. The wizards, particularly chief wizard Pavel Curtis/Haakon, were sick of sorting out communal and personal conflicts and had placed responsibility for conflict resolution back with the avatars, but had provided no means of resolving conflicts. In the wake of death and rape, Curtis sat down and created a system of ballots that allowed direct democracy to control LambdaMOO. Since this time a number of rules have been agreed at ballot and if you log on to LambdaMOO one of the rules you will find reads as follows:

> * Sexual harassment (particularly involving unsolicited acts which simulate rape against unwilling participants)
> Such behavior is not tolerated by the LambdaMOO community. A single incidence of such an act may, as a consequence of due process, result in permanent expulsion from LambdaMOO.[3]

Second, a new character appeared, Dr.Jest, with an almost unnamable familiarity and the disconcerting habit of stuffing avatars in a jar containing a tiny copy of Mr_Bungle. The penny dropped, with this reference and his familiar style it became clear that Dr.Jest was Mr_Bungle back from the dead. He had obtained a new Internet account and re-entered LambdaMOO with a new avatar. Immediately, a petition for Dr.Jest's toading was begun. Eventually, Dr.Jest chose to sleep and did not wake up.[4]

The moral of the Mr_Bungle cyberrape is often read as another confirmation of identity fluidity, renovated hierarchies and informational spaces, but the different moral it carries, and so its potency in teaching us the norms of cyberspace, is that social power in cyberspace is technically based.[5] All the actions described above appeared as text on screens and this was made possible by a combination of hardware – a particular physical computer located in the Xerox Parc Laboratory on the west coast of the USA – and software written and controlled by the wizards. The voodoo dolls, the gun that caged Mr_Bungle and the execution were all particular forms of software code. The fundamental form of power in LambdaMOO was/is technically based and consists of the ability to tinker with the machine – add memory, add speed – or to concoct software code that plays with forms of life – rape, guns, execution. This is demonstrated most clearly when, in response to these events, the chief wizard introduced balloting for decisions. The irony was of 'dictatorially imposing universal suffrage on an unconsulted populace' (Dibbell, 1994: 254) and the means of imposition were the voluntary refusal by wizards to use their powers and the coding into the software fabric of LambdaMOO of balloting. The socially embedded powers of LambdaMOO were technically based; they were forms of technopower.[6]

The social and the individual

The rape and execution of avatars are two of the most spectacular instances of technically based power in the societies of cyberspace and LambdaMOO is not the only place to have witnessed such attacks. There is a MUD called JennyMUSH designed to provide support for survivors of sexual abuse. In this virtual space, survivors use cyberspace's powers to create their own forms of help. One day a user changed their avatar from female to male, renamed it 'Daddy' and used a particular command to send graphic descriptions of violent sexual assaults to all members of the MUD. For half an hour there was no wizard on the MUD to stop the assaults. When a wizard finally logged on they changed the avatar's name to Vermin with the description 'This is the lowest scum, the most pathetic dismal object which a human being can become'. The users who were still in the MUD then wreaked virtual revenge on Vermin, raining down the most violent virtual punishments on the perpetrator (Reid, 1998). Or there is Wolf Grrrl, who chose her handle to meet head on the possibility of virtual sexual assault or harassment but still found:

> Muds were the absolute worst place on the net for me. I've had my character multiply raped, groped, kissed and passed around as a sexual prize (against my will). It was a completely humiliating experience. The dynamic began to echo power realities in real life so much that it tipped me into becoming more involved in feminism.
>
> (Cited in Chelmick, 1997)

Online harassment takes a number of forms: as ever it depends on which particular corner of cyberspace an avatar exists in, but includes harassing email, unsolicited pornographic pictures, online stalking and the already-mentioned forms of virtual assault.

> My daughter and I have been stalked for almost a year by a jerk who targeted me as his victim, apparently due to a newsgroup discussion of commercial advertising on the net. I wasn't one of the main participants in

that particular discussion, but I was the only woman – he didn't harass any of the men. (He is awaiting trial for stalking.)

(Cited in Chelmick, 1997)

A Web site has been set up to halt abuse of women online[7] and it offers policies and information to prevent harassment. It also offers a list of unsafe sites, which in mid-1997 was empty. While spectacular examples of harassment are not difficult to find, it is impossible to judge the extent of harassment online or to compare it to harassment offline because no substantial research has yet been done.[8] However, harassment remains important for present purposes because it points towards technopower:

> Unfortunately, the freedom to hide behind a phony name also contributes to a plague of on-line sexual harassment and rampant rudeness. A number of women I talked to in the public forums said they were constantly bombarded with crude private messages and sexual advances. These women said they did not engage in on-line sex, did not frequent sexually oriented public areas, and did not want to be approached via private messages.
>
> (Branwyn, 1993: 788)

Identity fluidity underpins certain forms of harassment both in the concealment of identity in favour of avatars and in new possibilities for harassment. The particular character of online harassment results from the same technologically based powers that make identity fluidity possible, because underneath the lives that occupy people online are cables, wires, terminals and line upon line of software code. When Wolf Grrrl was assaulted or when a male emails a picture of himself naked and aroused to a woman, these actions are made possible by the particularities of computer-mediated communication (Chelmick, 1997). The offline equivalent is a male harasser taking his nude photograph and taping it to the female's desk. The ease and seeming privacy of file transfer compared with such a public display makes cyberspace a more likely place for this form of harassment.

Renovated hierarchies are also underpinned by technical powers. This can be seen in attempts to create online hierarchies that negate virtual violence. In the flame war between alt.tasteless and rec.pets.cats there was no effective way within cyberspace of creating a hierarchy or barrier that protected rec.pets.cats, despite the use of electronic 'kill' orders, because the underlying technology allowed messages to flow around censorship. Similarly, during arguments over the effect of Mr_Bungle's rape some claimed a technical solution was the answer. A simple command (@gag) would prevent any of Mr_Bungle's messages being received by the person who used the command; Mr_Bungle is not censored and you don't have to deal with his fantasies. However, as Dibbell notes this would not prevent others seeing Mr_Bungle's messages, leaving the victim still attacked in the eyes of anyone else who happened to enter the room, even though the person being attacked would not know what is occurring (Dibbell, 1994: 247). Such commands or kill files may help in totally individualised situations: if one person is harassing another, then refusing to take their messages may neutralise the harassment. But in any social situation, where people participate as a community, individualised solutions have less power. The underlying technology structures power so that it seems to be a possession of individuals (set your own kill or gag orders), but power also circulates at a social or collective level and here it undermines individual actions. As happened in LambdaMOO, collective or social solutions to harassment are almost forced on virtual communities, whose members are implicitly operating with common sense notions of power as an individual possession. Finally, even the individual solutions of kill files are often all too easily evaded through Internet technology, simply by creating a new Internet account. The resurrection of Mr_Bungle as Dr.Jest was possible because the LambdaMOO software would have blocked any avatar formation by someone from the same email address or Internet account as Mr_Bungle but would not recognise that a different Internet account was used by the barred person. The software failed to recognise a Mr_Bungle reborn but other avatars did not.

The full significance of the third element of individualised cyberpower now becomes clear. It states cyberspace is informational space. Where beginning from the compelling perception of the individualism of cyberspace makes informational space seem the logical corollary of the more potent powers of identity fluidity and renovated hierarchies, the tales of harassment point in the opposite direction to the software and hardware that allow a world made of information to exist. Jones points out that 'the space of cyberspace is predicated on knowledge and information, of the common beliefs and practices of a society abstracted from physical space' (Jones, 1995b: 19), but the knowledge and information are themselves dependent on MUD software and servers, on TCP/IP, on telephone lines and personal computers, on optical fibres and ethernet. Jones goes from this passage to define online social life as the result of individuals sharing:

> But the important element in cyberspatial social relations is the sharing of information. It is not sharing in the sense of the *transmission* of information that binds communities in cyberspace. It is the ritual sharing of information…that pulls it together.
>
> (Jones, 1995b: 19–20)

Who shares? For Jones the avatars, all individualised online lives, share. But Jones is wrong, it is the transmission of information that makes possible ritual sharing and any powers built into the forms of transmission will structure forms of ritual sharing, such as the power to gag or the power to create voodoo dolls. Informational space points in one direction to identity fluidity and renovated hierarchies, but it also points in another to technopower and the structuring of online life by the technologies that allow cyberspace to exist. A transformation in the subject of power means shifting away from the typical objects that appear from the perspective of cyberpower of the individual. Moving into cyberpower of the social means that a new field and new actors will appear. First of all, the nature of technopower must be established.

Technopower[9]

Equally as compelling as entering cyberspace as an individual should be the fact that everyone enters it through technology. Yet, the compelling individualism of virtual lives seems to grip nearly all of its analysts. Descriptions of technology are often given in passing, to indicate the writer 'knows' it exists or to let others know how to become part of the life being described, or technology is mentioned to recount some of the truisms of cyberspace, such as that the Internet treats censorship as damage. These truisms appear as the endpoints of debate, establishing something that must be learned before anything sensible can be said about cyberspace. They are also often, at least implicitly, statements of technological determinism. For example, the Internet is a decentred, distributed, anti-hierarchical network and bombing one city will not stop other cities connecting. The technology is decentred and this leads to decentred virtual societies. Technology leads to society. As with all technological determinist arguments, these do not explore technology but demonstrate the effects of a technology. Technology leads to society in these arguments and, in this way, separates technology from society.

Technopower as it underpins society in cyberspace cannot be grasped from any of these viewpoints. Technopower has (in)human values, knowledge and technology welded together in ways that make them inextricable. The forms of society that are likely, or even possible, in cyberspace have technopower coursing through them, structuring the types of relations avatars develop. Each of the different corners of cyberspace – email, Usenet, MUDs – has a different form of technopower and all are laid over the forms of technopower that constitute the Internet itself. If we take one of the most novel and distinctive forms of society cyberspace has generated, MUDs, then we can immediately see several forms of technopower. At the simplest level, to the avatars in the MUD, there is the ability to build the MUD. Here is Hertz's description of building her first MUD home (remember, she is Rollergirl and she has found the helper Thorin/Shiro again):

> Thorin grins, growls, then morphs into his tiger character, Shiro, who gets on a sofa and lies down. As we talk, he tries to bite me and I smack him on the nose. 'Be nice, Don't bite.' He cringes
> 'So,' he says, 'what do you want to be able to do?'
> 'What do you mean?' I ask.
> 'Like morph, wear clothes, change size…'

'How about a Mudhouse?' I ask.
'Oh sure, got a name for it?'
'The Loft.'
'Type @dig The Loft'
Suddenly it exists and I'm there.

(Hertz, 1994: 279–80)

Thorin goes on to introduce Rollergirl to a number of other features, such as extra emotions, before making the pass at her that leads to their unhappy parting. Rollergirl gains access to greater power in the MUD by learning small pieces of computer code. Underneath the code that Rollergirl learns that is widely available to avatars is the code that wizards have access to that constitutes the MUD and allowed, for example, the execution of Mr_Bungle. This code accepts avatars logging in, maintains records of avatars' names, characteristics and the objects they build, defines the sorts of tools available to avatars and so on. Underneath this layer of technology is the Internet and computer technology that allows people to reach the MUD and log on, bringing their avatar alive. Technopower in MUDs is constituted out of at least these three levels, with each defining the sorts of powers individuals will have and the sorts of social structures that are likely to develop. Other corners of cyberspace will have similar layers of technology and expertise creating technopower.

In each part of cyberspace, technopower will be constituted around a constant, inescapable oscillation between what appears as inert technology and what seem to be social values. Rollergirl was taught a command @dig that allowed her to create a virtual home. This command was not written by her but picked up as if it were a hammer or wrench. It was something she used without having to think about it, neither did the command think about her. Inert, @dig lay there uncaring whether it was ever used, uncaring what name or type of home was built. @dig was a thing. This MUD was a social space constituted partly out of the ability of avatars to use the @dig command, leading to a society where people could construct personal spaces outside of communal spaces. This was a MUD that allowed a distinction between public and private, through @dig. One small element of the fundamental fabric of this virtual society resulted from a simple thing-like command but someone coded this command, it did not simply happen. Someone decided they wanted a home or that homes were a good idea in this or any MUD and they wrote the software code that allowed avatars to build virtual homes. The 'thingness' of @dig here opens up on values and beliefs of other people, no longer present when Rollergirl builds The Loft, who thought that @dig was a good idea. Those who wrote that command would have themselves employed a certain type of software code, the code that constitutes the MUD, and modified it to create @dig. The code to create the MUD would itself appear to the writer(s) of @dig as a tool, another thing, which could in turn be opened out to ask who wrote the MUD code. Who wrote the software code that creates online, real-time virtual environments capable of being extended and modified? At each point, there is an oscillation between the inert objectivity of software and hardware that has itself been previously constituted for human or social reasons out of other inert, objective tools. Both sides of this wavering are necessary, neither exists without the other. If no human had coded software or designed and built hardware, then no cybersociety could result and no cybersociety can be maintained if the software and hardware that support it are taken away.[10] Technopower is the constant shifting between objects that appear as neutral things – keyboards, monitors, email programs – and the social or ethical values embedded in these objects. Each questions the other. If email software allows easy many-to-many communication, we can ask: Why? Who made the software do this? What results come from this? And in asking we may open up the inhumane appearance of the program to find humans who embedded their ethics or ideals in a program. Technopower underpins the social structures of cyberspace through a constant shape-shifting between seemingly inert technology and alive-seeming values.

This does not mean that every piece of technology was created with a form of technopower in mind. Not every technological thing we encounter or rely on in cyberspace has been purposefully designed to constitute the social life it actually constitutes. The unexpected result is always possible, like the emergence of Teflon from the space race. But what will be found behind each thing will be human(s) in social spaces, making decisions within institutional and technological contexts. Dead technology always opens on the living. For example, consider perhaps the greatest icon of the digital age, the @ symbol, the single character that sits between your handle and your domain name to constitute your virtual address. The @'s place in cyberspace was created in 1972 by Ray Tomlinson, working for the firm Bolt, Beranek and Newman. Tomlinson was writing a small email program to be used on ARPANET, and almost as an afterthought it was going to be added to a new file transfer program. Tomlinson needed something to separate the name of a user from their machine. He was working on a certain keyboard, Model 33 Teletype, which only had around a dozen punctuation characters and he chose '@'. It had the advantage of meaning 'at', but any of the punctuation characters on this keyboard would have done. Indeed, several other email programs on other networks used different symbols, especially the '!' (Hafner and Lyon, 1996: 191–2; Quarterman, 1990: 216–22). The success of the Internet and its roots in ARPANET now ensure @ is as close to an undisputed thing as cyberspace may ever get. We can also see in Tomlinson's story various elements that appear as things, but which we could examine just as we have the @. Who designed the Model 33 Teletype? Why does it only have the punctuation characters it does? Certainly, it was never designed with the thought in mind that the @ must be included so that at some future time Tomlinson could turn it into an icon for the digital world. But, certainly, humans designed the Model 33.

Technopower is constituted like an infinite series of Chinese boxes, each opening onto another little model of itself, and each layer composed of the same elements: inert-seeming technology and alive-seeming values. Technopower can also be seen in offline life; from car engines (why are they made so powerful?) to ice cream, we live surrounded by technological artefacts that leak social values from every crevice. The difference between online and offline is that online social forms are constituted fundamentally, if not totally, from technopowers. The fundamental importance of realising that cyberspace is informational space is that it means technopower is dominant in online societies. When we adopt the perspective of the social in cyberspace, we lose sight of individuals and their powers and bring into focus impersonal powers based on particular technopowers that constitute the very possibility that cyberspace exists in the first place. But where do individuals fit in? How do they relate to technopower? And, if technopower is impersonal, why do so many experience cyberspace as a place where they gain greater power?

Individuals feel themselves both restrained and enabled by technology and these opposed feelings spring from the moment when technology is felt to be a thing that offers capacities for action. When using electronic mail, the @ helps us utilise a world-wide, cheap means of communication but the @ is also mandatory. If someone's @ key malfunctions, then the power of email will be immediately withdrawn. The oscillation in technopower creates moments when individuals can use the expertise or hardware others have provided, by using the technology that appears to them as a thing. Millions of email users have been able to use Ray Tomlinson's expertise by using the @. All the avatars in a MUD rely on the hardware and software provided by someone else and can do so with little thought because the MUD and its possibilities appear as things waiting for individuals to bring them to life. Anybody's place in technopower will be defined by the things they rely on and the things they are creating for others to rely on. Technical expertise, or the conviction of being powerful in cyberspace, is the individual resolution of all the pieces of technology someone can use or change. Everybody online is part of multiple webs or networks of technology, both ones that determine their actions and ones in which they are allowed to act and feel powerful. Expertise always builds on networks of other experts and on previous expertise. The ability to wield technical expertise is, then, not a personal attribute but a set of relations that situate certain individuals in positions as experts or as able to act.

The translations that continually position people in relation to technopower can be seen in the development of email systems. The first electronic mail systems were very simple. They delivered a message to a virtual mailbox, where the owner of the box could pick it up. There was no separation between the messages in the box: if you wanted one message printed out you had to print out all the messages you had received; if you wanted to see one message on the screen you had to look through all the messages. This was obviously onerous but users were still able to send email, utilising software and hardware designed by others to send messages. Soon, features like the separation of different emails was developed, the ability to reply automatically appeared and graphical versions arose. Now many email programs allow all these and other features, such as filtering mail (automatically sorting mail into different groups), options for storing mail, for developing complicated mailing lists and so on. At each stage of the development of email a certain form of software and hardware comes together to create a set of possibilities for users. These possibilities form the powers users feel they have, and these powers are reliant on the possibilities email software and hardware technicians were able to embed in the software and hardware that are being used. Individuals are positioned in technopower by their relationship to each of these stages: Which email program can someone use? Can they use all of a program's features? Could they modify the program to improve it or even write an entirely new program? Answers to such questions can be given for each individual in each particular context, again drawing our eye towards the power of individuals in cyberspace, but each question's answer springs from the form of technopower circulating in that context.

Such a relational form of power that situates individuals within contexts rather than looking to the power individuals wield mirrors the theories of Barnes and Foucault. Both see power as relations between individuals that situate the individuals, rather than as a possession utilised by individuals. The circuits of power are ones in which individuals act but over which no single individual has control, because Chinese box within Chinese box of thing-like technology next to value-laden human creativity creates a vast framework in cyberspace. All the pieces of technology constitute this framework, all the individuals and all the relations between technological artefacts and living individuals make up technopower. Nobody can hope to control or direct this vast web of power, even as everyone within it feels they are controlling or directing parts of it. The subjects of cyberspace are subjected to technopower, in the sense of both being constituted as creative, desiring individuals and being directed as dutiful, compliant individuals. Both Barnes and Foucault theorise power in this way; at this general level of analysis of technopower there is no real choice between their two theories of power. But there are differences between the two theories and one key difference poses a question to technopower that needs further analysis.

Barnes analyses power as the constituent of social order. The importance of seemingly trivial moments of social order to his work, like the red traffic light, is that they explain the micro-practices that maintain any social order, even the most insignificant. For Barnes, power is something that is normal as it is the constituent of social order. Power in the abstract is neither good nor bad; it only becomes good or bad when it is realised in particular societies. Foucault also analyses power and its micro-practices to explore how some of the most basic elements of social order are maintained, but he finds in power the explanation for domination. For Foucault, it is a fact that micro-instances of power aggregate into broad, society-wide strategies for domination and resistance. Where Barnes analyses power to explore the elements that constitute any social order,

Foucault theorises power to define the ways we are dominated, the ways we are subjected. So far, technopower appears to be the controlling circuits that underpin online life, that make it possible and structure its particularities, but we do not know whether this is simply the way order emerges online or whether inequalities will be its inevitable result. To define technopower more closely, its particular dynamics need to be outlined and assessed.

The spiral of technopower

What pattern does technopower in cyberspace have? It is not hard to guess that any such pattern will, first, be primarily concerned with the flow of information in cyberspace and, second, will largely define the underlying dynamics of online life. Cyberspace is constituted out of information, both in its material substructure of computers, software and wires and in its content, where information is constantly circulated to construct avatars and societies. This object can be understood as a reinterpretation of the third component of individual power in cyberspace – that cyberspace is informational space. From the viewpoint of the social the structuring factors that create informational space, and that then enable identity fluidity and renovated hierarchies, become the central topic for analysis, whereas from the viewpoint of the individual informational space is the result of individual cyberpowers. For social power in cyberspace to be fully explored, some of the fundamental patterns of information flows in cyberspace need to be outlined. Having done this, a more complex sense of how power distributes opportunities or abilities in online societies will also emerge. Information flows that offer capacities for action to some and not to others will largely define whether technopower constitutes a system of domination even as it constitutes online social order. The point to begin is information and its fundamental trends in cyberspace, while the point to aim for is social order and/or domination.

Perhaps the fundamental fact about information in cyberspace is that far more of it is available and moves at far greater speeds than ever before. As will be noted in the following chapter, the increase in both amounts and speed of information is true of both offline and online life. For example, on major network television in the USA between 1965 and 1995 the average advertisement shrunk from 53.1 to 25.4 seconds, the average news 'soundbite' shrunk from 42.3 to 8.3 seconds and the number of advertisements per minute increased from 1.1 to 2.4 (Shenk, 1997: 29). This represents shorter bursts of information, more often. Perhaps the most significant factor is the simple fact that in the overdeveloped countries the majority of workers now process and transmit information, increasing exponentially the amount of information that is available and the number of people using it (Webster, 1995; Castells, 1996). Cyberspace represents the most extreme example of this general acceleration of the production and circulation of information because it is constituted out of information. Further, cyberspace is not only subject to this acceleration but one of the factors creating it. Many-to-many communication, the multimedia Web, virtually instant world-wide document transfer, powerful search mechanisms to locate people, organisations and information – all of these, and more, are or are becoming essentially cyberspatial. Cyberspace also encourages people to produce more information rather than passively consume it. Producing television programmes and having them broadcast is expensive and difficult, but designing a Web page is as simple as word processing a document (if an appropriate program is used). Usenet has always encouraged production of information by many people, as has email with its ease of sending and replying to multiple addresses. Information moves faster, in greater quantities and in different forms in cyberspace. Most powerfully, cyberspace increases information by releasing it from material manifestations that restrict its flow and increase its price. Since the invention of printing presses allowed the mass distribution of information in pamphlets, books and newspapers, the form of information has determined the amount, cost and speed of the content of information. Ideas embodied in books have inherent costs and restrictions on the number that can be produced and the speed at which different people can obtain them, based on the simple fact that they have to be printed, bound and distributed. But ideas in cyberspace take advantage of the immaterial nature of ideas to alter radically the ability to spread information. Information is largely freed of its material form in cyberspace and can take advantage far more of the fact that in sharing information the original does not degrade and is not lost.

> The big error with information has been mistaking the container for the content....We're still focused on this idea that information is a product, a property, a thing, that it's made out of atoms and not out of bits....Trying to own information in the standard property model doesn't work. Property is something that can be taken from you. If I own a horse and you steal it, I can't ride it anymore, and its value has been lost to me. But if I have an idea and you steal it, not only do I still have the same idea, but the fact that two people now have that idea makes it intrinsically more valuable.
>
> (Barlow, cited in Brockman, 1996: 11)

An idea gains in value as more people use it, even if stealing it might mean the originator does not receive credit. Information is not its material form but its content and cyberspace alters the form to make the content infinitely reproducible. For someone to obtain the ideas in a book they must have the book. For many people to have those ideas many copies must be printed or the book must be placed in a central library where it can be repeatedly lent out to one person at a time. In contrast, information on a Web site needs only one version that many can view and take whatever copies they want. The same points can be made about file transfer or Usenet: one copy can be placed in cyberspace and virtually infinite numbers of copies can be taken. This distribution of information is only limited by the speed of access to the cyberspatial version. This analysis springs most famously from Marshall McLuhan's argument that '"the medium is the message" because it is the medium that shapes and controls the scale and form of human association and action' (McLuhan, 1995: 152). The message of cyberspace's medium is that information is freed from material constraints and becomes almost infinitely reproducible and available, or as Shenk puts it, 'Information, once rare and cherished like caviar, is now plentiful and taken for granted like potatoes' (Shenk, 1997: 27; Barlow, 1996b). Cyberspace plays a fundamental role in altering the nature of information's production, distribution and consumption by allowing radically greater amounts and speeds of information flow.

Information overload

A problem emerges here, however, because it is possible to have so much information that the ability to understand it is impaired: the important cannot be distinguished from the unimportant and too large amounts of information simply cannot be absorbed. While the notion of having too much information might seem paradoxical, it is also the case that only a certain amount of information can be dealt with at one time. Anyone buying all the Sunday newspapers will quickly find their Sunday disappearing into a day of newspaper reading or will have to contemplate wryly a pile of information they simply could not process. As early as 1985, Hiltz and Turroff estimated that computer-mediated communication resulted in what they call superconnectivity, whereby individuals' connections to each other increase ten-fold (Hiltz and Turroff, 1985: 688). Similarly, the GVU surveys consistently report around half their respondents feeling more connected to people who share their interests since coming online (Pitkow and Kehoe, 1996b; 1997). Hiltz and Turroff conducted a study of a computer-conferencing system that was dedicated to the 'design and evaluation of alternative structures for computerized human communication' and asked a sample of users how frequently they felt overloaded with information. In two surveys, 25.5 per cent of those who used the system for 10–49 hours per week felt overloaded always or almost always, while 48.5 per cent felt overloaded sometimes. Taken together these results mean that 74 per cent of people felt overloaded at least sometimes. Hiltz and Turroff argued that overload was mitigated by familiarity with technology because they found overload reduced for users with over a hundred hours per week on the system. However, a hundred hours per week is an extraordinarily high amount of time online, with GVU surveys indicating that only 22 per cent of Web users were online over twenty hours per week. Hiltz and Turroff's claims that overload decreases as users become more experienced appear highly optimistic (Hiltz and Turroff, 1985: 682). Shenk has an apocalyptic view of information overload, arguing that it is widespread, leading to new epidemics of stress and workplace injuries and threatening democracy:

Information overload threatens our ability to educate ourselves, and leaves us more vulnerable as consumers and less cohesive as a society. For most of us, it actually diminishes our control over our own lives, while those already in power find their positions considerably strengthened.

(Shenk, 1997: 15)

Shenk argues that in the last fifty years societies have gone from lacking information to becoming overwhelmed by it. The result of this is health problems, such as increased heart and blood pressure and weakened vision, weakened consumers because the glut of information is confusing, and a decline in people's behaviour, because their inability to manage information leads to frustration. Shenk also reports that too much information not only impairs decision making but simultaneously increases confidence in decision making, creating a world of poorer decisions held to more strongly. (Shenk, 1997: 35–50).

Two types of information overload can be broadly distinguished. First, there is too much information. Second, information can be so chaotically organised that it cannot be used – what Hiltz and Turroff call information entropy. The Web is an almost constant example of the first problem. If you searched the Web for 'information and overload' in 1997, one search service returned 45,910 possible connections. Examining all 45,910 is undoubtedly too much information. Shenk also notes the problem of cyberspace producing information overload:

here is a summary of what I've collected over four years of research. I have:

- purchased 40 books
- photocopied 600 pages from library books and journals
- torn out 575 newspaper and magazine articles
- recorded 80 hours of interviews

These numbers are normal and will not surprise anyone who has done a large research project. But my electronic access has brought me a mountain of information that has dwarfed my conventional research material.

Electronically, I have:

- conducted 481 Nexis searches, downloading 46.2 megabytes (the equivalent of 14,000 pages) of text
- visited roughly 1,000 Websites, downloading hundreds of additional pages of text.
All told, I have electronically amassed 700 separate text files, taking up 69.2 megabytes of memory space on my computer – that's 69 million 'bytes', the equivalent of 23,067 pages of text.

(Shenk, 1997: 46–7)

As Shenk notes, all this information is entirely practical from the computer's point of view, but is impossible for humans. There is simply too much of it to be useful.

The second problem of information overload, entropy, is indicated by the gap between 45,910 records returned by one search mechanism and a return of two records for the same words on another search mechanism. The gap between two records of interest and 45,910 records, for the same topic, indicates serious variation in the way records are organised. There are seemingly ever increasing means of searching cyberspace to find information or places, but they do not, even taken together, manage the information in cyberspace. For example, numerous means of searching the Web are available and results can be obtained by jumping between different search engines. For example, Yahoo! (http://www.yahoo.com) attempts to categorise all information into a taxonomy. This means that Web sites that track pollution will be categorised under 'Society and Culture: Environment and Nature: Pollution'. The obvious problem is that not all sites will cleanly and neatly fit into such categories (Steinberg, 1996: 62–3). A site like HotBot (http://www.hotbot.com) allows searches on key words rather than fitting all information into a pre-given taxonomy, as well as further techniques such as fuzzy logic. Between two such sites, or any of several others, reasonably powerful searches of the Web can be done, all at the cost of gaining familiarity with each site's particular interface and search philosophy. It is also unlikely that even taken together these search mechanisms organise and make accessible the Web's information. However, finding information in cyberspace is only the first problem of entropy. A second problem often emerges when so much information is found that it cannot be used in any meaningful way. Printing copies of useful documents found on the Web is an easy way of obtaining the information, but suddenly a researcher's room fills up with piles of loose paper that need to be organised. Some time later they are all placed into lever arch files but this needs to be done rationally so that information can be found, and by the time this has been done new piles of paper have appeared and also need to be filed. Entropy looms with the sensible researcher giving up becoming a full-time filing clerk. With so much information available in cyberspace, solving one problem of information overload leads to other, similar problems.

Between piles of paper or megabytes of files that would take a lifetime to read and those piles and megabytes being disorganised, there exists the constant problem of information overload. Either too much information or poorly organised information can lead to overload and both tend to lead to each other. The constant promise that a vital piece of information or a vibrant place of virtual life are just out there, slightly beyond our reach, often drives those in online life further into the embrace of information. Worse, these promises are often true. There is vital information on scores of topics, increasingly tending towards all possible topics, and there are vibrant communities in Usenet, on MUDs and elsewhere all waiting to be found. The result for most is at some point it will be too much, too disorganised and the burnout of information overload will become a virtual companion.

Pressures feeding information overload also come from cyberpower of the individual because access is a key political problem. As already argued, because of the advantages for individuals offered by cyberspace, access becomes a central political problem. The demographic profile of cyberspace users means access is largely defined as the problem of increasing access for those who are not yet able to go online. The result is that as the Internet and the Web gain greater publicity, more desire to go online is created and as various political forces align around issues of access then growth of the Internet can only be expected to continue. With Moore's law fuelling a continuous drop in prices or rise in power, barriers to access become ever lower. Yet, more people in an interactive environment means greater amounts of information circulating at the light speed of cyberspace; more people using and posting to Usenet, more people creating Web sites, more people sending and receiving email. Increased access will lead to more users suffering information overload and more users creating information that causes overload. The underlying power of cyberspace beginning from the social here touches cyberpower of the individual, with individualised cyberpower creating pressure to increase amounts and circulation of information, in turn leading to information overload.

The problem of information overload that seems inherent in cyberspatial communication, combined with political pressure towards greater access, produces ever increasing amounts and speeds of information and recurring problems of information overload. But if this were true, it seems obvious that cyberspace would already have ground to a halt, with burned-out information warriors simply giving up. The vast increases in numbers of Internet users mean that if the preceding claims were true, then some sort of information catastrophe should probably already have happened. Even a total melt-down should have already occurred, with users turning away from a medium that for all its seductions collapses under the weight of its own nature. That this has not occurred leads back to technopower, because it is increased management of information by technical tools that keeps information overload at bay. For example, for many people the initial use of email is attractive but then the amount of email they begin to receive becomes a burden. Worse, many people who send email can set their program to notify them that the email has arrived, when it arrived and when the recipient opened it. Suddenly, features that appeared to be an advantage become less attractive. Someone can easily send simple queries and know when they are received and read, ensuring the sender can police the receiver. Email boxes can become filled with inane queries that have to be answered, politely, or the person who sent them can produce evidence of slow or inadequate responses. People who have voicemail, pagers, mobile phones, faxes and email in personal digital assistants are never out of reach and must constantly respond or become known as rude or sluggish respondents. The answer to this problem for many people is an intelligent agent. Maxims is a program that learns to prioritise, delete, forward, sort and archive emails. Maxims monitors the conduct of the user and records different situations, such as which emails the user deletes and which the user archives, and creates rules that describe these situations. Maxims then uses these rules to control the user's email, appearing as an intelligent assistant who automatically performs some basic functions freeing someone from an overload of email (Maes, 1994). Similarly, there is a program called Smoky being developed that recognises insulting email or flames and there are programs that allow the user to bar access to various forms of information (Spertus, 1996). Placing a techno-logical tool in between the person and the flow of information can control information overload. People are rescued from information overload at the seemingly minor cost of greater reliance on technology.

Technological solutions to information overload are widely used. Maes lists intelligent agents that schedule meetings, filter Usenet news and recommend books, music and other entertainment (Maes, 1994). Another example is the idea of a personalised newspaper, delivered fresh to your computer every morning. A knowledgeable robot (know-bot, in fact another software program) can be taught your news likes and dislikes. It then searches news services or Web sites for information you are interested in and pieces all that it finds into a 'newspaper' that is delivered to your desktop PC (Maes, 1994). Various solu-tions to the glut of information that cyberspace produces have been created, from news services that email news bulletins once a day to ticker tapes that produce a constant flow of stock prices or news flashes across a browser. All these share a number of traits. First, they interpose some moment of technology between the user and information. This is always simultaneously a moment in which technopower is manifested and articulated because some technological tool, appearing as a thing yet operating according to values, is the way of controlling information overload. Second, the devices themselves produce information problems because they need to be installed and used properly. No matter how sophisticated such a device is, and many are sophisticated enough to 'learn' rather than having to be told what to do, the user will need to under-stand how to manage the device or risk being controlled by it. A device that sets up meetings or filters email conducts work too important to be completely out of users' direct control, creating further information needs. Third, tools that minimise information overload nearly always make cyberspace easier to use. This can be true to the extent that entering cyberspace is no longer needed for cyberspace to reach out and offer someone information. If someone simply cannot be bothered to overcome the barriers to going online, then they could still receive a personalised newspaper from cyberspace, simply by automating the whole procedure to the point of automatically printing out the newspaper every morning.

The fourth trait needs careful consideration because new tools nearly always make more information available, tending to create another problem of infor-mation overload. When users are overloaded they stop being able to use information sources effectively and when a technological device solves this problem it also increases the information someone is using. This seems too para-doxical to be true, as the goal of many tools for managing information overload is to reduce the amount of information received by focusing or managing it in some automated way. However, the very success of any such tool tends towards the production of more information because it makes gaining information more efficient and there is always more relevant information waiting out there in cyberspace. After an initial dip, when information seems to be being managed more efficiently and information overload reduces, problems can be expected to re-emerge with the devices that have become essential to information management producing too much information. For example, receiving emails from a news service every day means receiving one more email, one more possibly crucial piece of information, every day. Or having a browser on which stock prices tick across means being connected to your stock portfolio (assuming you have one) and to your possible wealth, every minute. Sell or buy becomes a permanent state. In this way, efforts to control information overload also produce new forms of overload. This spiral of overload, tools, more overload and more tools is fundamental to technopower in cyberspace and will be discussed in more detail below, but before that a more extended example will be useful, particularly because the greatest example of technological answers to information overload is the emergence of the Web itself.

To understand the fundamental importance of information overload to technopower it is important to see it at work in the chief cause of cyberspace's rapidly growing popularity, the World-Wide Web. The Web's fundamental breakthrough was to organise the resources of the Internet through a graphical user interface (GUI). Graphical user interface means exactly what it says and was invented initially, in the computer communications world, for personal computers. The interface is the means by which humans command computers. For most of us this is a screen that registers the changes we make as we type them (depending on the complexity of request and the relative obsolescence of the computer, of course). The first mainframe computers did not even have this sort of interface but received requests in the form of stacks of punched cards and responded in the form of printouts. This meant that anybody using a computer had to be able to code software, obviously a block to widespread computer use. Something similar was the case with early personal computers. By the late 1970s a microchip had been produced that was powerful and cheap enough to allow, for the first time, a personal computer. The result was something called the Altair, which had to be programmed by flicking switches and responded with flashing lights. Gradually a keyboard and a video terminal were added, particularly in the pioneering Apple II, and new forms of personal computers were created, but each communicated through words or commands typed on a keyboard that appeared on a screen that in turn showed the results (Levy, 1984: 187–92, 53–63). The next stage was to produce graphics on a screen that could be manipulated, negating the need to learn many different commands to run each piece of software. This was invented in the early 1980s by Xerox Corporation's Parc (Palo Alto Research Centre) Laboratory in a computer called the Alto. The Alto had a small box connected to the computer that controlled a pointer on the screen in addition to a keyboard, what we now know as a mouse, and it had graphical symbols on the screen. Examples of these symbols were a garbage bin for files that needed to be deleted or filing systems represented by images of filing cabinets (Rheingold, 1991: 69, 85–7). One of the founders of Apple Corporation saw this computer and applied its interface to the now famous Macintosh PC, whose popularity led to GUI becoming the normal computer interface (though by 1998 Microsoft's version of GUI, Win95/98, is the GUI most are familiar with).

The coming of GUI to the Internet occurred with the World-Wide Web and the Mosaic browser. These allowed all the different resources of the Internet to be organised behind the one common, intuitive interface that had the added advantage of using the same type of interface as most personal computers.[11] Familiarity and ease bred a sudden flowering. It was no longer a matter of knowing different commands on different computer systems, nearly always counter-intuitive, and the place of the Internet at the heart of a revolution in information speed and access was ensured. This change is also a technological solution. For most people, the Web and their browser are technological things, objects they use as tools. The emergence of a multimedia, GUI-based cyberspace is a quintessential moment of technopower, when vast numbers of people are able to use a technological resource because they have at their disposal a tool whose workings they need not worry about. This moment in technopower also answers problems of information overload because rather than needing to learn multiple information skills – how to log on, how to issue correct commands, which place to go for which information – only the ability to start a browser and then point and click is needed. A technological solution to a technical problem seems to have occurred. To prevent information overload in cyberspace more complicated tools were developed that helped organise information and offered greater control. At the same time, this ensured the development of a new context of technopower as new tools were generated, each tool embedded with certain values that appeared to users as things. The problem of information overload produced by the pre-Web Internet is answered by technological solutions that simultaneously and necessarily articulate technopower.

This can be further seen through the visionary and hyperbolic articulation of 'push' media as both the future and the end of the Web. The Web at its inception was essentially a 'pull' media, because Web sites had to be 'pulled' by people and did not arrive on someone's computer unless asked for. By 1997, a number of ways of information being pushed to someone's desktop computer were being developed. This has been interpreted by some as a new paradigm for the Web as a combined push–pull media and, ultimately, as the transformation of the Web and the end of the browser:

As things get more and more wired, media of all kinds are moving to the decentralised matrix known as the Net. While the traditional forms –

broadcast and print – show few signs of vanishing, the Net is being invaded by new species of media....Yet with each additional node, each new T1 line, the media that the Internet can support become richer, more complex, more nuanced. The Net has begun to offer things you simply can't browse....Technology that, say, follows you into the next taxi you take, gently prodding you to visit the local aquarium, while keeping you up-to-date on your favourite basketball team's game in progress. Another device might chime on your wrist, letting you know that the route home is congested with traffic, and flashing the address of a restaurant where you can eat cut-price sushi while waiting it out. On your computer at home, the same system will run soothing screensavers underneath regular news flashes, while keeping track of press releases from companies in which you own stocks. With frequent commercial messages, of course.

(Kelly and Wolf, 1997: 70)

Rather than having to sit at a desktop or laptop computer and laboriously search for information on local sites of interest, sports results or traffic, intelligent agents will have learnt to follow your needs, even to the point of anticipating that with traffic busy you might like to eat cheap food rather than drive. The underlying dynamic is that the information being generated on the Internet is becoming so complex that new means of receiving it are needed or useful information will be out of reach. This is a classic dilemma of information overload. The information is out on the net but there is simply too much and it is becoming too complex for individuals to reach out and take it with their browser. The answer is to interpose other technological tools that will push the information you 'really want' to different information-reading tools – personal digital assistant, laptop, pager, mobile phone or preferably all these things rolled into one device – that you can always have with you; 'a new medium is arising, surging across the Web in the preferred, many-to-many way: anything flows from anyone to anyone, from anywhere to anywhere, at any time' (Kelly and Wolf, 1997: 72). Kelly and Wolf's vision is undoubtedly hyperbolic, so much so that a year after publishing it *Wired* admitted push was coming slower and in less striking forms than they had anticipated (Boutin, 1998). However, their exaggeration is useful because it makes clear the pressure information overload brings to bear and because the changes they envisage relate to other changes occurring in browsers.

In early 1998 people normally entered the Web by starting a browser which automatically took them to a certain Web site; from there the user must use search mechanisms, hyperlinks or known addresses to navigate around looking for the information they need. Once they find what they want, give up out of frustration or simply become too confused by the links they have jumped around on to continue, people turn off their browser and return to their computer's other functions such as word processing or spreadsheets. It is possible to jump between the two, browser and desktop, and even to keep a window open to each, watching and working on them in quick succession, but in early 1998 it was normal that the two were distinct entities. A transformation being pushed by some of the largest Internet corporations is the merging of these two, so that information is constantly arriving from the Web even as you work on other things and if while working you need extra information you can automatically be transported to it, rather than having to launch a browser and search for it. Netscape is working on a 'wholly new interface, code-named Constellation, which serves both pull and push content straight from the computer desktop – in other words, without having to launch a browser' (Kelly and Wolf, 1997: 72). Another powerful push in this direction is coming from Microsoft, which is planning to embed hypermedia and the Web into its new operating system (Windows 98) and has released a browser (Internet Explorer 4) that can operate as a hypermedia desktop environment.

The importance of Microsoft's plan is measured by its dominance of operating systems in personal computers; these are the programs that make the computer run and allow the more useful packages, such as word processors, to operate. It is estimated that 80–90 per cent of personal computers use a Microsoft operating system, generally either Windows 3.1 or Windows 95/98. The way Microsoft organises its operating system leads directly to the way most individuals use their computers. Brad Chase is in charge of developing Microsoft's Internet Explorer and explains the new relationship between browser and operating system that Microsoft is creating this way:

> we're trying to solve the user problem that today you browse the hard disk [on your personal computer] one way, browse the network another way, and you browse the Web a third way…the key issue is that users are trying to get access to information, and what we're trying to do is make that simpler. So, for example, you might click on your C: drive to find…some information on your hard disk. And then you might single-click again – just like you do on the Web – on my documents to search through my documents, then go through your hard disk that way…and then decide 'Ooh, I want to go back to some proposal documents', and you would just click a Back button.…It will do other things as well, for example the ability to basically make your desktop a Web page…we are helping the broader issue of getting the user to the information they want more quickly. I could be browsing my C: drive and looking for information on, let's say, a proposal to sell some real estate to a customer, then I realize I needed some information about that that's on the Internet. I don't have to launch the browser, wait for the browser to click in, and do all that. I could type right in the Address bar the URL and go do it.
>
> (Chase, cited in McChesney, 1997)

The distinction between browser and desktop collapses, meaning that users can shift between their local C: drive and the Internet without noticing the distinction. Most have seen this as an attempt to use Microsoft's dominance of operating systems to win the battle with Netscape and make Internet Explorer the dominant means of exploring the Web.[12] A further reason for such a shift is the pressure to allow people easier and quicker access and the resulting extension of technological solutions that articulate technopower. Making the desktop akin to a Web page and then erasing the distinction between the desktop and the Internet makes computing one seamless search for information. This will undoubtedly make access easier for many, removing the need to set up separate connections,[13] and it will introduce many to the Web in ways that had not been expected. As push media have been integrated into this set-up as well, Kelly and Wolf's hope and expectation that everything and anything will flow to everyone at any time might appear close to coming true:

> In essence, what you want with a browser is to get information you want more quickly....For example,...[m]aybe you want to put your stock ticker on your desktop. Maybe you want to put the latest news headlines on your desktop. Maybe you want to be able to create a whole business desktop for my company that has information relevant to the business or industry I'm in, and have that right on my desktop.
>
> (Chase, cited in McChesney, 1997)

The difference between software project manager Chase and writers Kelly and Wolf is that the latter were hyping a new paradigm, while Chase was trying to build it. Kelly and Wolf also refer to the chief executive officer of Netscape, Jim Barksdale, because the makers of cyberspace's most used browser, Netscape Navigator, are moving in exactly the same direction as Microsoft. This is understandable not only in terms of information and the Internet but also because, as Bill Gates points out,

> Essentially, Netscape wants to take a browser and turn it into an operating system. We want to take an operating system and have enough Internet capability built in so that people continue to view Windows as the best way to use the Internet.
>
> (Gates, cited in Brockman, 1996: 99)

If the browser and the desktop collapse into each other, then Microsoft can try to use their dominance of operating systems to gain domination of browsers and Netscape can try to use their dominance of browsers to enter the operating systems market. The picture was further complicated in late 1997 because another powerful corporation, Sun Microsystems, developed another division of operating systems and Internet software, one that aimed at doing away with the powerful personal computer altogether. They claim their programming language Java makes it possible for people to order the computer tools they need when they need them. Rather than having a word processor sitting unused on a PC, they argue, why not download it when you need it? Cofounder and Chief Executive Office of Sun, Scott McNealy, puts it this way:

> You can deliver a Java-based computer that has no disk drive, no floppy, no CD, no operating system, and minimal memory; then you can use the network to store files, applications, data, video, audio, Web access, security and billing. All these activities can be handled in the server room by a trained professional....When you're on your network client, your Java client, you click on Word Processor and download a four-function word processor. It comes down in a heartbeat because there aren't many lines of code. It has four functions: Backspace, Delete, Cut and Paste, and Print. If I need right-hand justification, I can download that. If I need a new font, I can download that.
>
> (McNealy, cited in Brockman, 1996: 211, 213)

Instead of a powerful desktop computer that always has complex programs waiting to be used, Java allows simple, cheap terminals on desktops that are served via cyberspace. Here Sun undercuts any discussions about operating systems by virtually doing away with them. A desktop that can be personally designed for each individual also offers potential for handling information overload by reducing the complexity of desktops and leaving all the complications of setting up and maintaining software to a computer professional.

Sun, Microsoft and Netscape – in each case pressures of information overload create a demand on the basis of which the competition for control of your desktop computer and your access to cyberspace is being played out. It is always possible that the problems of building such systems will mean they will not work or that people will reject a system that removes the personal property of their C: drive for communal vistas of information, but the fact that three of the major corporations constructing cyberspace were all heading in the same direction in mid-1997 means that certain underlying forces were being felt. The breakthrough that allowed people to navigate cyberspace with simple point and click devices, which opened up the information world to computer novices, has given way to pressures to deliver more information faster. The pressures of information overload are nowhere more profoundly registered than in these two shifts, first to the Web and GUI browsers and, second, to the need to reinvent browsers felt by Sun, Netscape and Microsoft. A new paradigm for computer-mediated communication has been articulated because more information might be gained more quickly. If anyone needed proof that technopower in cyberspace is fed by a constant spiral that begins when information overload is felt, that continues with the invention of new tools to manage overload and starts again when those tools lead to new forms of overload, then a few moments of reflection on both the emergence of the Web and the mid-1997 hype for push and the collapse of the browser/desktop distinction are all that is needed.

The complete spiral

All the elements of technopower in cyberspace have been articulated in the preceding examples. First, information overload is an automatic result of entering cyberspace; the world of information is the world of too much information. Second, problems of information overload are normally dealt with by introducing new technological tools that both manage information and place further technological distance between user and information. Third, the new technological tools simply return users, after varying lengths of time, to the first step because new forms of information overload emerge. Round and round the spiral goes, continually layering greater amounts of technology between users and the information they seek, claiming to make information gathering simpler but always producing too much information. It is not that people are paralysed by too much information, though they can be, but that there is always the conviction that just around the corner, with some new technology, we will finally be able to master this world of information and truly know what we want, when we want to. An abstract hunger for a virtually infinite amount of information is created and that can never be satisfied.

Technopower in cyberspace is governed by the ever increasing reliance by users on technological tools that time after time appear as neutrally pointing the way to greater management of information, but time after time result in different forms of information constituted by the values inherent in tools that can never satisfy the abstract need for information. The direction of technopower in cyberspace is towards greater elaboration of technological tools to more people who have less ability to understand the nature of those tools. Control of the possibilities for life in cyberspace is delivered, through this spiral, to those with expertise in the increasingly complex software and hardware needed to constitute the tools that allow individual users to create virtual lives and societies. The ultimate direction of cybersocieties is towards increasing control by elites empowered within technopower and decreasing control of the fabric of cyberspace for individuals. The irony is that greater elaboration of technology is demanded by individuals and appears to them as tools for increased control of information. The pressure to control information overload comes from users who suffer from it or who are frustrated by the information they cannot obtain. This pressure produces tools that simultaneously answer one problem of information overload while producing new forms of it: that which sets infon(a)uts free enslaves them. The continual elaboration of technopower delivers the fabric of life in cyberspace to an elite and is called for by individuals seeking answers to information overload. Individuals strive to free themselves in cyberspace with the tools of an informational world. As a consequence, we have become dedicated to the endless task of forcing information's secrets from cyberspace, of exacting the truest confessions from a shadow. The irony of this deployment is in having us believe that our 'liberation' is in the balance.

The spiral of technopower defines the particular nature or direction of technopower in cyberspace. Particular structures and pressures in cyberspace feed into the creation of technology according to values and its use or appearance as inert things. These pressures point towards growing control of cyberspace by elites who are defined by their technical expertise, that is their ability to delve into and alter the 'thingness' of the technology that constructs online life. The possibilities of cyberspace are created, modified and controlled by the actions of technically sophisticated individuals. In *Snow Crash*, Hiro Protagonist always wins his sword fights in the metaverse but then as someone wryly reminds him, he did program the ability to have a sword fight in the first place. Further, it is not pure knowledge or thought that is at stake here. Even the most expert individual cannot affect cyberspace by pure thought alone; it is the oscillation between tools and values that constitutes technopower and even experts have to rely on some tools. Individuals may work in the most powerful computer languages and may use the most powerful computers, but they still must use these things to create cyberspace. Online life is increasingly affected by networks of experts who rely on expert tools to delve beneath and modify the tools used in online life. Those who benefit from the spiral of technopower by having greater freedom for action, because they can delve deeper into layers of technology, are themselves caught in networks of things and people. Barnes and Foucault both understand the way people's possibilities for action are determined by the place they have in networks and neither allows things to stand outside of these networks. However, Foucault more clearly grasps the dynamics of domination that can emerge when power is a distributed network. Foucault argues that dominations are necessary corollaries of networks of power and this accords more closely with the nature of technopower in cyberspace than Barnes' understanding of power. It is not that domination is necessarily absent from Barnes' account, but that in seeking out the foundations of social order Barnes offers answers to questions about the existence of social order, whereas Foucault attacks the question of unequal orders. While both analyses of power are relevant, at this stage Foucault's bleaker vision of power as the generation of domination and elites is closer to the nature of technopower in cyberspace.

But one implication of this analysis seems mad. If greater technological complexity is delivering cyberspace to an elite, then why not get rid of this greater complexity? But who wants to go back to computer systems that do not have GUI? GUI makes computers simple enough that 3 year olds can play interactive books, whereas computers without GUI always need dedication simply to make them work properly. Who wants to go back to an Internet that does not have GUI or even Gopher? Before these two, a reasonable knowledge of the computer language UNIX was almost mandatory for successful navigation of the Internet. Who wants to return to a time when emails simply attached themselves to each other in a long list, making one giant email? Nobody wants to go back to these times, back to when the Internet was a place of experts because you had to be an expert to be able to use it. Considering the advantages computer-mediated communication offers the individual, particularly against large institutions, it seems naïve to suggest anything except that removing technical barriers is a fundamentally good thing. Here the perspective of the individual arises again in relation to the social. From the perspective of the individual, continual elaboration of the technical infrastructure of cyberspace makes particular forms of social interaction and information utilisation possible, extending the advantages the individual gains from cyberspace. The claim that providing simpler tools for entering and using cyberspace is an elaboration of technopower that favours an elite based on technical expertise seems foolish when viewed from the perspective of the individual, implying as it does that greater capacity for action for individuals is bad. However, it remains true that creating greater complexity in the underlying technology of cyberspace distances individual users from cyberspace's fundamental fabric and transfers control of that fabric to an expertise-based elite. The simultaneous elaboration of the control of the fabric of cyberspace by an elite and of the powers of individuals within that fabric emerges as one of the complexities of life in cyberspace. This will be discussed at length in the conclusion, when the connections between all three levels of cyberpower are analysed; at present it is only important to note that individuals and elites seem to gain power simultaneously.

Another related, and seemingly false, conclusion might be that anybody with expertise becomes powerful in cyberspace, but all the programmers working in the great programming factories appear far more like cogs in corporate or government wheels than as powerful individuals. It is as if the importance of the car is taken to mean that every mechanic is a powerful person in industrial society. Such counter-intuitive conclusions deserve some elaboration to develop further the implications of the spiral of technopower, and the place of the car in modern life is a good analogy. The technology of cars permeates modern, industrialised countries. It is impossible to imagine almost any aspect of modern life without realising that cars have had some effect on it, while there are aspects of life that seem entirely constructed around cars (e.g. large out-of-town shopping malls). Of course, this does not make each individual mechanic a powerful person in car-based societies – despite the feeling of helplessness that car failure induces in many people – but the system of technopower based around cars does position certain people as powerful actors based on their expertise or control of expertise. For example, pollution problems created by car-based transport are now widely recognised and feared, yet nation after nation has extreme difficulty in changing its private and public transport systems to mitigate this world-wide danger. A whole coalition of nations was willing to go to war to protect oil supplies from the Middle East, largely because of the importance of oil in producing the fuel cars need. And if actors with a wide range of actions are needed to prove the power of cars, then the heads of car-making corporations or road-building companies or ministers of transport need only be thought of. The technopower system based around cars is one that constitutes an important part of the fabric of most modern societies; it structures people's everyday options for living. This does not make the individual mechanic all powerful, any more than technopower in cyberspace makes the individual programmer all powerful, but it points to the embedded nature of technopower and the way individuals are situated by technopower as being able or not able to act. These systems produce the conditions for living, they structure and control the range of choices most people have. Part of the specificity of technopower in cyberspace is that cyberspace is almost entirely constructed out of technopower and this makes technopower the dominant form of power in constructing virtual lives and communities, whereas technopower based on cars is only one system among many others conditioning offline lives. This dominance of technopower also means that individual programmers have greater potential for action in cyberspace than any mechanic working on their own might have in car-based societies. Hackers provide one example, explored later in this chapter, of individuals with far wider choice of action in cyberspace derived from their expertise. Another example is the often-voiced expectation that the 'next big computer thing' will come out of some unknown programmer's garage rather than from established corporations. Here the belief is that programming on your own or in small groups can lead to more innovative programs that will then become important in cyberspace, transforming the programmers into corporate giants on the basis of their expertise (of course, the emergence of Apple computers from a garage is the archetypal version of this story). The individual programmer may not be all powerful in cyberspace but the system of technopower in cyberspace offers greater choice of action to an elite based on technical expertise.

The form of cyberpower from the perspective of the individual has here connected to the different form of cyberpower from the perspective of the social and it has already been argued that cyberpower holds both these perspectives. Cyberpower, in its totality, will be made up not only of the particular forms of cyberpower that come into focus when a certain perspective is taken, but the complex relations that are generated between these perspectives. It has already been seen how the politics of access generated from cyberpower of the individual fuels information overload by creating pressure towards greater access. For example, Esther Dyson is an important analyst of the Internet both in terms of business and its social consequences. She is a venture capitalist, technological/business futurist and recent chair of online civil rights group the Electronic Frontier Foundation, and she argues:

> The key to thinking about the Internet is this: the Internet changes the economies of scale in favor of the little guy. It used to be only big guys could send stuff, only big guys could advertise, only big guys could have newspapers. Suddenly everybody can reach the audience they deserve, more or less for free....People think that being rich means having power. If you sell a million copies of Windows, you get a lot of money, but you don't

control what people see though Windows, and that's a fundamental difference....The real issue regarding the Net is going to be people's ability to use
it, their education, and their literacy.

(Dyson, cited in Brockman, 1996: 84–7)

Here is an almost perfect enunciation of the effects of cyberpower from the
point of view of the individual. Dyson claims cyberspace makes individuals
stronger; it matters not a bit which tool you use except that those tools should
help educated use of the Internet easier. It does not matter how many
computers run Microsoft operating systems because what we do with those operating systems is in our control. This argument would similarly apply to the
previous analysis of push media and the collapse of the desktop and browser
distinction. Any integration of desktop and browser does not matter except to
the extent that it helps greater use of cyberspace, because each individual at
each computer chooses what the new desktop/browser will do and where it will
take them. But considered from the social, Microsoft and Windows do matter.
The technology used to access and create cyberspace is not neutral, it is constituted within cycles of technopower that embed various values into the
technology that people use. The collapse of the desktop and browser results
from certain beliefs about how cyberspace can best be structured and if this
structure becomes dominant then there is no individual choice about using it.
Microsoft and the other dominant corporations of the Internet, like Netscape,
Sun, Cisco and more, all wield the power that constructs the possibilities that
underpin Dyson's optimism. If these corporations or the governments that also
fund cyberspace's development begin to shift, then individuals will have little
power to resist because the social fabric shifts around them. Control for individuals, from this perspective, can only come from an ability to unlock the things
technopower constitutes to reveal the values embedded in them and to rema-
nipulate those values, creating new things dancing to new tunes. In short,
resistance must be generated from within technopower otherwise it relies on it.
This is the problem with Dyson's optimism – it relies on technopower – and also
the truth of her optimism – the technopower that exists delivers much of what
Dyson claims. The clearest example of technopower being actively pursued to
bend cyberspace's social fabric is the US government's attempt to mandate
eavesdropping in cyberspace. This battle springs from new methods of encryption, which require a short explanation.

Encryption is the art of scrambling messages to a predefined code or key,
ensuring only those who know the key can read the message. For example,
NJDSPTPGU is Microsoft encrypted according to a key that says replace each
letter in the message with the next letter in the alphabet, or EPACSTEN is
Netscape encrypted according to the even simpler key that says reverse the
letters in each word. These are both easy keys to break, meaning that if I send
messages using those keys and someone else wants to read the message then it
would not be hard to do. The first problem with encryption is how to generate a

code that is difficult to break. The answer is that larger keys create more complex codes and computers provide essential number-crunching machines for creating ever-larger keys. This is the source of strong and weak encryption, which is defined by the length of the key[14] (Libicki, 1995a; Loen, 1993). The second problem with encryption is how to share the key between the sender and receiver. Both reader and writer must have the key to encrypt and then de-encrypt messages, but this means the key must itself be sent as a message and can be intercepted. The second revolution in encryption is the invention of public key encryption. This involves having two different keys, a private one for decrypting and a public one for encrypting.[15] If I want to send an encoded message to someone I simply encrypt it with the public key of the recipient and they can decrypt the message with their private key. Certain mathematical procedures ensure a private key cannot be guessed from a public one, completing a system that removes the problem of transferring keys between sender and recipient (Rawlins,1996: 9–21; Loen, 1993). These two answers to the long-standing problems of encryption combined with widespread use of computers have led to the appearance in the last twenty years of widespread, easily available encryption that can secure messages. The emergence of a free program to conduct strong public key encryption, called Pretty Good Privacy (PGP), in the early 1990s meant that anybody in cyberspace could download an encryption system that is thought to be nearly unbreakable. Further, the widespread use of encryption is necessary for safe financial transactions online. The only way credit card numbers can be sent safely across the Internet is if strong encryption is available (Barth and Smith, 1997). With these forces behind it, strong encryption might be thought of as an essential element of cyberspace.

The revolution in cryptography is essential background to the early 1990s when many governments began to consider ways to defeat the spread of strong encryption.[16] Law enforcement agencies in the USA are extremely worried about the possible consequences of widespread strong encryption. One of their most potent weapons in the fight against crime, the phone-tap, suddenly looks out of date. What would it matter if criminals' emails could be intercepted if their contents could not be decrypted? Unsurprisingly, a number of US law enforcement agencies have reacted to this possibility. The Chief Counsel with the National Security Agency argued:

> What worries law enforcement agencies – what should worry them – is a world were encryption is standardized and ubiquitous: a world where anyone who buys an US$80 phone gets an 'encrypt' button that interoperates with everyone else's; a world where every fax machine and every modem automatically encodes its transmissions without asking whether that is necessary. In such a world, every criminal will gain a guaranteed refuge from the police without lifting a finger.
>
> (Baker, 1994: 132)

But standardised and ubiquitous encryption is encryption everyone can use, meaning that law enforcement agencies were attacking anybody's right to secure communication. The means with which this goal has been pursued demonstrates the workings of technopower and has gone in two phases: Clipper chip in the USA and key escrow internationally. First, something called the Clipper chip was propounded. This was a particular microchip that would be placed in every communications device – fax, modem, phone, etc. – approved for use in the USA. The chip would provide, first, encryption and, second, a backdoor by which law enforcement agencies could decrypt all communication passing through any Clipper device. With Clipper, phone and data-taps would be pre-installed throughout the USA[17] (Jordan, 1998; Van Bakel, 1996; Barth and Smith, 1997; see also Clipper archive at http://www.eff.org). The fabric of cyberspace is here subject to change. The question of whether this change is good or bad needs to be put aside to grasp that the implementation of a certain technology affects the nature of online societies. US law enforcement with the Clinton government developed another proposal that they are trying to have implemented world-wide, the key escrow system. Key escrow means that all encryption keys would be held 'in escrow' by two government agencies, with possible sentences of five years' imprisonment for failure to supply your key. Law enforcement could then obtain a copy of any key through a warrant and decrypt messages with it. The UK government generated a similar proposal whereby the keys would be held by a 'trusted third party'. As civil libertarians have pointed out, the thought of everyone having to lodge a copy of their front door key with the police is worrying, particularly as it will not stop criminals or terrorists using keys that are not lodged with the proper authorities (they are, after all, criminals). As the police point out, they may be crippled without some such system and they can only obtain keys with proper warrants. And, as Internet industries point out, first, the Internet cannot grow financial services such as shopping unless strong encryption is made widely available legally and, second, few people are happy with the idea of handing the police both their front door key as well as the right to look at their credit card purchases (Campbell, 1997a; 1997b; Vesely, 1997). It is entirely unclear, in early 1998, which side of this debate will win within the USA or internationally. All that is certain is that key civil rights and law enforcement changes are being implemented through technological changes in cyberspace.[18]

The tale of encryption demonstrates that eavesdropping is being mandated through the construction of certain technological tools according to the values of governmental security agencies. It is an exercise in technopower. The point for the present context is that this long, complicated and important battle will define certain basic facts of online life and there can be no doubt that the battle centres on different values being embodied in different technological tools. The very fabric of social life in cyberspace is at stake in such battles – what it is possible to do and not to do. This does not undermine or destroy all the claims those such as Dyson make, it simply points to another perspective. Even if US law enforcement agencies obtained everything they wanted and implemented it on a global scale, then it would still be possible to use strong encryption and refuse to deposit a key with trusted parties. The individual would still be able to subvert key escrow. Of course, doing so would make these outlaw communications stand out from all those that complied and would then lead to a possible jail sentence. Perhaps mass non-compliance could undermine the system. Would the US government really lock up Bill Gates, other industry leaders and thousands of net users if they refused to comply? After all, US Internet industries are heavily in favour of liberalised encryption because it is the only way to ensure safe commercial transactions are possible on the Internet. The point for cyberpower is that it matters which software and hardware underpin social life because within this mass of code, wires and microprocessors, values are embedded that structure the possible forms of online life.

Technopower in cyberspace is subject to a spiral in which the demand to increase access to an almost unlimited amount of information results in new technological tools that in turn result in a further set of demands to improve these tools, resulting in new tools and so on. At each twist and turn of this spiral, particular values inform choices that are then embodied in software and hardware. The embodied values appear to most users not as social or human values but as the inherent abilities of certain thing-like tools. These inherent abilities then predetermine possible forms of social life in cyberspace and these abilities are open only to the most technically literate or sophisticated. Even as the Internet becomes easier to use, literally becoming child's play, the conditions for acting as an individual increasingly come under the control of a technical elite.

The technopower elite

> Technology does not invent, install, or maintain itself, but needs human beings to bring it out into production. It is thus not the technology that matters but the human skill and social organisation that lie behind it. In other words, it is the professional experts who have constructed the system, which in turn has created them. And among the professionals most responsible, the key players are the professional managers of the great corporations and their counterparts in government, the state bureaucrats. They stand at the apex of the new society, controlling its economy and administering its policies and, increasingly, distributing the income and arranging its social relations.
>
> (Perkin, 1996: 6)

If an elite is generated in cyberspace, what is its nature? The only clear conclusion so far is that being a member of the cyberspatial elite means having wider possibilities for taking action based on the ability to delve within layers of software and hardware. Within this software and hardware cyberspace itself is constituted and having greater control over more elements of this allows greater choice of action. The technopower elite has an intimate relationship to the constitution of technological tools because it is from this constitution that its powers flow. Like all elites, the technopower elite comes in many guises, from the shareware programmer who releases their game for free to the controller of Microsoft's operating system development and to the hacker illicitly gaining control of others' machines. And, of course, it is not necessary to be an expert to control and direct experts. No one believes that Bill Gates wrote every line of Windows 95/98 but everyone knows that he gains great choice of action from its widespread success in constituting most people's computing environment. Before outlining this elite and its relation to technical expertise, a further myth of the electronic frontier becomes relevant because there is no more compelling or newsworthy exponent of technical power than those who appear to have gone over to the dark side, those who use their expertise to break into computer systems and subdue corners of cyberspace to their own purpose. The technopower elite includes hackers.

MYTHS OF THE ELECTRONIC FRONTIER 6: KEVIN MITNICK, SUPERHACKER[19]

Originally, being a hacker meant being obsessed with developing computer technology, but now it often means illicitly entering and taking control of computer systems. Most computer systems have security that should allow only authorised people to use them. Only the user and computer system administrator should know passwords. However, passwords can be guessed (remarkably high numbers of people still choose simple passwords like 'hello' and remarkably high numbers of systems administrators still forget to turn off widely known passwords that come pre-installed in some computers) or passwords can be stolen (trojan programs can sit in a computer watching and recording everyone's log-in name and password or someone can watch over your shoulder as you log in). Using all manner of such tricks and exploiting all manner of security lapses, hackers have siphoned $10 million from Citibank, changed the title of the CIA Web site to Central Stupidity Agency and altered the UK Labour Party Web site so that the 'Road to the Manifesto' read 'Road to Nowhere'. Hackers have rigged phone contests, winning more than one red Porsche from a Los Angeles radio station, and have broken into the secrets of a reputed US National Security Agency software writer. In fact, the last is part of a complicated story that led to the capture and imprisonment of the most famous, feared and perhaps typical hacker,

Kevin Mitnick, superhacker. Mitnick has a long hacking history. Early on he developed detailed knowledge of the telephone system, allowing him to explore it for free. Then he extended his knowledge into computers – after all computers control the telephone network. With this combination Mitnick was inside the fabric of cyberspace, with powerful knowledge that only needed complementing with a laptop computer and a phone line to open up a world of choices.

Mitnick's story reached its last climax with a series of attacks on telephone companies in which it appears he sought out the source code of mobile phones. The source code is the fundamental software that controls any computerised device and with it Mitnick would have been able to understand the deepest secrets of mobile phones and, perhaps, be able to reprogram them creating untraceable calls. As part of this effort, Mitnick appears to have had a hand in, if not perpetrated, an attack on a National Security Agency computer security programmer and analyst, Tsutomu Shimomura. The attack exploited a weakness in IP and demonstrates the way Mitnick had gained powerful control of the fabric of cyberspace. IP spoofing depends on the fact that many computers are tied into networks where they trust other computers on that network, but do not trust computers outside the network. For example, computers A and B are connected to the Internet and have various security measures that prevent unauthorised access to them, but they are also part of the same network and are open to each other, still using IP. The IP spoofing attack on Shimomura's home network happened this way. First, the intruder queried the computers on his network to find out which computers trusted which others. Two computers were defined as having an open relationship; Shimomura had called them Osiris and Rimmon. Next, a rapid series of messages were sent to Rimmon, effectively gagging it by continually saying to it the computer equivalent of 'hello, hello, hello'. Then a series of 'helloes' were sent to Osiris in order to gauge the sequence in which Osiris expected to receive messages from Rimmon. Having done this a message could be sent to Osiris that appeared to come from Rimmon but actually came from an outside computer, because the counterfeit message had both Rimmon's identifying number and appeared in the sequence Osiris expected. Osiris trusted the message and suddenly was open to the attacker. The first thing the attacker did was to issue the command that made Shimomura's network open to any other computer on the Internet.

The IP spoofing, or TCP/IP packet prediction, attack dramatically demonstrates the control over the fabric of cyberspace, the ability of one computer to communicate with another, that Mitnick was involved in. Having been hacked and then finding not only confidential software tools but his email spread across the Internet, Shimomura took up a chase to try and track down the culprit.[20] The trail was picked up when Shimomura's stolen files were discovered hidden on the WELL, which Mitnick had infiltrated. From there Shimomura and the FBI were able to track Mitnick's calls back through the Internet to the phone connections he was making, finally leading literally to his door. The stream of electronic communication Mitnick needed to connect to cyberspace also pointed straight back to him. The subversion of this trail seems to be the reason Mitnick was pursuing cellular phone software and had attacked Shimomura in the first place, but he clearly had not yet made himself invisible in cyberspace. Mitnick was arrested in Raleigh, North Carolina, on 15 February 1995.

With his capture Mitnick became the most famous hacker of all time, the first hacker to appear on the front page of the *New York Times*. In the immediate aftermath of his capture wild estimates of the cost of his illegal activities flew around, in one case reaching into billions of dollars. However, the case against him unravelled leading to an eight-month sentence, but he was returned to California to face further charges. If Mitnick's power and damage were measured against many criminals, his cost to the community would appear as at most middle range. Though he stole valuable software, there is no evidence that he sold any software and because stealing in cyberspace means taking a copy, not denying access to the object, little of real damage seems to have been done. Mitnick also used up $100,000 of phone time but, though this is an easily identifiable expense, it is similar to illicitly copying software because it represents phone capacity that would have gone unused, meaning that no one was prevented from using the phone, though a phone company missed substantial payments. There was only one documented instance of Mitnick attempting to destroy a computer by reformatting the hard drive and, of course, there is the expense and time both of catching Mitnick and making systems secure. This last cost perhaps points towards the real fear that Mitnick and other hackers generate that causes their demonisation, because skilled hackers have far greater capacity for action in cyberspace than many others. Hackers sit in strong positions within the webs of technopower because many of the thing-like mechanisms that make up cyberspace are open to their manipulation.

The moral of Kevin Mitnick, superhacker, is that the fundamental material of cyberspace circulates within a form of technopower that places everyone in relative positions of control or subservience defined by their ability to open up the fundamental material of cyberspace to manipulation. Journalist Jon Littman once asked Mitnick if he thought he was being demonised because new and different fears had arisen with society becoming increasingly dependent on computers and communications. Mitnick replied 'Yeah....That's why they're instilling fear of the unknown. That's why they're scared of me. Not because of what I've done, but because I have the capability to wreak havoc' (Mitnick, cited in Littman, 1996: 205). The ability to wreak havoc is an ability constituted out of technopower, the fundamental social power in cyberspace.[21]

Kevin Mitnick, and any of a number of other hackers whose exploits have become known, such as Kevin Poulsen or Phiber Optick, are powerful in cyberspace. One of the most often made comments about them is the disjunction between offline lives of low-rent apartments, little hope of good jobs and unthreatening personal appearance and online lives of power and threat, of the ability to phone-tap the FBI, to see everything and go anywhere in cyberspace. Hackers seen through these eyes appear to many as demons of cyberspace, carrying off credit cards, reading email, selling secrets and siphoning millions out of bank accounts. Yet, hackers are also consistently found not to have damaged the systems they entered or to have done anything much but explore. Even the famed $10 million Citibank hack appears to have been carried out by a criminal gang, who bought the secrets of Citibank for two bottles of vodka and a hundred dollars from a drunk, depressed hacker, who had created the ability to steal but was interested in the ability and not the money (Gow and Norton-Taylor, 1996). Hackers also undoubtedly form communities that support their hacking. They publish newsletters, hold conferences, create Web sites and chat online (Jordan and Taylor, 1998). Hackers are some of the most dedicated and powerful inhabitants of cyberspace and their ability to act in cyberspace is defined almost entirely by their expertise. There are numerous examples of hackers using astonishingly outdated equipment to control the most powerful resources of cyberspace. After all, telecommunication does not need a powerful computer and a simple machine can control a powerful one. Hackers demonstrate the extreme end of the technopower elite, where material resources are close to zero, though never actually zero, and expertise is monumental. With this combination, in a world made from information, extraordinary capacities for action open up.

At the other end of the spectrum of cyberspace's technopower elite stands the familiar figure of Bill Gates and all other heads of institutions that command expertise by controlling the work of many. As already argued, it does not matter that Bill Gates did not write every line of Windows 3.1 or Windows 95/98 for his position at the head of Microsoft to confer on him enormous power in cyberspace. Where hackers have the power to manipulate whatever exists in cyberspace, Gates and those like him have the power to wrench the fabric of cyberspace in new directions. The possible collapse of the desktop/browser distinction is a clear example of this, as is the emergence of the Web and browsers; Netscape came from nowhere in 1993 to become a $2 billion corporation in 1997. One way of generating expertise in cyberspace is not to code software yourself, not to learn obsessively the intricacies of the phone network or a computer system, but to hire many people and put these skills together under your control. Douglas Coupland's tongue-in-cheek account of programmers working at Microsoft captures the aggregation of technical expertise when his protagonist muses about life on Microsoft's campus/factory:

> There was mist floating on the ground above the soccer fields outside the central buildings. I thought about the email and Bill and all of that, and I had this weird feeling – of how the presence of Bill floats about the Campus, semi-visible, at all times...Bill is a moral force, a spectral force, a force that shapes, a force that molds. A force with thick, thick glasses.
>
> (Coupland, 1995: 3)

Gates is an easy target because of both the power of Microsoft and the extraordinary way he is personally identified with the company, but there are a number of people who are in similar positions because of their control of corporations or government investment or research.

Then there is a third group in the technopower elite. Somewhere between the institutional giants and the underground hackers are people who join together to create and distribute free software. Again, groups of technically sophisticated individuals pool their expertise to create software or hardware that implements the fabric of cyberspace. No greater example of this exists than the program UNIX, which more than any other program controls the computers that create and maintain cyberspace. In particular, the way UNIX has been rewritten into an operating system called Linux by groups of volunteers demonstrates this component of the online elite. Linux is distributed free and is free of copyright, so it can be continually copied. Software idealists created it because they believe software should be free, particularly operating systems because they define the computer environment. This project pursues goals perhaps most clearly enunciated by programmer Richard Stallman in the Free Software Foundation. Stallman helped set up the Foundation to promote the distribution of free software, arguing that making software proprietary stopped the free flow of ideas essential to building better software. Software should be freely distributed and anybody should be allowed to alter programs to customise or improve them (Freedman and Mann, 1997: 54–6, 73, http://www.gnu.ai.mit.edu). Within this ethos, Linus Torvalds wrote the core of Linux. To be useful Torvald's kernel needed various other components such as communications software. This was waiting in the Free Software Foundation's Gnu program. Here Torvald's central kernel could be supported by numerous necessary other parts of an operating system and in 1994 Linux officially appeared. As part of it, there could be found one file that listed more than a hundred names of the major programmers who had, free of charge, created Linux. Torvalds became the centre of the co-operative creation of the key component of software for cyberspace, the operating system of computers. The distributed nature of Linux's development means it continues to grow and change, often at a far quicker rate than software coming from institutionalised corporations (Moody, 1997). Linux is not a dominant operating system, but it is a powerful one. It demonstrates the ability in cyberspace to co-operatively generate expertise and embody that expertise in programs that form cyberspace.

Personifying the technopower elite offers us the three linked figures of Kevin Mitnick, Linus Torvalds and Bill Gates. These three demonstrate that controlling expertise in one way or another offers the key to riding the spiral of technopower and controlling many of the myriad choices that form cyberspace. The spiral of technopower also implies that such expertise will play an ever greater role in constituting the nature of cyberspace and the individuals who use cyberspace will be ever more reliant on the technopower elite.

Beginning from the assumption that there is a social fabric to cyberspace leads to the conclusion that an elite has appeared within cyberspace. Moreover, pressures partly generated from the politics that empowers individuals also fuels a spiral of technopower that offers this elite ever greater control over the social fabric of cyberspace, even as it provides individuals with ever greater ease of use. The shift from the perspective of the individual to the social has also led to the addition of a second type of cyberpower. First, there is power as the possession of individuals, whose use in cyberspace favours individuals, and, second, power as patterns of social relations that create systems of domination, whose articulation in cyberspace fuels an ever more dominant elite. To pursue cyberpower further it is essential to pursue the elite further, into the offline world. The social in cyberspace is now clear, but what of the social between online and offline life? What pressures and circuits of power might become clear if the line between cyberspace and meatspace, virtual life and real life, on and off, is moved to the centre and sets the questions?

Chapter 5

The virtual social II
The social between online and offline

Key concepts

Global

> Global refers to activities or resources that are lived or managed on a world-wide basis. Global does not mean planetary, in the sense that it does not mean everyone on the planet is involved with each global resource or activity. Cyberspace is global: it does not exist within any national boundary and information within it is available world-wide. Cyberspace is not planetary: only a small part of the planet's population uses cyberspace.

Real time

> Real time means activities or resources whose actions and reactions occur immediately, with no delay. Speaking with someone in person is a real-time conversation. Many of cyberspace's resources and activities can be experienced in real time.

Never ending

> Never ending means activities or resources that never cease or that are available twenty-four hours a day, seven days a week. Many activities or resources beat to the rhythm of the week: sport at the weekend, work in daylight hours and play after dark. Most activities or resources of cyberspace never end, they never close and are always available.

Informational space of flows

> Cyberspace provides a particular sort of information control and management that is necessary for the new type of socio-economy that is often called an information socio-economy. This is a space in which information is controlled and managed globally, in real time and never ending. This space provides the essential resources offline life demands from cyberspace.

Introduction

Beginning from the assumption that online life is collectively created allows a particular form of technopower to be defined, but so far it is the technopower of online life alone. The problem emerges that technopower points to the rise of a new elite which has, at first sight, connection to offline elites – corporations enmeshed in markets, governments interested in regulation – but it is unclear how cyberpower of the social extends to this intersection of online and offline life. The task of this chapter is to focus on the intersection between online and offline societies to articulate fully cyberpower of the social. The uses and effects of cyberspace on non-virtual societies will be articulated by focusing on the particular importance of cyberspace to social changes in global societies since the 1970s, often called the change to information societies. The drive for governments and corporations to spend billions of dollars, ecus and yen on constructing and elaborating cyberspace cannot be found solely in the intrinsic values of cyberspace. Rather, cyberspace is also constructed in the search for certain effects in already existing reality. However, the focus of cyberpower is the nature of cyberspace and analysis of the intersection of online and offline must, accordingly, be directed to the effect on cyberspace of the demands made on it by offline societies. Any other plan would mean that these analyses would have to make their object the definition of global or information societies, rather than the definition of power in cyberspace. This does not mean that changes in or the current nature of offline societies will be ignored, only that such changes will be introduced because of their relevance to online life and its contribution to offline societies. Cyberpower of the social here pursues the nature of power that both allows cyberspace to reach across into offline life and answers demands made on cyberspace by offline life.

The areas that cyberspace is already crucial to in offline life are, broadly understood, production, consumption and politics. It is not that other areas of socio-economies are unimportant to the emerging information age, but that cyberspace is not a crucial element of changes occurring in such areas. Production breaks down into three different changes in which cyberspace is closely involved. First, finance capital has grown in size and speed by migrating into cyberspace. Second, production processes can be split into functional sections that can be located in different parts of the world because all the components of a geographically dispersed production process can be co-ordinated through cyberspace. Third, the component of production processes least able to shift on a global basis is labour, which being constituted by humans is particularly attached to place. However, a new international division of labour has arisen alongside new, global forms of finance capital and production and consists of two axes (core and periphery workers) and four categories of workers (high-value producers, high-volume producers, raw materials producers and redundant producers). As with production processes the co-ordination needed to create and maintain such a system is essentially provided via cyberspace. There are two changes in consumption. First, informational socio-economies try to expand markets for goods through increases in world trade and to generate greater consumption within existing markets by targeting goods ever closer to individual desires. Second, the nature of information as a commodity, as a thing to be bought and sold, alters fundamentally with the integration of audio-visual information into textual and the gradual convergence of different types of media (such as radio, TV or text) into one multimedia. Finally, the role of cyberspace in political structures in informational socio-economies is discussed in relation to changes in the power of nation-states, the emergence of different democratic possibilities and new opportunities for grassroots organisations. Changes here are less certain than in production or consumption because they are often resisted by offline political elites who are threatened by cyberspace's potential. When the roles of cyberspace in production, consumption and politics are taken together it will also be seen that a particular type of space emerges that supports all three. Following leading theorists of current global socio-economies, this space will be called the informational space of flows. This space provides global, real-time and never ending communication, without which the changes that cyberspace creates for information societies would not be possible. Offline societies need this space of flows to continue the trends identified in production, consumption and politics and will demand that cyberspace be structured to deliver the informational space of flows. This means that offline socio-economies do not focus on all the possibilities that cyberspace offers but demands the resources cyberspace creates in the space of flows. It also means that offline demands can only be met through further articulations of cyberspace's technology – that is, through technopower – and this places the technopower elite in the complex position of meeting offline demands for the informational space of flows but also having its own interests in cyberspace. Cyberpower of the social between offline and online points towards the critical co-ordinating and constructing role of the technopower elite in creating and maintaining both cyberspace and the informational space of flows.

If cyberspace is crucial to areas of offline life, then those that control or manage these areas will want some reassurance that cyberspace will continue to provide its services. Producers, consumers and others will all, in different ways and through different representatives, want to ensure the space they depend on is reliable and secured. To do this governments will legislate about cyberspace, corporations will build and rebuild it to their design, politicians will apply it to electioneering and consumers will demand its support. All these pressures also coalesce into a general attempt to construct cyberspace so that it maintains and extends the informational space of flows. However, cyberspace (as outlined in previous chapters) is not just a function of offline life but has created its own social structures and forms of community. The desire of consumers to make cyberspace into the ultimate home shopping network runs directly counter to the desires of many communities in cyberspace to be decentred, anti-hierarchical and devoted to the full range of virtual pursuits. The desire of governments to control a medium with unprecedented possibilities for freedom of speech runs counter to the censorship-evading ethics and technology of cyberspace. These and other desires to create a certain form of cyberspace by offline powers do not automatically translate into a restructured cyberspace, but become the ground of conflict between the cyberspace that exists and the cyberspace offline powers would like to see. Articulating cyberpower between offline and online societies also defines a battleground.

Beginning from the simple point that societies as well as individuals cross the boundary between online and offline allows a further elaboration of technopower to be reached. This elaboration connects competing powers in offline life to the differing positions of virtual individuals, as possessors of power, and virtual elites, as managers of technopower. Cyberpower becomes further complicated by this exploration that allows us to see the ongoing direction various offline forces will attempt to compel cyberspace towards and the ground on which offline and online forces battle, ally and betray each other.

Cyberspace and production, consumption and politics in information societies

A growing body of theoretical and empirical work in all areas of the social sciences argues that sometime in the 1970s a fundamental shift in the nature of society was initiated. At its simplest, this is portrayed as the third great shift in human society, from agricultural to industrial and now to informational societies.[1] The unifying thought behind all the various theories of this change is that a move began in the 1970s that took the globe's socio-economies away from industrial forms that emerged in the nineteenth century and towards socio-economies in which information plays a central role. It is claimed that the key resource at the beginning of the twenty-first century will be knowledge and universities and research facilities will play the role that mines and foundries did in industrial times. Even with only this vague description it seems highly likely that cyberspace, a place made of information, will be important to societies based on information. To understand the shifts of power between online and offline life, it is important to define the relationship between cyberspace and informational socio-economies. By focusing on this relationship, certain factors can be drawn out from theories that posit the dawn of an information age. These factors will then allow a clear definition of the relationship between online and offline social structures. This means that the present task is not to define the informational society or the information age, but to take up the now widespread and well-founded work arguing for the emergence of informational socio-economies and see where cyberspace plays a significant role.[2]

In the following discussion, it also needs to be kept in mind that it is trends and not stable structures that are identified. The informational age, society or city is not an established fact but a series of trends that lead from industrial to informational socio-economies. One of the complications when discussing this transition is that it can often be plausibly claimed that whatever is supposed to have disappeared is in fact still present. The problem here is that some assume industrial and informational economies are mutually exclusive, rather than different socio-economic models one of which is moving towards the other. For example, one indication of a socio-economy becoming informational is often thought to be the decline of manufacturing industries and the rise of service and information-based industries. However, taken as a global economy it seems that manufacturing has not disappeared, indeed may even be on the rise, but has shifted away from countries where it was previously located. If manufacturing has not disappeared but has become global, does this mean socio-economies are still essentially industrial (Castells, 1996; Perkin, 1996)? Rather than expecting manufacturing to disappear entirely, implicitly arguing that informational economies cannot include manufacturing industries, it is the remaking of industry around different principles that makes informational different to industrial. It is clear that information played an important role in industrial socio-economies – it is difficult to imagine any socio-economy in which information would not be important – but it is the specific place of information in recent socio-economic change that marks the rise of information societies. As Castells claims:

> I argue that information, in its broadest sense, e.g. as communication of knowledge, has been critical in all societies, including medieval Europe which was culturally structured, and to some extent unified, around scholasticism, that is, by and large an intellectual framework. In contrast, the term informational indicates the attribute of a specific form of social organisation in which information generation, processing, and transmission become the fundamental sources of productivity and power, because of new technological conditions emerging in this historical period.
>
> (Castells, 1996: 21, fn. 33)

It is not that information did not play a role in industrial or earlier economies, critics of the information age hypothesis have sometimes pointed out that research laboratories were invented in the late nineteenth century. As Castells argues, such claims miss the point. The substantive trends identified below are part of a different type of socio-economy, not because they utilise information but because information becomes centrally important to these socio-economies. Further, what has occurred is a shift between the two that takes place over time, rather than suddenly, and it should be expected that an informational socio-economy will retain pockets of industrial, just as industrial socio-economies have retained pockets of agricultural. It can also be expected that different societies with different histories and cultures will develop different forms of the information society. Trends will be realised in different ways. Japan and Germany are undoubtedly different to the USA and UK, but this does not undermine the claim that they, and much of the rest of the world, have shifted towards information-based societies.

The overall change can be reasonably simply stated, though what it means exactly is a far more difficult question. The fundamental belief is that developed and developing socio-economies have been restructured from using information as a key component in industrial forms of production and consumption to information becoming both the central resource for and key driving force of socio-economies. As part of this transition socio-economies have also become global in ways they were not previously. By changing from industrial to informational it is also claimed that capitalist or market economies and their accompanying states have been reformed within different structures but not destroyed. Castells argues that 'what is specific to the informational mode of development is that here knowledge intervenes upon knowledge itself in order to generate higher productivity' (Castells, 1989: 10) or, more succinctly, 'For the first time in history, the human mind is a direct productive force, not just a decisive element of the production system' (Castells, 1996: 32). Information societies are called this not because previous societies did not utilise information but because information has become the central principle by which production, consumption and, more generally, power is distributed across a global socio-economy. What this claim means exactly can only be defined by exploring the changes themselves and the task here is to focus particularly on those changes involving cyberspace. What are identified below are the major trends towards information societies that involve cyberspace: production, consumption and politics.[3]

Production

Production refers to the myriad processes by which commodities (the things that we buy and sell) are created. A production process may involve a single cobbler, tapping out hand-made shoes, or huge assembly lines of thousands of people turning out cars. All these different forms of production can be broken down into three simple component parts. First, capital or the accumulated money that buys raw materials or parts, technology and labour. Second, the type of process in which raw materials or parts, technology and labour are organised so that commodities result. Third, there is labour, or the workers who provide skills. All three have undergone change over the last thirty years and each has a different relationship to cyberspace. These changes will be outlined in turn to establish the first set of trends towards the information society that involve cyberspace.

There are a number of different forms of capital.[4] Money may be accumulated in the bank, it may be invested in stocks or bonds or it may be used to buy and sell currency. Taken together these forms of money can be called finance capital. Or money may be invested in land or property or in the technology, land and buildings needed to create a production process, what can be called fixed capital. Finance capital has altered fundamentally, in a way that is entirely dependent on cyberspace, and its changed powers have come to dominate fixed capital. Of all the different elements of a socio-economy, finance capital has become the most closely integrated into cyberspace and has three characteristics. It is truly global, played out in real time and never ends.

As one financial exchange closes another opens, with Tokyo, New York and London having become the three biggest, and stocks on one exchange can be traded on another. A change initiated in one market can ripple around the world as different markets open and close. Even when a particular market is closed its traders can utilise other open markets. Computers have also automated many aspects of trading, making shifts in markets ever faster. At the same time a number of changes in the regulatory regimes of finance capital have significantly liberalised flows of money. At the end of the 1970s exchange controls on many major currencies were abolished allowing significant investment by many outside of their national 'home' and placing the relative positions of currencies under the control of currency markets. There was also significant deregulation of stock exchanges, allowing a more diverse range of institutions to deal in different exchanges, often across national borders (Lash and Urry, 1994: 20–1; Harvey, 1989: 160–1; Castells, 1996: 434–7; Hirst and Thompson, 1996: 40–4). The effect of these changes has been to increase vastly the volatility, power and independence of finance capital. Harvey calls it the co-ordinating power of informational production (Harvey, 1989: 164). The seven largest economies in the world, the G-7 countries,[5] all increased their transborder financial flows (i.e. money flowing in or out of a national border) at least ten-fold from 1980 to 1992. For example, in the USA, transborder financial flows went from 9.3 per cent of its gross domestic product (GDP) to 109.3 per cent, in Germany from 7.5 to 90.8 and in Italy from 1.1 to 118.4. The amount of money being traded and the sheer amount of trading have also skyrocketed in this period. The average borrowing on international capital markets grew from an annual figure of $95.6 billion in 1976–80 to $818.6 billion in 1993. The 'Eurodollar' financial market, that is beyond any national government's control, grew from $50 billion in 1973 to $2 trillion in 1987. The average daily transactions on the UK, US and Japanese stock exchanges rose from under $200 billion in 1986 to nearly $1,200 billion in 1992. If we take just the New York Stock Exchange, the total capital of firms trading on that exchange grew from under $5 billion in 1960 to over $35 billion in 1987 and the amount of shares traded daily grew from under 5 million in 1960 to nearly 160 million in 1987 (Castells, 1996: 94, 434–7; Harvey, 1989: 160–4, 334–5; Lash and Urry, 1994: 17–22; Hirst and Thompson, 1996: 40–4, 51–75). As an indication of the extraordinary strength and reach of finance capital, we need only remember the UK during 'Black Wednesday' when international currency markets forced the pound out of the European Exchange Rate Mechanism, or Thailand, Malaysia and other Asian countries in 1997 when their currencies came under sustained pressure.

The immense strength of finance capital and its emergence as global, twenty-four hours a day and always in real time occurred because it migrated to cyberspace. Banks and markets are connected via dedicated computer networks that transfer money, stocks or bonds and report prices. Money and information flow ceaselessly and at extraordinary speeds around the world, pushing trillions of dollars globally both in cash and other forms such as stocks or bonds. All this frenetic activity occurs in cyberspace. Traders in all sorts of finance capital trade by looking at glowing screens through which they ask computers to buy or sell and then to communicate those commands to other computers. Decisions to buy and sell are also mediated by the screens, through which dealers take in the latest information essential to efficient operation. This is often not the Internet but other, more shadowy, world-wide computer networks such as SWIFT, which is an international network that links over 1,000 banks, or the X.25 networks run by many telecommunications companies (Lash and Urry, 1994: 22; Dreyfus, 1997; Quarterman, 1990). But this is cyberspace and the role of the virtual lands is to annihilate both time and space, allowing finance capital a global reach that never stops and always operates at its cutting edge. Cyberspace can do this with finance capital because money can become digital, enabling it to merge into cyberspace. Money can be represented by numbers on a screen or stored within a computer's memory, as can the number of stocks owned in a certain company or the type and number of bonds or most other financial instruments. Finance capital can take full advantage of the global, unsleeping and instantaneous powers of cyberspace because it can make itself into the very stuff of cyberspace: the ones and zeroes that a computer understands and can process. The ability of finance capital to make itself digital is the basis of cyberspace's ability to remake finance capital in informational socio-economies.

Finance capital is the liquid form of capital; it is the capital that is available for investment or any other use. Its growth in reach and strength in the last thirty years makes it a crucial element in informational societies. It is not the only element of informational societies to shift to a global regime, but different versions of this path can be expected because not all the elements of socio-economies can become digital. In fact, with the sole exception of software and perhaps expertise, which live as naturally in cyberspace as money seems to, all commodities must be rendered in some non-digital form to be useful. Even computers must be put together out of silicon, steel and plastic before their users can bathe in virtual light. The second key area of change is in factories or the processes by which goods are produced. Changes in the creation of commodities are, essentially, that a process that used to be largely unified in one location or in closely linked regions can now be split and spread all over the globe. Labour-intensive elements of production can be taken to countries where labour is cheap and trade unions weak, while knowledge- or expertise-intensive elements can be taken to the most qualified. One process producing one commodity can now be a world-wide venture (Castells, 1989: 33–125; 1996: 386–94; Harvey, 1989: 141–72; Lash and Urry, 1994: 60–74). For example, there are five distinct operations in the production of semiconductors that can be separated in time and space. First, research and design is needed and generally requires research scientists and engineers. Second, engineering the design into a circuit that constitutes the chip requires the skills of applied scientists and engineers. Third, embedding circuits into the 'wafers' that form their material support requires skilled labour. Fourth, chips are assembled into electronic components, requiring routinised, low-skill labour. Fifth, the final product must be tested, which is usually automated (Castells, 1989: 73). Each of these five different elements could be located in different parts of the world, perhaps keeping research work close to a university in the developed world but sending the assembly of electronic components to a newly developing country where wages are lower (in fact, often Mexico or South-East Asia) (Castells, 1989: 79). Information technology commodities were among the leaders in introducing such world-wide production systems, but the principles extend to any commodity whose creation can be broken into distinct parts. The processes by which commodities are produced (factories) can now be globalised on the basis of functional separations between the different parts or processes needed to create a particular commodity.

Any distributed process depends on efficient co-ordination. If scientists design a different chip, engineers must make the design into a template, skilled workers must embed the template in chips, labourers must put the right chips in the right components and machines that test must test to new standards. All along the process co-ordination is needed between all elements. Further, such production processes must react to demand for the commodity under question. If Ford is selling large numbers of two-door cars but few four-doors in the same model, it must alter its production process to reflect this. Breakdowns in supply from one element of a process to another also demonstrate global interdependence. When there was an explosion at the factory that produced the world's largest supply of high-grade epoxy resins, an essential component in semiconductors, suddenly manufacturers of semiconductors world-wide faced a 50 per cent shortfall in a necessary element to produce many electrical goods (Brown, 1997: 204). Information must flow between the different elements of the production process and to managers for globalised factories to be successful. Of course, cyberspace again provides a unique and essential resource for conducting such communication. Whether a company sets up its own dedicated communications network or connects its company networks to the Internet, computer-mediated communication plays a vital role in maintaining the flows of information that allow distributed production systems to be successful.

Cyberspace is deeply embedded in both finance capital and the creation of commodities. In both cases, cyberspace provides essential communication without which it is hard to imagine new informational forms existing. The difference between them is that with finance capital there is virtually a merger between the object (money, stocks) and its communication, whereas the material nature of a production process means such a merger is impossible. Instead, communication allows a more flexible and spatially dispersed set of relations between the material elements of a factory. This union between object and communication is even less pronounced for one key element of production processes, labour. Whereas raw materials, machinery, designs or any of the other inanimate elements of a production process could generally not care less where they are being processed, labour tends to care passionately. People live in certain places not just as labouring units or as elements of global production systems, but as humans with histories, friends, families and lovers related to the place where they live. Labour is also a crucial element in any production system. Its distinctive relationship to globalised production and its importance to any production system mean labour should be considered by itself as an element in the creation of commodities.

The first point to note is that labour has not been literally globalised along with production processes. 'Only 1.5 percent of the global labour force (about 80 million workers) worked outside their country in 1993, and half of them were concentrated in Sub-Saharan Africa and the Middle-East' (Castells, 1996: 232). People do not disperse themselves around the world, chasing jobs wherever they are available, and the human reasons why this is so should be obvious. However, this does not mean that labour has not been affected by globalised production or that there are not important, if numerically small, categories of labourers who do chase work around the globe. Instead, a global division of labour has emerged in which certain types of labour are significant and which moves finance and other elements of production to that labour, wherever it is situated. There are two layers to this informational division of labour, a general structure of cores and peripheries and four functionally different types of labour. In general, informational socio-economies produce a split within corporations between a core of workers whose employment is secure and reasonably well rewarded, and part of whose responsibility is to ensure the corporation maintains some sense of unity, and a periphery of workers whose employment is usually insecure and variably rewarded, depending on the skills they offer (which can range from the most menial and repetitive labour to highly paid consultants) and who are used by the corporation to maintain flexibility. Workers of the periphery can be brought in or turned out depending on the fortunes of the company, while core workers maintain the fact of a company. This flexible labour force follows from the segmentation of the production process that is part of informational socio-economies. Corporations are based on rapid responses to information flowing in and out of the company facilitated by equally flexible finance capital and this means maximum flexibility must be created in the workforce to allow the corporation to take advantage of its information based adaptability (Harvey, 1989: 147–58; Lash and Urry, 1994: 60–110; Castells, 1996: 272). Within this general framework, Castells identifies four distinct types of labour that informational production systems utilise and that are distributed globally:

> What I call the new international division of labour is constructed around four different positions in the informational/global economy: the producers of high value, based on informational labour; the producers of high volume, based on lower-cost labour; the producers of raw materials, based on natural endowments; and the redundant producers reduced to devalued labour....The critical matter is that these different positions do not

coincide with countries. *They are organised in networks and flows, using the technological infrastructure of the informational economy.*

(Castells, 1996: 147, emphasis in the original)

Each country contains some of these four different types of labour, even the most marginal nation includes some of the highest-value labour, if only 'to ensure the transfer of whatever capital or information is still accumulated in the country' (Castells, 1996: 147), and even the most advanced informational socio-economies include devalued labour living in marginalised areas. Labour is globalised in the sense that different types of labour are utilised by corporations across the globe, not in the sense that workers move across the globe.[6] The human attachment to place here clashes with the informational erasure of space. Production systems interrelate labourers on a global basis, labourers who will have virtually no knowledge of each other and little contact with each other. The different types of labour also produce different strengths and weakness within socio-economies. High-value labourers, unsurprisingly, often command higher wages and control over their work. The way many corporations have attempted to accommodate such workers within university-campus-like facilities in attractive locations clearly indicates their privileged status. Sometimes material privileges are allied to cultural markers, reinforcing the notion that these workers are special. The most famous example of this is perhaps Microsoft's leafy, wooded, campus in which soft drinks with high caffeine levels are provided free, playing into the belief that good software coders are like artists who have passionate 'runs' at their coding during which stimulants are needed to keep them going as long as possible (Levy, 1984; Stross, 1996; Coupland, 1995). Castells and Hall identify a world-wide trend towards 'milieux of innovation', such as Silicon Valley, in which high-value workers are accommodated (Castells and Hall, 1994). The other three types of workers can expect to receive less in the way of parkland and free cola. High-volume workers are typically required also to be low paid and poorly protected, raw materials producers have variable wages but almost universally dangerous and often isolating conditions of work and all societies have felt the emergence of the marginalised and dispossessed who have no place in informational socio-economies (Lash and Urry, 1994: Part Two; Castells, 1997: 108–47). Labour in information socio-economies is structured according to two principles: a division between core and peripheral workers, and a four-fold division between types of work.

When finance capital, production systems and labour are considered together, the overall direction of informational production appears clearly to serve the interests of those who can most closely relate to the new flows of information. High-value information workers can expect high rewards, though they have also fallen under demands for harder work and more 'flexible' working practices. Corporations that can afford to spread their factories across the globe and maintain effective communication can reap benefits. However, the emergence within informational socio-economies of entirely dispossessed peoples, who have little hope of entering any component of the informational socio-economy, accompanies the heightening of some international inequalities. Some nations have been able to attract, in particular, high-volume work and use this to lessen international inequities, while some nations seem to face the possibility of structural irrelevance to the globalised informational socioeconomy. For example, Africa's international economic position has dramatically worsened since the 1960s, with Sub-Saharan Africa's share in world trade in primary commodities dropping from 7.2 per cent in 1970 to 3.7 per cent in 1989 and its share in manufactured goods dropping from 1.2 per cent in 1970 to 0.4 per cent in 1989 (Castells, 1996: 134). In terms of cyberspace, we need only note that Sub-Saharan Africa has only 0.59 per cent of all Internet hosts, and that its share drops to 0.016 per cent when South Africa is excluded, to see that the informational space of flows and cyberspace have barely arrived there.[7] Parts of Latin America have suffered similar problems and the fate of areas of the former Soviet Union also seems potentially bleak (Castells, 1996: 115–45). The phenomenon of similar irrelevance *within* successful informational socio-economies has become known as the emergence of 'dual cities', in which many cities are both enriched beyond previous dreams and impoverished beyond worst fears. Ghettos, 'no-go' areas and deeply impoverished housing estates have become features of the most advanced, globalised and richest cities in the most advanced, globalised and richest nations in the world. Gaps between richer and poorer in developed countries have widened during the early stages of the informational revolution, with the USA and UK leading the way[8] (Castells, 1989; Sassen, 1991; Lash and Urry, 1994: 145–70).

Cyberspace is intimately involved with these changes, forming an essential supporting structure to globalised production, the international division of labour and finance capital. However, production is only part of the tale of informational socio-economies and before the place of cyberspace in the informational social revolution can be fully grasped the areas of consumption and politics must also be outlined. Cyberspace's contribution to production is clear in its creation of a new space that facilitates global, instantaneous and continuous communication through which forms of production can and have been remade.

Consumption

The reverse and necessary complement to production is consumption. For example, the system that informational socio-economies are held to be replacing has sometimes been called Fordism. Henry Ford's name was taken for this system because he is thought to have invented both the new form of production, in mass assembly lines that generated vastly increased numbers of commodities, and the new form of consumption, by paying higher wages and offering financial instruments that allowed workers to buy the commodities they were producing. Mass production needs mass consumption or it becomes over-production and eventually a failed corporation (Harvey, 1989: 125–40; Hall and Jacques, 1989). Mass consumption remains a key element of informational socio-economies that may have created even more productive ways of generating commodities than under Fordism.[9] Though informational socio-economies are sometimes thought of as ones that produce information and so have done away with manufacturing industries, the shift has rather been the alteration of manufacturing industries through the integration of information processing as a central structuring principle alongside the creation of information-producing industries. This has led to faster increases in manufacturing productivity during the 1980s than during the previous twenty years.[10] Given that manufacturing in the late industrial period, the Fordist period, was already dependent on mass markets, increases in the productivity of manufacturing industries mean that even larger markets are necessary or failure through overproduction will become one of the features of informational socio-economies. Understanding the conjunction of informational production with informational consumption means understanding what systemic answers have been found to this problem. The first important area of informational consumption for cyberspace stems from two related solutions: increasing markets world-wide and promoting increased consumption through niche marketing. The second important area of informational consumption for cyberspace is one easily ignored because it is obvious in cyberspace – the consumption of information. Because cyberspace is centrally concerned with information, it is sometimes easy to miss the key point that cyberspace takes part in wider shifts in the way information is consumed. Changes here are so fundamental that while some compare them with the first emergence of printing presses, others go further back to compare them with the creation of the alphabet or even the domestication of fire.

The two broad changes in consumption are fundamentally different because there are commodities whose consumption is, in the first case, dependent on their material embodiment and, in the second, is not dependent on their material embodiment. The idea or design of a car cannot be consumed as a car without being made real in glass, plastic and steel, but the idea of an idea can be consumed no matter whether it is carried by paper, computer terminal or the voice of a friend. These two types of commodity will be called essentially material and essentially immaterial commodities. These awkward terms indicate that some commodities are inherently dependent on their material embodiment, whereas other commodities can be embodied in different ways, meaning their essence as a commodity does not lie in their embodiment. A book may have many covers, but a Ferrari has to have one shape made out of one material. The opposition is not between material and immaterial commodities because all commodities need some material embodiment, even if that embodiment is as ephemeral as the electricity in a computer. The often made slippage that posits information as an immaterial substance is unacceptable because information always needs some form of material embodiment whether that is paper, screens or even human flesh. The point is that the essence of some commodities inheres in a particular material form, whereas some commodities can take many forms and remain the same commodity. These two forms of commodities will be examined in turn.

A dual process of quantity and quality marks the development of informational consumption of essentially material commodities. Quantitative processes are simply the effort to create larger and larger markets for commodities. From the eagerness with which companies are hoping China's billions of people will become consumers to the efforts of governments to broker open trade agreements, such as the USA's demand that Japan open up its internal markets, there are many ways in which it might be assumed that the informational age will be marked by increasingly open markets and burgeoning trade:

> We have entered a period of sustained growth that could eventually double the world's economy every dozen years and bring increasing prosperity for – quite literally – billions of people on the planet. We are riding the early waves of a 25-year run of a greatly expanding economy that will do much to solve seemingly intractable problems like poverty and to ease tensions throughout the world. And we'll do it without blowing the lid off the environment.
>
> (Schwartz and Leyden, 1997: 117)

At present, this is only wishful thinking. A drop in the expansion of world trade has marked the shift from the period following the Second World War to the informational period. Between 1950 and 1973, world trade grew at over 9 per cent per annum, but from 1973 to the mid-1980s it expanded at only 3.6 per cent per annum (Hirst and Thompson, 1996: 21). Rather than increasing world trade, the picture to mid-1995 is one of the continuing importance of home markets for multinational corporations and of increasing regionalisation between the three economic powers of Japan/East Asia, USA/NAFTA[11] and the European Economic Area. In terms of home markets, informational consumption is related to niche marketing strategies that are discussed next. Regionalisation means that trade has increasingly developed between the three already advanced regions, with some parts of Latin America being drawn into USA/NAFTA, the developing Asian economies and China attaching to Japan and Eastern Europe and poorer or smaller European countries attaching to Germany and other major European nations in the European Economic Area. As with international financial flows there are potentially severe problems with some countries or regions becoming irrelevant to this triad that underpins informational socio-economies. For example, the amount of foreign direct investment into the developing regions of Asia grew from an annual average of $1.3 billion in 1973–6 to $19.8 billion in 1990–3, Latin and South America grew from $2.2 billion to $11 billion, but Africa remained relatively stationary with a shift from $1.1 billion to $1.4 billion, and the Middle East and developing Europe grew from minus $1 billion to $1.6 billion (though it fell from $2.6 billion in 1983–9). As with finance capital there is a danger of some regions of the world becoming structurally irrelevant to the informational economic system (Hirst and Thompson, 1996: 67, see also 21–40, 67–72; Castells, 1996: 99–102). Nevertheless, whether trade develops as regions or more openly between nations, cyberspace provides the necessary communication for trade to change or develop. Cyberspace's ability to co-ordinate trade between the three regions and their satellites and to react quickly to changes makes it an integral component of quantitative changes in informational trade.

The qualitative change in consumption can be summarised by the emergence or creation of niche markets (Hall and Jacques, 1989; Harvey, 1989; Mort, 1996). These involve targeting commodities ever more closely to particular socio-economic groups, thereby splitting the mass market into smaller and smaller units until, in a perfectly consumptive world, each person would have commodities so perfectly tailored to their desires that they would simply have to buy them. While perfect individualised consumption seems a fantasy, there are some points where the collection of information about individuals allows individualised commodities to be produced. You can now, if you live in the right area, have yourself measured for personalised jeans. The process is simple. You go to the right shop where all the necessary measurements are taken and then transferred, utilising computer-mediated communication, to the factory that will produce and then mail you the perfect set of jeans. The information is then retained for any future orders. The circle is squared and bespoke tailoring meets mass production. Or there is the example of information collected by supermarkets, particularly through 'reward' cards that offer some refunds on goods in exchange for personal details and allows the automated recording of purchasing. With this data, the supermarket can know not only what its daily needs are but also what each individual shopper's purchases are. 'Smart' shopping trolleys have been developed as one application of this. Once such a trolley is loaded with details held on your reward card (by swiping the card in a trolley) it could map a path around the store or beep a warning if you inadvertently pass by your normal purchase of free-range eggs. The database might register your fondness for chocolate ice cream and discretely point out the current special offer, just as your smart trolley passes the appropriate aisle. However, the more common and achievable aim than consumption designed for individuals is to generate information that allows the targeting of areas or particular stores to particular socio-economic groups (Davies, 1996; Lyon, 1994).

The generation of such information, either at individual or more commonly at group or area levels, allows the creation of smaller markets within mass consumption that aim at particular types of people who are more likely to want and be able to afford particular commodities. Firms can then be designed to meet these consumption patterns even as they change. For example, the clothes firm Benetton was overtaken by the Gap in 1995 largely because it could not

match the Gap's ability to put new types of clothes in shops every two months –
Benetton was only able to change every six months (Castells, 1996: 437). Here
the ability to shift consumption quickly, to follow the information being generated about changes in consumption, is a crucial factor and the firm's production
line must be engineered with this in mind. Niche markets are part of consumption patterns moving towards fragmentation and the closer integration of
production with consumption. This is a different shift to the previous discussion
of changes in production processes. It involves a firm organising itself to
produce 'just-in-time' for its particular markets. A firm does not want a huge
backlog of stock because it is trying to respond swiftly to market changes and
opportunities and this means producing the required goods for the identified
market just in time. Such a production system may also be globalised, as previously discussed, but it need not be and certainly will not be if the global
distribution of production means goods cannot be transported to their market
quickly enough. Whereas the changes in production already outlined may serve
either mass or niche consumption, the development of just-in-time production
systems results from a revision in the nature of consumption (Castells, 1996:
157–66; Lash and Urry, 1987: 198–201; Hall and Jacques, 1989; Mort, 1996).
All these elements are tied together with flows of information. Which store is
selling which goods? What line is proving successful and how does it relate to
which socio-economic group? What materials are needed and where, to produce
which parts, and where must these parts be sent and when to produce which
commodity in what colour? All these and other questions are continually asked
by firms to enable the identification of specific consumer groups, the definition
of their likely desires and the production of goods to meet those desires.
Cyberspace again forms a basic substructure that allows these flows of information to reach around the world in the cause of ever shorter gaps between the
identification of a market opportunity and its fulfilment in sales. The whole
system revolves around enormous amounts of information continually speeding
to and fro, a role cyberspace is ideally suited to. Again, altered socio-economic
conditions depend, in large part, on the particular nature of cyberspace as the
place of information.

   The problem of increased production potentially leading to firms producing
too many commodities and then going out of business is answered in two ways
within informational socio-economies: the extension of mass markets and the
creation of niche markets. These two revisions of consumption combined with
changes in production provide a potentially solid basis for stable informational
socio-economies. And cyberspace is an essential component in almost all major
elements of these changes, providing a way of making vastly greater amounts of
information swiftly available.

   The second component of informational restructuring of consumption in
relation to cyberspace now becomes relevant, for cyberspace is not just a
conduit down which information can be poured but also participates in restructuring what information itself is. This is clearest in the reconstruction of

world-wide media, the industries that offer commodities whose essence does not reside in their material embodiment. Mirroring the shift in essentially material goods from homogeneous mass to fragmented mass markets is a shift to fragmented media:

> Newspapers were written, edited and printed at a distance, allowing for simultaneous editions of the same newspaper tailored to several major areas....Walkman devices made personally selected music a portable audio environment....Radio became increasingly specialised, with thematic and subthematic stations....Radio's hosted talk shows filled the time of commuters and flexible workers. VCRs exploded all over the world....Film survived in the form of video-cassettes. Music video, accounting for over 25 per cent of total video production, became a new cultural form that shaped the images of a whole generation of youth....The ability to record TV programs and watch them at selected times changed the habits of TV audiences and reinforced their selective viewing....People started to tape their own events, from vacation to family celebrations....For all the limits of this self-production of images, it actually modified the one-way flow of images and reintegrated life experience and the screen.
>
> (Castells, 1996: 337–8)

During the 1980s in the USA, the number of independent TV stations grew from sixty-two to 330, while the share of prime-time audience held by the three major networks dropped from 90 per cent to 65 per cent. The growth of cable and satellite networks means the choice of TV grows on a world-wide basis, leading to such cultural anomalies as the US TV soap opera *Falcon Crest* gaining 450 million viewers in China. From hand-held video cameras that allow the production of home entertainment to the creation of hundreds of different TV channels, the mass audience that once constituted the consumers of immaterial commodities has been shredded. It has, however, at the same time shifted into fewer hands, increasing the concentration of ownership of a more diverse media (Castells, 1996: 229, 341; Lash and Urry, 1994: 111–43; Bender and Druckrey, 1994; Schiller, 1996). The underlying change in media, of which this massive diversification is essentially a sign, is a change whose nature and significance is still being disputed (even more than the nature and significance of information socio-economies). Castells claims it is a change to information structures first established in 700 BC by the invention of the alphabet. Marshall McLuhan saw it as the end of the era begun by the Guttenberg printing press in the fifteenth century. Paul Levinson sees it as the most recent evolutionary shift in information following on from the alphabet, the printing press and industrial media (telephone, telegraph) (Castells, 1996: 327; McLuhan, 1995: 216; Levinson, 1997). The common thread in these arguments is that the invention of the alphabet prioritised written discourse over sounds and images in the construction of rationality. It is claimed Western discourse prioritised abstract, literary forms of reasoning, relegating arguments from sound or image to the emotional:

> The electronically induced technological extensions of our central nervous system...are immersing us in a world-pool of information movement and are thus enabling man to incorporate within himself the whole of mankind. The aloof and dissociated role of the literate man in the Western world is subsuming to the new intense depth participation engendered by the electronic media and bringing us back in touch with ourselves as well as with one another. But the instant nature of electric-information movement is decentralising – rather than enlarging – the family of man into a new state of multitudinous tribal existences.
>
> (McLuhan, 1995: 248–9)

The new realm of multimedia finally does away with the dominance of the alphabet, fully reintegrating the audio-visual with the written. Cyberspace emerges here as a strategically significant component of these shifts, because it both introduces new forms of communication and provides a fantastically complex application of multimedia. Further, the Web may be gradually absorbing other forms of media, despite being a small medium in early 1998. Nowhere is this clearer than the investments TV networks have begun to make in Internet technology that allows video to run across the Internet. It has been reported that two of the USA's main TV networks, ABC and CBS, have invested $80 million and $100 million respectively in companies working on Internet video. Still at a primitive stage in early 1998, Internet video often consists of small boxes on the screen containing a grainy, jerky (if you're connection is fast enough, if not it becomes a still) image that is recognisable as video but only just. But if communications pipelines continue to get bigger and if Moore's law holds (ensuring computers become exponentially faster) then proper full-motion video of TV quality on the Internet might just be within reach. The key example is audio on the Internet. The software RealAudio provides sound across the Internet and when it

> debuted in April 1995, it was an ear-wearying squall, compromised enough to squeeze through a 14.4 modem. Eyes rolled. But those who dismissed it sneered too soon. Today's RealAudio 3.0, on just a 28.8 modem, can compare with FM radio. Over a broadband connection, it can approach the fidelity of a compact disc.
>
> (Reid, 1997: 125)

Assuming video follows the path blazed by audio, the Internet could become the site of serious competition to TV. This change also emerges from a different direction with the idea of network computers, as already noted in the plans of Sun via their computer language Java. Rather than buying a fully powered computer, a cheaper simpler model that includes the most common tools used on a PC (word processor, spreadsheet and Internet connection) and that could function as a TV can be produced. Or a set-top box that connects to a TV and allows the TV to be used to surf the net might be produced. In a less radical way than full-motion video on the Internet, these two examples still show TV and cyberspace converging towards each other (Schofield, 1997). With all forms of media reborn within multimedia and new forms growing, such as online gaming, cyberspace is strategically placed to implement a fundamental McLuhanesque revolution in information consumption. This change amounts to a new commodification of information, because it redefines the nature of immaterial commodities and their role in socio-economic life.

It should be clear that if the Internet can provide both audio and video of comparable quality to radio and TV and provide it already embedded in multi-media – and thus already connected to text, other sites, sales possibilities and so on – then the revolution McLuhan envisaged in the 1960s will have in some form happened. It is also not that network TV or even mass audiences can be expected to disappear, if only because industrial forms can be expected to remain attenuated within informational ones, but that their nature will be altered by existing as only one means of delivering information commodities alongside radically new forms. Cyberspace here appears not, as it does in production, as the supporting structure of a component of informational socio-economies but *as* one of those components. The delivery of informational commodities, including music, writing, images, video and all these integrated in multimedia, may be fundamentally structured by cyberspace. The ultimate media deconstruction seems possible with the Internet making everyone not only a publisher but also a TV network owner as well. Here the hope, for some expectation, is that the Internet will finally prise open the hitherto closed doors of film, video and TV to everyone. Enough has been said in previous chapters about cyberspace's populist possibilities for the opportunities to be clear. Rob Glaser, once a vice-president at Microsoft and developer of the key audio appli-cation for the Internet RealAudio and video application RealVideo (combined in Realplayer), argues 'Content will no longer be limited to three networks or thirty-six cable channels, but rather by production economics' (Glaser, cited in Reid, 1997: 127). Simply put, the cost of running a TV network will be the cost of making the show and placing it on the Web, all of which will be far lower than is presently the case for setting up a TV network, even if meeting the production quality of existing TV may be difficult.

There is, however, no certainty that this undoubted possibility will come about. The two sides of this coin are expressed first by Eric Lee, a union activist, and second by Jane Metcalfe, President of Wired Ventures:

> The Internet has made it easier than ever before for transnational corpora-tions to outwit and outmanoeuvre unions....But ironically, the very technology which has given corporations such a great advantage over

unions…has become cheap enough and accessible enough to allow unions to move toward a new internationalism.…Thanks to the Internet, a century-long decline in internationalism has already been reversed.

(Lee, 1997: 12–3)

Lee claims the communication possibilities of the Internet devolve the ability to provide information so radically that it provides an effective tool with which to combat the newly globalised forms of production that offer great benefits to capital and employers over labour. However, some are not so optimistic about the populism of the Internet. Jane Metcalfe is the president of Wired Ventures, the company that runs *Wired* magazine, Hotwired Web site and other Wired ventures, all of which are dedicated to exploring the revolution cyberspace brings or is part of. She notes the technical difficulties of publishing and using the Web will grow as it becomes more sophisticated:

Until now the tools have been very accessible.…Anybody can learn HTML. But the emergence of object-oriented programming languages like Java will make much more complex applications available.…The explosion of people who are learning HTML and creating personal homepages is great, but those pages aren't going to look nearly as exciting or sensational as those made by engineers who can do the Java programming.…There will be jags of technology, when a new thing that only engineers can use is designed and then filters down through an interface-design process until it becomes accessible to a larger public. Meanwhile the pioneers are out developing the next edition of the latest technology which will be difficult to use and therefore inaccessible to the bulk of Web users.

(Metcalfe, cited in Brockman, 1996: 225)

Metcalfe reintroduces the spiral of technopower and notes how it will mean that the most advanced and attractive means of creating Web-based multimedia will always be out of reach of those who are not part of the technopower elite. This does not mean that more modest Web sites will not serve some purposes equally as well as more advanced sites, but it does point out that the hope that the Web might function as inherently democratising or populist is dependent on technopower. Hopes that the new commodification of information will redress the balance towards individuals, after informational production has tilted it toward corporations, is both real and dependent on technopower in cyberspace.

In relation to both types of commodities, cyberspace is an essential substruc-ture that ensures flows of information that make possible elements of the information age. However, whereas cyberspace's role in production seems to unambiguously support the already powerful, its role in consumption both aids production in helping develop fragmented markets and provides tools for spreading information and developing opposition. Before consolidating this analysis of the importance of cyberspace to the new international socio-economic structure by abstractly defining the space that cyberspace constructs, it is important to consider one final area in addition to production and consumption.

Politics

Politics does not need to be given the depth of analysis devoted to production or consumption because changes in offline politics related to cyberspace are essentially a result of the new commodification of information. Politics appeared in the analysis of consumption with Lee's identification of a new Workers International and further analysis of both governmental and popular politics will show that cyberspace's already outlined remaking of information constitutes its key contribution to remaking politics. It is also the case that changes in politics related to cyberspace are less clearly established. In politics, trends can be identified but they appear more as possibilities, whereas trends in production and consumption are already firmly instituted.

The one area where cyberspace has undoubtedly brought political change is in the emergence of a global system that restructures the power of the nation-state. Finances flowing across national borders show little regard for the interests of the nation-state they flow through. Information spreading instantly throughout cyberspace evades controls that are more easily put in place on nationally based, centralised broadcast media. For example, emails came out of Russia describing the attempted coup against Gorbachev, providing a commentary 'as it happened' that eroded state censorship. Any national law concerning goods or information that can be digitised is in danger of being trumped by cyberspace. The obvious example here is pornography, which can be accessed globally in cyberspace by users in countries that outlaw it from servers located in countries that do not outlaw it. Another example is the decision to locate a Web site critical of McDonald's in the Netherlands because of more liberal laws there. It is not that nation-states are necessarily disappearing, as some claim, but many of them have failed to come to terms with the inherently international nature of cyberspace. Castells argues that nation-states must try to establish relative advantages for their nationals within the web of interdependent nation-states and also to reconsider attitudes to international agencies, through which some international competition can be played out (Castells, 1996: 80–90). Cyberspace undermines nation-states to the extent that nation-states can no longer exist in isolation, simply pursuing policies congenial to their national constituencies. However, the end of nation-states in a new, necessary internationalism also seems a distant prospect. Instead new forms of competition between nations – for jobs, media centres, favourable treatment from international bodies and so on – have emerged as nation-states become interdependent because of the international flow of information (Castells, 1996: 80–103; Freidan, 1991; Held, 1995).

A second area of political change wrought by cyberspace is claimed by some to lead from the revision of information distribution and production to devolution of control from highly centralised electoral dictatorships to involved citizens:

> The political significance of CMC [computer-mediated communication] lies in its capacity to challenge the existing political hierarchy's monopoly on powerful communications media, and perhaps thus revitalise citizen-based democracy....Which scenario seems more conducive to democracy, which to totalitarian rule: a world in which a few people control communications technology that can be used to manipulate the beliefs of billions, or a world in which every citizen can broadcast to every other citizen.
>
> (Rheingold, 1994: 14)

And since Rheingold wrote this large amounts of government and government-related information have appeared on the Internet. Yet there is little evidence of structural alterations in political processes resulting from cyberspace's reinvention of information. Cyberspace has at times been co-opted within political processes, for example Jonah Seiger of the Center for Democracy and Technology noted that the 'Christian coalition at the Republican Convention had this war-room organised, where each state organiser had a cell-phone and a laptop computer and then there was a command centre' (Seiger, 1996). Such innovations are enhancements to existing political processes and are not fundamental changes. Compared with the migration of finance capital to cyberspace, little has occurred in governmental systems world-wide that restructures them around informational principles. Sadly, more information, available more quickly, does not add up to restructured governments (Casey, 1996). Of course this does not mean that fundamental changes are not going to occur, as some are claiming, only that they have not by 1998. John Katz argues that in the USA the 1996 presidential election marked the death of the political system and the birth of

> a new kind of nation – the Digital Nation – and the formation of a new postpolitical philosophy. This nascent ideology, fuzzy and difficult to define, suggests a blend of some of the best values rescued from tired old dogmas – the humanism of liberalism, the economic opportunity of conservatism, plus a strong sense of personal responsibility and a passion for freedom....Where freedom is rarely mentioned in mainstream media anymore, it is ferociously defended – and exercised daily – on the Net. Where our existing information systems seek to choke the flow of information through taboos, costs and restrictions, the new digital world celebrates the right of the individual to speak and be heard – one of the cornerstone ideas behind American media and democracy. Where our existing political institutions are viewed as remote and unresponsive, this online culture

offers the means for individuals to have a genuine say in the decisions that affect their lives. Where conventional politics is suffused with ideology, the digital world is obsessed with facts. Where our current political system is irrational, awash in hypocritical god-and-values talk, the Digital Nation points the way toward a more rational, less dogmatic approach to politics. The world's information is being liberated, and so, as a consequence, are we.

(Katz, 1997a: 49–50)

Katz argues that the Digital Nation is the site of a new elite which will eventually remake democratic politics according to the values he sets out. The possibility that the new commodification of information will form a new elite capable of taking over offline government is not pure fantasy, but there is still no clear evidence that Katz's expectation is coming about (despite a 1997 survey that claimed to identify the elite Katz speculated on (Katz, 1997b)). This does not mean that electoral and governmental politics will not be remade in the way that Katz and Rheingold suggest, perhaps it is simply a longer time changing than production or consumption, but it is suggestive that Katz in 1996 claims changes are in train that Rheingold in 1994 also identified and in neither case is there strong evidence that the change has occurred. Another example would be Josh Quittner's analysis of the Electronic Frontier Foundation's move to Washington, when he confidently argued that the online civil rights organisation would be able to 'reverse-engineer government, to hack Politics down to its obvious component parts and fix it' (Quittner, 1994c: 80–1). EFF subsequently ran into difficulties, both internally and externally, that led its online constituency to question its judgement, its policy and lobbying staff to split away to form the Center for Democracy and Technology, and EFF to relocate to San Francisco nearly bankrupt in order to, as one of its founders John Perry Barlow said, 'save our mortal souls' (Barlow, 1996a, also cited in Jordan, 1998). The disjunction between Quittner's expectations and EFF's experience demonstrate how difficult it might be to apply software or Internet principles to established power structures.

The obvious explanation for the slow effect of the new commodification of information on politics is that while offline elites were largely beneficiaries of informational changes in production and consumption, meaning an alliance of informational innovation and financial and governmental muscle ensured change, in politics established offline elites have much to lose from cyberspace's potential democratisation of information, ensuring their resistance. The USA's Communications Decency Act is probably the clearest example of this, with a number of supposedly pro-Internet legislators – including such powerful figures as Democrat Vice-President Al Gore and Republican Speaker of the House of Representatives Newt Gingrich – failing to oppose legislation that would have severely undermined free speech in cyberspace. These erstwhile champions of cyberspace stood aside while legislators sought to fundamentally undermine the possible benefits of cyberspace-based free speech by making vaguely defined 'indecent' speech illegal in cyberspace. When push came to shove, pro-Internet members of offline elites were happy to restrict cyberspace's democratising potential, possibly because it would have undermined their offline powers, while they simultaneously promoted cyberspace's other benefits for informational socio-economies. Similar comments could be made about the encryption wars in the USA, where supposedly pro-Internet legislators have attempted to mandate government surveillance of cyberspatial communication. Again, cyberspace's potential populism is restricted in favour of shoring up existing offline elites. Offline political elites can be expected to resist some of the effects of cyberspace on informational socio-economies, which perhaps helps explain why some of the obvious changes that have been expected in politics have so far not appeared. It is also a possible pointer forward that where Rheingold talked about a democratic benefit potentially open to all citizens, Katz talks specifically about a digitally based elite:

> Here is a growing elite in control of the most powerful communications infrastructure ever assembled. The people rushing toward the millennium with their fingers on the keyboards of the Information Age could become one of the most powerful political forces in history. Technology is power. Education is power. Communication is power. The digital young have all three. No other social group is as poised to dominate culture and politics in the 21st century.
>
> (Katz, 1997a: 191)

Perhaps changes to governmental politics as part of cyberspace and informational societies are likely to come not from a populist source but from the technopower elite.

Whatever the future of governmental politics, it can be seen that the underlying power for change that people like Katz or Rheingold argue results from the net relies on what has already been called the new commodification of information. The new means of making and distributing immaterial goods such as ideas is the power that cyberspace throws at established bureaucracies and representational governments. Change that may come can therefore be seen as closely related to aspects of consumption in informational socio-economies that have already been discussed. One articulation of this is Castells' argument that democratic politics has become entirely dependent on the 'rules, technology and interests of the media' (Castells, 1997: 314). Castells does not mean that the media decide political issues, as if TV anchormen and women voted for or against legislation, but that for democratic politicians to gain power they must receive the votes of people whose main, if not sole, source of information about politics comes from the media. Popular media are then the arena in which politicians are forced to make their claim on votes and then on the support needed to govern effectively. Further, because of the glut of information that floods over people, the simplest forms of information have a disproportionate power to influence people's understanding of politics: 'Audiovisual media are the primary feeders of people's minds, as they relate to public affairs' (Castells, 1997: 314). For politicians to make an impact within this field requires vast amounts of money. For example, in the 1996 US national elections it was believed serious candidates would need $40 million for their campaigns and that less than $25 million meant it was not worth trying. Even in a country like the UK, where paid political TV is illegal and major parties are given free air time, the amount spent on making the free air time as powerful as possible and on pursuing other avenues – such as the 'billboard wars' in the 1992 and 1997 elections, where the two main parties spent large amounts on billboards – means that more and more money is required to run a successful media campaign (Schiller, 1996: 40; Castells, 1997: 317–28). Democratic politics is played out in a field where reality is defined by the dominant forms of media, particularly the short, sharp shock of audio-visual soundbites, and this ties parties into increasing demands for funds that in turn leads to a culture of corruption and scandal. If the media have become the main arena in which democratic politics is fought out, then Rheingold's and Katz's claims of a fundamental shift in politics might well come from the already discussed shift in media that cyberspace brings.

Similar arguments can be made about populist politics. Perhaps, politics outside of governmental boundaries in non-government organisations (NGOs) or, more broadly, in social movements will also be restructured by shifts in information commodification. Most commonly discussed in this context is the Zapatista revolt in Mexico, where what initially looked like a guerrilla war quickly became a media war. Instead of fighting in the jungles, though there has been fighting and deaths, the Zapatistas used their weapons to create media events. On the day that the North American Free Trade Agreement (NAFTA) began, which joined Mexico, Canada and the USA into a free trade zone, the Zapatistas occupied an area of the Chiapas region in Mexico. When the army arrived they withdrew to the rainforests. They successfully created such a media event that they were able to force the Mexican government into negotiations and avoid a full-scale war. They did this by full use of the new possibilities for information flow, including the Internet (Castells, 1997: 72–83). Castells makes similar arguments about the Patriot Movement in the USA and the *Aum Shinrikyo* cult in Japan, while comparable points have been made about Greenpeace and other social movements (Castells, 1997: 84–109; Pearce, 1996; Jordan and Lent, 1998). This alternative sphere of politics may be undergoing serious changes with the rise of informational socio-economies but, again, the role cyberspace plays results essentially from the altered forms of information production and distribution.

It is not yet clear exactly how politics, in both its populist and governmental forms, is changing within informational socio-economies and in relation to cyberspace. All that is clear is that changes that can be identified result from the new commodification of information. The conviction of many that politics is becoming different, and of some that cyberspace is important to those changes, seems as yet not clearly supported. This is complicated because changes that appear inherent to cyberspace are not necessarily welcome to the political elites dominant in offline politics. The ability of those who are already subordinate offline to use the new commodification of information to become more powerful has also emerged, with the Zapatistas providing the most famous and striking example. As with production and consumption, change in politics in informational socio-economies closely related to cyberspace rely on the creation by cyberspace of a new space in which information flows in ways previously unknown.[12] It is the nature of this space that now needs to be outlined.

The informational space of flows[13]

Informational socio-economies involve cyberspace in a number of key elements of production, consumption and politics. By themselves, these analyses provide a number of suggestive connections between offline and online, whose pursuit would almost certainly lead to a number of pressures crossing between virtual and non-virtual lands. In particular, the battle between an elite and a grassroots emerges yet again, with the elite gaining significant power in the realm of production and consumption only to find the new commodification of information providing weapons to the subjected. This clash of dominant and subordinate, witnessed in different ways in the circuits of cyberpower so far identified, is strong enough that in democratic politics informational changes appear stalled, because the political elites face a clash between defending their authority and attracting votes. However, rather than pursuing each individual connection it can be noted that common elements run across production, consumption and politics. By articulating the common ground that cyberspace opens out for informational socio-economies, the particular insights into production, consumption and politics can build an overall view of the relationship between cyberspace and informational socio-economies:

> the various subjects and objects of the capitalist political economy circulate not only along routes of greater and greater distance, but also – especially with the rise and increasing capacities of electronic networks – at ever greater *velocities*. This faster circulation of objects is the stuff of 'consumer capitalism'. With an ever quickening turnover time, objects as well as cultural artefacts become disposable and depleted of meaning. Some of these objects, such as computers, television sets, VCRs and hi-fis, produce many more cultural artefacts or signs ('signifiers') than people can cope with. People are bombarded with signifiers and increasingly become incapable of attaching…meanings to them.…Contemporary global order, or disorder, is…a structure of flows, a de-centred set of economies of signs in

space. But alongside and against these asymmetrical networks of flows there is increasing evidence of a radically other set of developments. There is evidence that the same individuals, the same human beings who are increasingly subject to...such space economies are simultaneously becoming increasingly *reflexive* with respect to them. Alongside the silent majorities, the small-screen addicts, the 'black hole' of Baudrillard's semio-scape, there are large numbers of men and women who are taking on an increasingly critical and reflexive distance with reference to these institutions of the new information society.

(Lash and Urry: 1994: 3–4)

Cyberspace offers to informational socio-economies a space in which flows of information reach globally, operate in real time and never stop. Three concurrent elements create a particular informational space that underpins the new informational forms of production, consumption and politics. This is a space, at its heart, of flows, of seas of data transmuted into the universal digital language of ones and zeroes and then sped around the world so quickly that time and distance are erased. Cyberspace provides to offline life a unique space of information flow. Not only does cyberspace create its own particular forms of life, but it contributes an extraordinary form of space that is indispensable to the new form of global socio-economy that looks likely to dominate the twenty-first century. The informational space of flows has three components. First, it structures a global form of communication. Second, it operates this global communication in real time or, put another way, communication ignores distance to work nearly instantaneously. Third, it never stops, never sleeps and never tires or rather, if it does stop, sleep or tire then this is a malfunction in the communication system. These three components will be discussed in turn.

The informational space of flows is global. It connects far-flung elements of socio-economies by transferring information across wires and satellites, through computers and onto various screens. These networks are not all integrated into the one network, but the Internet increasingly absorbs this information flow. Global is also not planetary; not all pieces of information in all places are integrated and made available to all other places. Rather a space that spans the globe, while ignoring places in all parts of the world, has been created, and within this space national boundaries are constantly crossed. Money that is flung down the cables of international financial networks is rarely marked by national boundaries and with one click on a Web site a user can be carried from a server in one nation to another, with no indication this has occurred. This also does not mean that the space of flows is international, in the sense of treating all nations the same. As discussed in Chapter 2, the language of cyberspace, and consequently of this space of flows, is Anglo-American. For some time Asian characters could not be represented at all within cyberspace and even today, many essential elements of European languages are difficult to use within cyberspace. The space of flows is also unevenly distributed, again

following cyberspace, much of it is located in the advanced or quickly industri-
alising nations with a disproportionate amount located in the USA. Still,
utilising the informational space of flows means assuming a global perspective.

The informational space of flows is real time. Flows of information occur
virtually instantaneously. Price changes in New York are registered immediately through the space of flows to all that can utilise it. Online discussion can
take place with the immediacy of a phone call. Posting new information on
the Web means it is immediately available throughout cyberspace. The space
of flows frees information from time by erasing the gaps between production,
transmission and consumption of information. However, there is a second
articulation of real time in the space of flows, because one of the powers of
cyberspace is asynchronous communication. In email, newsgroups and many
other online forums, information is not dealt with in real time but is posted,
leaving a gap for others to respond. This gap means the flow of information
passes in stops and starts – a message is posted and then replies come at inter-
vals. Ironically, asynchronous communication relies on real-time flows – as
soon as someone composes their message and presses the send button then
that email or newsgroup post appears at its destination. Asynchronicity
produces different benefits to simultaneity. Most obviously, email's asynchronicity allows it to combine some of the intimacy of the phone with the
store and retrieve capabilities of answering machines and letters. Time in asynchronous communications is slowed down or speeded up depending on the gap
between message and response; it can be real time – with email being replied
to instantaneously – or it can wait for long periods of time – on Web sites or
in newsgroups as people respond in their own time. The fundamental power of
the space of flows is to pass information in real time, but this also results in
particular forms of asynchronous communication. The informational space of
flows erases the regular passage of time – the constant ticking of one equal
minute after another – either entirely, by being instantaneous, or asyn-
chronously, by alternately compressing or extending it.

The informational space of flows never sleeps. Whether the sun is setting or
rising has no effect on the servers and wires that shift information around the
globe, and someone or something, somewhere, is always awake in a global
system producing more information. Web sites do not close for the weekend at
5 p.m. on a Friday, they simply carry on running. Financial markets migrate
around the world, carried by the space of flows to whoever is awake. Email and
postings wait for whoever will find, read and react to them. Information is
always on the move and always there, waiting to be moved. The steady
rhythms of time are dispersed, no longer carrying people through days in
which lunch and leisure are part of daily routines. The space of flows disrupts
routine with the certain knowledge that a new piece of information is out there:
a new email has arrived, a Web site has opened or altered, a stock price has
changed or a new design has arrived to be implemented on the factory floor. The

informational space of flows never stops, never slows down and respects no routine or rhythm.

The informational space of flows allows information to be moved and manipulated according to these three abilities: global, real time and never ending. However, the informational space of flows must not be thought of as the cause of informational socio-economies. The informational space of flows is the space that cyberspace provides to informational socio-economies that makes certain elements of those socio-economies possible. It is a significant and important part, making possible all the elements of informational socio-economies that rely on global, real-time and never ending information flows. These underpin the 'space-time compression' that Harvey, among others, has identified as crucial to these new economies and it is difficult to imagine informational socio-economies without the services of the informational space of flows (Harvey, 1989: Part III). But it would be a mistake to shift from the importance of the space of flows to any belief that it causes or is the sole force behind the rise of informational socio-economies. Such a belief is tempting because it provides a simple understanding of why informational socio-economies emerge that implicitly relies on the comfort of technological determinism. However, far more forces than the technopower spirals of cyberspace are at work in the creation of informational socio-economies. For example, the rise of East Asia as a significant economic force[14] does not result from any simple inclusion within the informational space of flows. It has its roots in the Cold War, first through widespread US funding of socio-economies in South-East and North-East Asia and, second, through US tolerance of government policies of internal protection that nurtured local industries, both in the cause of containing communism. Towards the end of the Cold War, East Asian socio-economies gradually opened to the outside world and regional organisations have emerged that look to continue the growth of East Asia. However, the collapse in late 1997 of currencies and then socio-economies in East Asia perhaps points both to problems when removing protection from local socio-economies and to ongoing capitalist weaknesses of boom and bust in informational socio-economies (Berger and Borer, 1997b). The story of East Asia involves the informational space of flows – massive and abrupt fluctuations in currency markets have been part of its 1997 crisis just as much as elements of production systems relocated to East Asia have been part of its success – but it would be false to take this space as the determinant ignoring government policies, international relations and wider economic and cultural forces.

Finally, it needs to be kept in mind that cyberspace, the Internet and the informational space of flows are different things. Cyberspace includes the Internet and the space of flows but it also includes a number of other computer networks that may not be connected to the Internet and contains resources that are not part of the space of flows. Some businesses create dedicated networks to service their own information needs avoiding the Internet, and world-wide computer networks that are not connected carry some services, such as financial transactions. Cyberspace includes all these, as well as the Internet. The chief example of this is the emergence in the mid-1990s of intranets. These are networks set up by particular organisations that utilise Internet technology – TCP/IP, servers, HTML, browsers and so on – but are not necessarily connected to the Internet. Many intranets allow only certain communications in and out, blocking access to parts of the intranet that are confidential to the organisation but allowing email or Web surfing in and out to the Internet. Intranets are like small, dedicated Internets and are clearly part of cyberspace and the informational space of flows, though they may or may not be part of the Internet. The space of flows, in turn, includes all parts of cyberspace and the Internet that contribute to the three core elements of the space of flows: global, real time and never ending. Some important parts of cyberspace will not be part of the informational space of flows. MUDs and Usenet immediately spring to mind as significant components of virtual lives but inessential to the informational space of flows. These disjunctions are important because, as will be explored below, they form some of the issues around which struggles over the nature of cyberspace can be expected to erupt. Offline elites seeking to utilise the informational space of flows will have little interest in sustaining the identity experimentation available in MUDs, while individuals attempting to enhance their powers may see little advantage in cyberspace becoming the home of niche marketing. To explore these more fully, the interrelations of offline and online elites now need to be analysed.

Online and offline

Strictly speaking, the space of flows is the peculiar set of abilities to manipulate information that cyberspace offers to offline space. All the previously discussed changes in offline life that derive from or depend on changes in the production, manipulation or distribution of information can also be seen to depend on cyberspace, simply because the space of flows depends on cyberspace. But the two are distinct. Cyberspace generates its own forms of life and its own circuits of power, as well as generating the changes in information that make the space of flows possible. But the space of flows only deals with the aspects of cyberspace that leap across the barrier between online and offline life. The informational space of flows is the part of cyberspace that informational socio-economies need. And a particular myth of the electronic frontier has emerged to articulate cyberspace in a way that allows offline life to grasp and exploit the advantages of the informational space of flows.

MYTHS OF THE ELECTRONIC FRONTIER 7: CYBERSPACE IS THE ELECTRONIC FRONTIER

Frontiers are the line between what a culture or society knows about itself, often called its civilisation, and what a culture or society does not know about some other place, often called barbarian. This line can be stable or it can move, but it is always a boundary between the known and the unknown. Cyberspace is just such an unknown – a place that many know exists, that many believe holds great promise, but whose contours, ecology and natives seem exotic and strange. Reports back from over the frontier seem to confirm this is a foreign place. It is full of people who can change their bodies, it is full of extraordinary amounts of information about anything, you can talk to people from all over the world there but can never be sure they are who they claim they are and, the greatest hope of all, perhaps there is gold out there – perhaps creating a Web site, advertising your software online or some other vague, unspecified project will make you a lot of easy money. You can be a pioneer there, a frontier-breaking colonist finding excitement and adventure out in unknown places. Cyberspace has often been described as the electronic frontier. Other metaphors have been applied to cyberspace, famously the information superhighway, but also a living organism, a spider's web, a galaxy and a city, but the electronic frontier has a particular importance.

Unlike most of the myths of the electronic frontier, the myth of cyberspace as a frontier is not a story but a metaphor, perhaps the founding metaphor for cyberspace. It has defined many people's understanding of the virtual lands.[15] This myth does not have a beginning, middle and end, but a set of images through which the strange world of cyberspace can be grasped by those familiar with offline life:

> The early days of cyberspace were like those of the western frontier. Parallel, breakneck development of the Internet and consumer computing devices and software quickly created an astonishing new condition; a vast, hitherto-imagined territory began to open up for exploration....This vast grid is the new land beyond the horizon, the place that beckons the colonists, cowboys, con artists, and would be conquerors of the twenty-first century.
>
> (Mitchell, 1996: 109–11)

The electronic frontier has also been a particular type of frontier that reflects the overwhelmingly US origins of the Internet, the Wild West. Hackers and their pursuers can be thought of as cowboys, law and lawless in a land where justice is often summary or non-existent. Black-hatted hackers will steal into your email, strip away your credit records, rob you of your newest software products and even hold the metaphorical gun of logic bombs or destructive viruses to your head. White-hatted hackers will give up their skiing holidays and pursue the black hats out of a sense of honour,[16] bringing order where there was chaos. A rich vein of images and stories is available to those who use the electronic frontier metaphor, allowing the strangeness of cyberspace to be translated into terms that anyone who has seen Hollywood's version of the Wild West will be able to understand. For example, in the early 1990s a number of large US corporations became interested in cyberspace and began to construct proprietary networks that would not necessarily connect to each other or to the Internet. This occurrence easily and elegantly became the equivalent of the railroad companies in the West, who encouraged people to settle in frontier lands near the railroad, resulting in the pioneers' total dependence on the railroads for all communications and supplies. Existing in one of the proprietary networks would have meant being as dependent on that corporation as pioneers were on a railroad company. Take almost any situation in cyberspace and a cowboy metaphor will not be far away – which makes it extraordinarily appropriate that one of the influential voices of cyberspace is a cowboy.

John Perry Barlow used to own and run a ranch in Wyoming, USA, and he still wears the hat, boots and scarf that mark him as a Western man. The organisation he co-founded, which has been mentioned several times already, bears the appropriate name of the Electronic Frontier Foundation (EFF), not Freedom but Frontier. Barlow bears other distinguishing experiences, as lyricist for the Grateful Dead and Republican state senatorial candidate (failed), but his life as a cowboy has a powerful resonance in cyberspace. His co-founders all came from the world of software: Mitchell Kapor, co-creator of the breakthrough spreadsheet program Lotus 1-2-3 and founder of Lotus Corporation; John Gilmore, UNIX software expert and early employee of Sun Microsystems; and Steve Wozniak, co-founder of Apple. When EFF was founded in 1990 the sense of being at a frontier, of existing in wild lands, was strong and the name resonated. The fundamental mission of EFF was articulated as 'civilising cyberspace', though since then Barlow has suggested that the arrival of some large corporations in cyberspace means they should consider 'frontierizing civilization'. The metaphor fits so comfortably with organisations trying to represent the grassroots of cyberspace that EFF's name has been used all over the world for organisations such as Electronic Frontiers Italy, Electronic Frontiers Norway, Electronic Frontiers Australia, Electronic Frontiers Texas and so on. The frontier metaphor rests easily with the spokesmen and women of cyberspace.

The moral of the myth of cyberspace as the electronic frontier is two sided, just as frontiers themselves give rise to two different understandings. The first moral is about the nature of human society. A frontier is an outlaw region, where governments or states have little power and individuals are left to themselves. From this basis people may create communities or choose to live solitary, self-determined lives. The frontier spirit is libertarian and from this basis genuine communities may be created. Frontiers provide genuine, authentic forms of existence, where you may have to struggle simply to survive, but you also know that what you create is entirely yours, including whether you participate in a community or not. In frontiers people may be forced together by a common commitment to provide human necessities. Frontiers, by their nature, do not include all the organised amenities of civilisation; often things necessary for survival are absent and this draws people into authentic social relations. Barlow has noted that where he farmed cattle you did not pass by a broken-down car because, in winter, those in the car would freeze to death, and the ex-Executive Director of EFF, Lori Fena, similarly noted that she came from Alaska (the last frontier, as it says on Alaskan number plates) where people have a frontier spirit but are unified by the harshness of weather to provide communal support. Frontiers provide the ultimate state of human liberty and social relations emerge from the desire of people to be together or from needs that cannot be ignored. Frontier societies have no need of government because social relations are either freely chosen or are a response to basic human needs.

The second moral draws on a different history and appreciation of frontiers, one of conquest, war and extermination. Many point out that the story of the Wild West was not simply one of brave explorers self-generating authentic societies but of gold fevers, land grabs, exaggerated machismo and the annihilation of communities that previously existed there. They note that many people's idea of the Wild West is not 'what it was really like' but comes from Hollywood's string of Westerns in which Amerindians were there to be shot at or to inflict torture on innocents, where women and children had to be looked after by strong, gun-wielding men and profit motives were held only by those in black hats. They further note that frontiers are not the boundary between civilisation and the unknown but between one civilisation and another, and in all places where Western countries have created frontiers the already existing civilisation has been severely damaged, if not annihilated. Frontiers existed not just on the Wild West but in Africa, Asia, Australasia and the Americas – in fact almost everywhere has been subject to invasion by the West, an invasion many argue is still occurring in post-colonial times with the imposition of free market economics on a world-wide scale. The reason for these frontiers had little to do with the creation of libertarian communities, but with power and profit. Resources have been plundered, civilisations destroyed and the frontier societies that implemented these changes were violent and male centred. Calling cyberspace a frontier marks it out as a place to be plundered that will be alien to those who cannot 'take the heat' of macho abuse or dislike the dominance of Western values, like free market individualism and its political soul-mate, libertarianism.

Calling cyberspace a frontier offers these two morals and many will believe the one closest to beliefs they already hold. Those attracted to libertarianism will point out that they are aware of all the problems with frontiers, but these problems do not hold in cyberspace because there are no already existing civilisations and any civilisation that feels excluded need only develop its own corner of cyberspace. For liberty lovers, cyberspace is all the positive elements of frontiers because cyberspace's nature as literally man- and woman-made means it has infinite amounts of space, enough for all, and no existing civilisations to be pillaged. Those fearful of cyberspace point to the low participation of women or the prevalence of abuse, the dominance of Western culture or of the English language and frenzied attempts to find gold in cyberspace, to claim that cyberspace is a frontier in the full sense of the word. Cyberspace for them is simply the latest frantic page in the long, appalling story of Western colonisation. These two interpretations do, however, hold a moral in common. In both, cyberspace is a place that people can move to and occupy. It is simply the interpretation of what this means that divides the two sets of moralists. Cyberspace imagined as the electronic frontier is cyberspace imagined as a place available for possession.[17]

The fundamental power of the metaphor of the frontier is to take as protean a form of communication as cyberspace and conceive it as space. This is, perhaps, the reason why the metaphor of the frontier is the foundation metaphor for cyberspace, because it conceives virtual life fundamentally as a place, and nearly all other metaphors for cyberspace follow this conception. Grasping cyberspace as a place allows notions of control and domination of purchase on the virtual lands. The informational space of flows becomes something that elites and the grassroots can try to control as 'their own'. The final component of social power in cyberspace is to grasp these interrelations and understand their relationship to technopower. This will articulate the connection between social cyberpower between online and offline and social cyberpower in online life, to complete the definition of the second circuit of cyberpower.

It is clear that cyberspace creates communications that are essential to informational socio-economies. It is also clear that much of this communication in the informational space of flows favours the already powerful. It is also clear that the commodification of information offers new ways of those attached to place to organise themselves to regain some strength in the face of globalised elites. Both these possibilities depend on the peculiar powers of cyberspace as they are applied to the boundary between online and offline societies, and this means that the fundamental source of social power, of the ability to act, 'in between' cyberspace and meatspace will be technopower. Global, real-time, never ceasing communication depends on the interplay of technological things and social values that characterise the social in cyberspace. This is simply because the changes cyberspace effects depend on the peculiar nature of its social relations. If a company has engineers dotted around the world but needs them to discuss matters then they will, if sensible, turn to email. Offline problems will be worked on with online resources. If a trade unionist wishes to track a corporation's world-wide organisation and contact workers in far-flung places, then both the information-searching abilities of the Web and the communications of electronic bulletin boards or email will be relevant. In each case, cyberspace's resources are utilised. Offline comes to online for the space of flows. That means technopower becomes the fundamental form of power underpinning the space of flows, just as it defines the cyberpower of the social in cyberspace. Technopower becomes the medium through which the space of flows can be managed or directed. The resources of technopower offer the possibility of directing the space of flows towards particular ends, through the construction of tools with values that promote those ends. The metaphor of the frontier helps create an understanding that the resources technopower creates are available for occupation and use. The metaphor of the frontier ensures that the advantages of the informational space of flows, based on technopower, are not lost because of the strangeness of virtual life.

Here we find a two-way connection between the construction of offline and online societies in technopower. The fundamental pressure from offline interests will be towards the construction, elaboration and maintenance of the informational space of flows. Powerful forces will focus on cyberspace to ensure that the space of flows remains capable of the functions informational socio-economies rely on. This process will not be simple or linear; there are offline elites of the industrial era who can be expected to fear the effects of informational socio-economies and seek the restriction of cyberspace's development. Further, the elements of cyberspace that do not aid the space of flows can expect little or no support from offline interests. All these elements would need to be examined one by one to see what their effect on offline is before the attitude of offline interests to them could be confidently outlined. There is not the space to do this here, rather the important point is that cyberspace and the informational space of flows should not be confused, because any such confusion can lead to the assumption that offline elites must support cyberspace because they need it to continue constructing informational space. This is not so. Cyberspace is of little importance to informational socio-economies except where it makes the informational space of flows possible. This fundamental conclusion identifies one trend in political and cultural struggles between online and offline.

To understand the attitude of offline interests towards online politics the question must be asked, how does this politics affect the informational space of flows? And not, how does this politics affect cyberspace? This conclusion is complicated by the fact that any attempt by offline elites to structure online life must flow through technopower, which means it must flow through the online elite and online elites have an interest in cyberspace and not just the informational space of flows. A second trend in pressures between online and offline can therefore be identified in the ability of online elites to mediate the pressures of offline interests on cyberspace. This suggests online elites might act as the protectors of online life but this is not necessarily so. The wider ability of the online elites to act flows from their place in networks of technopower and is based on their expertise in cyberspace technology. This may mean their interests are in resisting or facilitating demands from offline, depending on the nature of those demands. No assumption of the essential benevolence of the online elites towards cyberspace can be assumed, only – like all elites – their essential benevolence towards themselves. However, a further basic trend in the intermingling of online and offline is here established in the ambiguous position of the online elite towards the disjunction between cyberspace and the informational space of flows.

The present task is to identify some of the fundamental pressures resulting from the cyberpower of the social, but any actual developments from these pressures can be expected to reveal the complex nature of elites and grassroots. While conclusions about the pressures and interests of these elites and grassroots seem valid, they could never be applied to the actual development of cyberspace or informational socio-economies without great sensitivity to particular interests, actors and contexts. Cyberpower identifies basic, abstract pressures and forces that could only be applied to cyberspace and socio-economies with empirical sensitivity. The essential point is that the importance of cyberspace to offline societies lies in the informational space of flows and this space is dependent on the ebbs and flows of technopower. Whereas the individual in and between cyberspace can possess power and utilise it, the social in and between cyberspace situates individuals according to their technical expertise or their control of expertise in relations of dominated and dominator. The second circuit of cyberpower is a circuit of technopower.

Chapter 6

The virtual imaginary

capture of the imaginary is enough to motivate all sorts of behaviour in the living beings.

Jacques Lacan (1977: 207)

Key concepts

Collective imagination
People who never know or meet each other can become committed to a common cause by articulating a vision they all understand and support. Nationalism is based on a collective imagination because every member of a nation cannot possibly meet every other member, but they can believe in similar pictures of the nation. All communities have some sort of collective imagination.

Utopia
A society or place that is perfect or ideal.

Dystopia
A society or place whose imperfection is perfect or who's evil is ideal.

Virtual imaginary
The collective imagination of cyberspace is called the virtual imaginary. Two poles of a utopia of immortality and heavenly cyberhosts and a dystopia of total surveillance and perfect social control structure the virtual imaginary. The virtual imaginary always appears to be almost true, because the technology needed to realise a virtual utopia or dystopia always appears to be almost ready.

Introduction

Cyberpower has so far emerged as circuits of power that constitute the possibilities for individuals and societies in virtual spaces. If you begin by examining cyberspace either from the individual or from the social, then a particular type of cyberpower emerges. From the perspective of the individual, the power of cyberspace places weapons in the hands of individuals, which they can use to renovate identities and social positions both online and offline. From the perspective of the social, the power of cyberspace rests on the constant dance of technological thing with social value and produces an ever increasing reliance on complex technical systems that, in turn, offer greater control of action to those who wield technical expertise. The two circuits connect to each other because the drive for greater and faster access fuels the development of more and more complex technologies to deliver that access. Put another way, increased access increases the power of individuals to demand even faster and more widespread access, thereby restarting the process of creating more complex technology. This connection means that the power of a technically based elite grows as demands for access grow and that further articulations of technopower enable greater access and greater individual rights in cyberspace. Individual powers and social power expand together in cyberspace. Yet this complex of powers is not the whole story of cyberpower because individuals and communities are bound together by more than just their individual capacities or social structures. Lying across these two are the hopes and dreams, fantasies and nightmares, the collective imaginations or the imaginary[1] of those with virtual lives.

This chapter will examine the two sides of cyberspace's imaginary. First, it will analyse the utopian side of the imaginary by examining cyborgs and the fantasy of information codes that underpin them. Cyborgs are the connection of human to machine and everyone in cyberspace is a cyborg, as their virtual self only comes to life through keyboards, screens, wires and computers. Cyborgs transgress boundaries and give rise to hopes that previous categories – such as women and men or human and animal – will be overcome. It will then be argued that the mingling of human and machine in cyberspace, which underpins the creation of cyborgs, relies on a deeper fantasy in which everything is governed by information codes. This fantasy is explored with particular emphasis on its connection to the mapping of the human genome and understandings of the nature of information in cyberspace. At its most rhapsodic, the heavenly imaginary of cyberspace offers both immortality and godhood to humans through the translation of life into information held in cyberspace. The dystopian side of cyberspace's imaginary reverses these hopes and pictures a Superpanopticon of total surveillance, which results from the archiving of all social interactions in distributed databases interrelated through cyberspace. From bank transactions to newspaper purchases to car travel, it is feared that all social actions will be translated into digital records that can be assembled to form a complete account of someone's life. The Superpanopticon will be defined through Michel Foucault's analysis of disciplinary power and will be exemplified through three tactics for its realisation. First, hellish cyborgs is the fear of social control through joining human and machine together, for example through the implanting of tracking devices in humans. Second, the collection of minutiae is the dread of social control through recording and collecting every small transaction that occurs in someone's life. Third, fear of cyberspace is the anxiety that all the individual powers offered by cyberspace can be turned to evil purposes. The imaginary's hell relies on the transmutation of human lives, as they are lived minute by minute, into information that is collated through cyberspace. Both sides of cyberspace's imaginary rely on the belief that everything is made of information or can be turned into information. This type of power is then defined as being similar to Barnes' notion of power as social order because participating in cyberspace's imaginary, whether in hope or fear (or both), means becoming part of the imagined community of cyberspace. The meaning of cyberspace's imaginary is not its spectacular content of heaven or hell, but that the process of working for or against cyberspace's heavens and hells means individuals become part of cyberspace's community.

The collective imagination

People believe in imaginary relationships that help define collectives. Anderson defined a nation as 'an imagined political community – and imagined as both inherently limited and sovereign' (Anderson, 1991: 6). It is imagined because it is impossible for all members of the community to meet; they must hypothesise their commonality. It is limited because there are always borders and beyond those borders there are other nations. It is sovereign because it creates its own rules within its borders. Finally, it is a community because, regardless of actual inequalities between members of a nation, it is always conceived as a 'deep, horizontal comradeship' in which all are equal as members of the nation (Anderson, 1991: 6–7). Though Anderson uses this definition to explore the nature of the nation-state, something cyberspace helps to undermine, a similar imagined community exists in cyberspace. One obvious sign of this is John Perry Barlow's Declaration of Independence for Cyberspace, written in anger as a response to the passage into law of the USA's censorious Communications Decency Act but also enunciating wider principles. Barlow begins by naming the enemy, establishing a boundary:

> Governments of the Industrial World, you weary giants of flesh and steel, I come from Cyberspace, the new home of Mind. On behalf of the future, I ask you of the past to leave us alone. You are not welcome among us. You have no sovereignty where we gather.
>
> (Barlow, 1996c)

In the middle, he provides a definition of his new world and its fundamental political tenets:

> Cyberspace consists of transactions, relationships, and thought itself, arrayed like a standing wave in the web of our communications. Ours is a world that is both everywhere and nowhere, but it is not where our bodies live.

We are creating a world that all may enter without privilege or prejudice accorded by race, economic power, military force, or station of birth.

We are creating a world where anyone, anywhere may express his or her beliefs, no matter how singular, without fear of being coerced into silence or conformity.

(Barlow, 1996c)

And at the end he establishes the new community of cyberspace and its sovereign rights, against the Other of the industrial world:

Your increasingly obsolete information industries would perpetuate them-selves by proposing laws, in America and elsewhere, that claim to own speech itself throughout the world. These laws would declare ideas to be another industrial product, no more noble than pig iron. In our world, whatever the human mind may create can be reproduced and distributed infinitely at no cost. The global conveyance of thought no longer requires your factories to accomplish.

These increasingly hostile and colonial measures place us in the same position as those previous lovers of freedom and self-determination who had to reject authorities of distant, uninformed powers. We must declare our virtual selves immune to your sovereignty, even as we continue to consent to your rule over our bodies. We will spread ourselves across the Planet so that no one can arrest our thoughts.

We will create a civilization of the Mind in Cyberspace. May it be more humane and fair than the world your governments have made before.

(Barlow, 1996c)

Barlow declares there is a community with particular values in cyberspace. From some perspectives, Barlow's pronouncement may seem utopian – cyberspace becoming independent? – but from Anderson's perspective it is a textual version of the 'exemplary suicides, poignant martyrdoms, assassinations, executions, wars, and holocausts' that a nation fashions its biography out of (Anderson, 1991: 206). It was a moment when the collective imagination of cyberspace was articulated and forced people to recognise themselves as part of a particular imagined community. Barlow commented on the effect and intention of his declaration in the following way:

The main thing that happened was that it made people think, which was the idea in the first place. I knew it wasn't going to have any affect on the people to whom it was addressed. To the extent that they ever encountered it all, which was unlikely, they were going to find it utterly ludicrous because nothing could be further from their reality framework, whereas for a lot of people it was going to seem like a dangerous statement of the obvious that we weren't ready to make. But I felt, and I still feel, that it was time somebody stated that obvious fact or planted a flag of some sort, not on behalf of any government because there couldn't be one, but on behalf of a reality saying 'this is inherently extra-national, inherently anti-sovereign and your sovereignty cannot apply to us. We've got to figure things out for ourselves.' And I really think we do, I don't know how anybody else can. I think that a lot of people who reacted to it negatively are gradually starting to respond to it by saying 'well, all right, he's got sort of a point here, maybe we do have to start thinking about how we create systems of our own governance'.

(Barlow, 1996a)

Barlow's attempt to plant a flag on behalf of cyberspace is the result, and not the cause, of an existing imagined community in cyberspace, not necessarily a nation (though some use the term digital nation), but a political community. Other such indications, few as grandiloquent, can be found. For example, at the end of an early piece exploring the relationship between the Electronic Frontier Foundation and virtual communities Mike Godwin wrote:

One of the things you often see when you read discussions about EFF on the WELL or on Usenet is a sense that the EFF has become a representative body. While this is misleading – EFF is not yet a membership organization – it's still the case that EFF is regarded as an advocacy group for electronic communities generally. You'll often read comments from Usenet folks who think the most appropriate pronouns when talking about the EFF are 'we,' 'us,' and 'our.'

And if that neighborly sense of belonging doesn't prove the existence of a community, I don't know what does.

(Godwin, 1991)

Here the emergence of certain crucial pronouns marks the sense of a community lurking behind an organisation that did not even allow membership.[2] There seems little doubt that alongside the virtual lives that individuals construct and the virtual societies technopower conditions, another layer of cyberpower exists in the fantasies and nightmares that collectively constitute the imagination of cyberspace. Here will be found the common beliefs of individuals who never meet each other that will move them to fight for their cybercommunity, believe in their cybercommunity and even love their cybercommunity. To complete the identification of the complex structure of cyberpower, this third level needs to be explored and its particular form of power distinguished.

One further characteristic of imaginaries needs to be noted because they often appear to be on the verge of coming true; they are in a constant state of almost becoming real. Imaginaries offer hopes and fears that often do not appear as hopes and fears, but as real projects just one or two steps away from completion. Much of the urgency that people draw from imaginaries stems from this sense of being nearly but not quite finished, meaning that people feel a need to act quickly to prevent the imagined disaster or bring on the imagined benefit. Cyberspace's imaginary strongly reflects this aspect, particularly as technological solutions always appear on the verge of reality. There is one recurrent source for this in cyberspace, as all through its history radical new possibilities are thought to be coming within the next five to ten years because Moore's law results in exponentially increasing computing power that will deliver the fantasised possibility. Rheingold's description of future cyberspatial sex is one example of this. In 1991, he described the possibility that bodysuits will become available that have the 'intimate snugness of a condom' (Rheingold, 1991: 346) and allow touch and sensation to be simulated creating a virtual body that can be plugged into cyberspace. Once in cyberspace the technology Rheingold dubs teledildonics will allow virtual sex that includes full physical touch between physically separated people. Having noted that this technology is twenty to fifty years from realisation, Rheingold then goes on to list all the different technological barriers that need to be overcome and finds that they are all being overcome. Fibre optic networks are being built, he quotes an experiment that allows touch to be transmitted at a distance and he mentions the massive increase in computing power that is needed, which of course Moore's law defines will be answered at an exponential rate. The overall effect is of being told about a radical, transformative technology that is coming quickly and of a need somehow to grasp the change before it occurs (Rheingold, 1991: 345–53):

> Given the rate of development of VR [virtual reality] technologies, we don't have a great deal of time to tackle questions of morality, privacy, personal identity, and even the prospect of a fundamental change in human nature. When the VR revolution really gets rolling, we are likely to be too busy turning into whatever we are turning into to analyse or debate the consequences.
>
> (Rheingold, 1991: 350)

Rheingold on teledildonics is only one example of possibilities in cyberspace that seem almost realities and because of this we must concern ourselves, as a matter of utmost urgency, with the radical changes that are coming. Cyberspace's imaginary is filled with the nearly real fantastic.

Cyberspace's imaginary is structured by two opposed conceptions of its future, heaven and hell. Cyberspace has given rise to many exaggerated hopes and fears that indicates its twin-sided imagined community. In Barlow's Declaration of Independence can be seen the heavenly side in a new world of 'Mind' that is inherently free from almost any discrimination you can think of. David Brown's analysis of cyberspace is advertised as a 'more sober, alternative perspective' that turns out to be almost entirely negative: 'I see a world in which technical connectivity starts to subtly undermine the essentially ethical ties needed to bind and sustain communities, economies and entire political systems' (Brown, 1997: 4). Cyberspace's collective imagination exists on these two poles of a new, radically egalitarian world of pure thought and the destruction of ties that make civilised, humane societies possible.

Visions of heaven...

MYTHS OF THE ELECTRONIC FRONTIER 8: COMMUNITY OF
MIND OR IMMORTALITY IN SILICON

Perhaps the oldest desire of human society is to cheat death, the dream of immortality. Even with all the efforts of smart drugs, elective surgery and personal trainers, the best human body will run out after some time. An alternative would be to separate the body from whatever is believed to be our essence, that indefinable sense of self, and to make the essence live allowing the body to rot. Separating the mind and spirit from the body allows the possibility that the essential 'I' could be translated to something less fallible, less terminal than the human body. If translation could be made two way, then there is no reason why the I could not be placed again in a body, if an I wished. The chosen body could then, in turn, be discarded to be replaced or not, as the I might want. And many believe that just such a place for the I is emerging on silicon and in cyberspace.

The first part of this story is the belief that computers can be used to model or mimic, first, intelligence, and, second, the human mind. The academic discipline and software industry of artificial intelligence is dedicated to these ends and it spreads in both directions. Computers are taught/programmed to act intelligently, leading to such shocks to human pride as a computer finally unnerving and beating the human world chess champion. The mind is also modelled to see if its workings can be explored through simulation. Both these directions point to the possibility that more complex programs and more powerful hardware will come closer and closer to acting just like the human mind. The important result is not necessarily the actual work that is produced, often far short of the fantasies that drive it, but the ontological shock that comes with the realisation that computers might be considered, in some sense, alive:

Although many philosophers in the past have suspected one could abstract the laws of life and apply them elsewhere, it wasn't until the complexity of computers and human-made systems b ecame as complicated as living things, that it was possible to prove this. It's eerie how much of life *can* be transferred.

> So far, some of the traits of the living that have successfully been transported
> to mechanical systems are: self-replication, self-governance, limited self-
> repair, mild evolution, and partial learning.
>
> (Kelly, 1994: 2–3)

The significant point is not the list of life's parts that have been transferred to machines or any concern whether the parts will ever add up to
a whole, but the belief that life can be transferred to complex computer
systems.

The next step in the story is easy. Why not put my life, your life, our
lives on complex computer systems? Hans Moravec is head of
Carnegie–Mellon's mobile robotics laboratory and he looks forward to a
time when the information stored in his brain will be downloaded into a
computer. Marvin Minsky is a pioneer in artificial intelligence who has
similar hopes. The Extropians are a group dedicated to achieving this
end and expect to do so within their lifetime. Much cyberpunk science
fiction explores these possibilities, the most obvious version being the
end of Gibson's trilogy that begins with *Neuromancer*, where a number
of humans finally manage to inject themselves entirely into cyberspace.
The collapse of the human/machine barrier is here constituted by the
collapse of the barrier between human behaviour and complex computer
systems. Once this obstruction is removed, more than intelligence or
the mind can be encoded onto silicon; we can look forward to the I, in
all its complexity, becoming immortal.

Of course, there immediately appears to be a land fit for the I and all
its friends – the virtual lands is the obvious place for virtual selves to go
and live. All the different immortal souls can then create and destroy in
their new limitless world. It would be the ultimate MUD, populated by
fully realised human virtual subjects, the halls of the immortals. This
leads to the fourth and last step in this story. The collapse of the
distinction between humans and computers leads to the encoding of
consciousness, which leads to its uploading into cyberspace where the
immortals can mingle, which finally allows the ultimate joining
together of all human consciousnesses. Perhaps cyberspace will allow all
the coded consciousnesses to mingle in a more fundamental way than as
if at the ultimate cocktail party. Perhaps something will emerge that
points to a higher stage of being, beyond individuality. Many call on the
philosopher–theologian Teilhard de Chardin's concept of the Omega
Point, the point at which all human minds become one, and dream of

cyberspace's community of mind becoming that point. Michael Benedikt expresses nearly all points of this myth of the electronic frontier:

> the resentment we feel for our own bodies' cloddishness, limitations and final treachery: their mortality. Reality is death. If only we could, we would wander the earth and never leave home; we should enjoy triumphs without risks, eat of the Tree and not be punished, consort daily with angels, enter heaven now and not die....In counterpoint to the earthly *garden* Eden...floats the image of the Heavenly City....In fact, all images of the Heavenly City – East and West – have common features – weightlessness, radiance, numerological complexity, palaces upon palaces, peace and harmony through rule by the good and the wise, utter cleanliness, transcendence of nature and of crude beginnings....The image of the Heavenly City, in fact, is...a religious version of cyberspace.
>
> (Benedikt, 1991a: 14–16)

There we have it, the ultimate dream of humanity. The moral of this myth of the electronic frontier is that freed from our bodies, our Is will be able to mingle, join and finally create the heaven that rests within us now only as a dimly perceived potential. Cyberspace offers the ultimate fantasies of both individual immortality and collective transcendence. The body's dominance over the mind is the stranglehold broken by complex computer systems. The mind comes to dominate the body, to the extent that the mind will pick and choose its bodies. Made into the informational codes that live so well in cyberspace, all the Is finally have a chance to become We. Cyberspace allows the becoming of a transcendental community of mind.[3]

Cyborgs

Central to the vision of heaven that inhabits cyberspace's imaginary is the cyborg, the fusion of human and machine already mentioned in Chapter 2 as one of the key figures of cyberpunk science fiction. All who enter cyberspace become cyborgs because they depend on machines for their online life. The cyborg offers a number of transformative possibilities that have come to invest it with extraordinary hopes. Donna Haraway has developed perhaps the most influential theorisation of cyborgs and she traces their emerging significance as radical reinventors of humanity to three simultaneous breakdowns in human culture. First, the barrier between human and animal has been breached. Centrally, Darwinian evolutionary theory has demonstrated the connection between all humans/animals rather than human uniqueness. Humans share common roots and many close connections to animals, 'language, tool use, social behaviour, mental events, nothing really convincingly settles the separation of human and animal' (Haraway, 1991: 151–2). Second, the distinction between organic (human–animal) and machine has collapsed. Machines now appear to play chess with greater intelligence than humans do:[4]

> Late twentieth-century machines have made thoroughly ambiguous the difference between natural and artificial, mind and body, self-developing and externally designed, and many other distinctions that used to apply to organisms and machines. Our machines are disturbingly lively, and we ourselves frighteningly inert.
>
> (Haraway, 1991: 152)

Third, the boundary between physical and non-physical is unclear. Ample evidence of this has been given and more will follow:

> Our best machines are made of sunshine; they are all light and clean because they are nothing but signals, electromagnetic waves, a section of a spectrum, and these machines are eminently portable, mobile....People are nowhere near so fluid, being both material and opaque.
>
> (Haraway, 1991: 153)

With changes as momentous as these already in effect, it is not a matter of choosing to be a cyborg but:

> The body must become a cyborg to retain its presence in the world, resituated in technological space and refigured in technological terms. Whether this represents a continuation, a sacrifice, a transcendence or a surrender of 'the subject' is not certain.
>
> (Bukatman, 1993a: 247)

Cyborgs are one of our last, greatest hopes. The cyborg asks us, what is it to be human? Cyberspace is central to this question because we are all cyborgs in cyberspace. We are not necessarily the fully immersed cyborg of teledildonics but at the very least we can be attached to keyboards being drawn through the screen into virtual lives. Cyborgs offer revolutionary hope because they transform what it means to be human. For example, Haraway sees cyborgs as a source of hope particularly for feminists because 'The cyborg is a creature in a post-gender world' (Haraway, 1991: 150; Holland, 1995: 165). Similarly, Chela Sandoval argues

> cyborg consciousness can be understood as the technological embodiment of a particular and specific form of oppositional consciousness that I have

elsewhere described as 'U.S. third world feminism.'…Haraway provides new metaphoric grounds of resistance for the alienated white male subject under first world conditions of transnationalisation, and thus the metaphor 'cyborg' represents profound possibilities for the twenty-first century.…An oppositional cyborg politics, then, could very well bring the politics of the alienated, white, male subject into alliance with the subaltern politics of U.S. third world feminism.

(Sandoval, 1995: 408–9)

Here cyborg consciousness appears to be the medium through which the divisions between the oppressed may be healed and on which a new politics able to confront and resist globalising capitalism, patriarchy and racism can be based. Others have different hopes. Col. Frederick Timmerman Jr, US Army, director of the Center for Army Leadership, talked of the future warrior as:

In a physiological sense, when needed, soldiers may actually appear to be three miles tall and twenty miles wide. Of course, in a true physical sense nothing will have changed. Rather, by transforming the way technology is applied, by looking at the problem from a biological perspective – focusing on transforming and extending the soldier's physiological capabilities…can we not achieve the superman solution?

(Timmerman, cited in Gray, 1997: 210)

Even as some hope the metaphor of the cyborg may help overthrow the fundamental oppressions of the world, others see it as the salvation of a military struggling to come to terms with the end of the Cold War. Soldiers that always know where they are, that have weapons with unerring aim and defences of unbreachable solidity, all these are the hopes of a cyborg military (Gray, 1997; Shukman, 1995). What is common between the uncomfortable bedfellows of Third World feminism and hyper-advanced military systems is the belief that the transgressions Haraway identifies – human/animal, human/machine, physical/non-physical – offer revolutionary possibilities. Other areas could be similarly explored. For example, the possibility of cyborg doctors conducting operations through cyberspace using mechanised arms that touch the flesh of the patient is only one of the more spectacular possibilities of cyborg medicine (Gray, 1995: Part 3).

The cyborg becomes in all these different stories the metaphoric medium through which hopes and dreams are articulated that drive people forward. For example, the response of the US Marines to problems brought about by budget cuts at the end of the Cold War that restricted the amount of training marines could undergo was cyborgian. Some officers were asked to look for a cheap solution that would provide individual soldiers with team training and the result was the conversion of one of the most popular ever computer games, Doom, into a virtual marine-training machine. In Doom you play the role of the last space marine (ironically) capable of defeating an alien invasion; to do this you race through halls killing all aliens in your way and the screen presents a first-person view in which your weapon is at the centre. Doom's attractions for the Marines were that it could be networked, meaning a number of people could play in the same environment at the same time, it could be customised, because the company that made Doom had released game editors so that individuals could build their own versions, and being an off-the-shelf game it was cheap. The Marines took it, replaced Doom's weird array of alien monsters with human enemies, replaced Doom's array of fanciful weaponry with pictures and sounds of Marine standard rifles and machine guns and then taught teamwork to real marines over networked systems. The first version of Marine Doom was produced mainly in the free time of one of the two marines working on the problem of cheap team training. Now with a working system that appears to do much that is asked of it, these two marines have the interest of the US Army, Secret Service, FBI and more, and have left the Marines to market their game commercially (Riddell, 1997). Here soldiers were inspired to work in their own time to utilise networked game playing to overcome budgetary problems that undermined the training of marines. Of course, the story does not finish here. New games keep emerging that allow more soldiers to interact online and the final goal of virtual training for all armed forces always hangs in the air. With Marine Doom it was the military cyborg that was driven one step further by the possibility of actually creating something new, but this is similar to other branches of the cyborg world. Technology emerging every day seems to promise, any minute now, the realisation of the dreams of cyborgs and drives people to work in the service of their collectively imagined cyborg.

Information codes

Cyborgs are a central component of the myth of immortality in silicon and of the heavenly side of cyberspace's imaginary, but they are also only the expression of a deeper fantasy. Cyberspace is a world made of information, we live in an 'information age', in information socio-economies, and all of these, along with any other 'information this and that', are enabled by computer code. All the different commands typed in by a software programmer that tell a computer what to do are the instructions that make an information age possible. One cautionary tale underlines this. In 1985, as part of Star Wars research, the USA's Space Shuttle was programmed to pass over a mountain in Hawaii that had a powerful laser on it. The Shuttle had a mirror on it and the laser would hit the mirror, bounce back to Earth and allow scientists to measure distortion caused by the Earth's atmosphere. Unfortunately, the programmers coded all distances as nautical miles and forgot to convert the height of the mountain from 10,000 nautical miles to its real height of 10,000 feet. When the Shuttle passed over the mountain the software code ordered it to flip over on its back and point the mirror at deep space, where 10,000 nautical miles would be, leaving the laser to bounce harmlessly off the top of the Shuttle (Chapman, 1993: 827–8). It is often when things go wrong that we see most clearly what we take for granted and the upside-down Space Shuttle underlines both the control software code has over computers and that it is fallible humans that create the code. Grasping the importance of information codes leads to one of the imaginative leaps that inhabit cyberspace's imaginary, because there is another information code of increasing importance.

In biology, the basic substance of life is now understood to be made of the information code of DNA. The analogy between life as coded information and software codes running the 'body' of cyberspace is too close for the conjectures of an imaginary to miss. The fantasy beneath the cyborgs of cyberspace is that everything, even or especially life, has become information:

> The third regime of the control revolution, seeded two centuries ago by the application of information to coal steam, is the control of information itself. The miles of circuits and information looping from place to place that administers the control of energy and matter has incidentally flooded our environment with messages, bits, and bytes....Genetic engineering (information which controls DNA information) and tools for electronic libraries (information which managed book information) foreshadow the subjugation of information.
>
> (Kelly, 1994: 162)

Here life is just information with no fundamental, ontological distinction between it and library databases. As with all other components of the imaginary this collapse of life into information also appears to be occurring before our eyes, driving the urgency that many feel in understanding this change. That DNA is the information code of life is an established fact of biological science. But further, the secrets of DNA are the subject of a billion-dollar investment by the US government that has unleashed the Human Genome Project to unfurl finally the complete, detailed code of information that makes up DNA. A detailed analysis of the Human Genome Project is beyond present concerns;[5] its importance here is that it confirms the belief that the secret code of life will become one more piece of information:

> The ultimate purpose of this program is to write down the complete ordered sequence of As, Ts, Cs and Gs – the four nucleotides – that make up all the genes in the human genome, a string of letters that will be three billion elements long.
>
> (Lewontin, 1994: 107)

There is no need to explore the complex biology or the vast funding of this project to be able to see that the result will be an extremely long sequence of letters that claims to unravel the mystery of life. Within the grasp of humans, or so the promoters of the project say, will be therapies for all sorts of genetic disorders and a profound knowledge of what it is to be human. And what better to manipulate and explore such a code than computers? Life will enter computers as a long code of As, Ts, Cs and Gs.

In addition, and from the opposite direction, computers are giving birth to life in the form of self-replicating software programs that can pass many tests for being alive. Intelligent agents have already been discussed in Chapter 4, and they are one version of what are becoming called 'bots', software programs let loose in cyberspace that seem to be alive:

> A bot is a software version of a mechanical robot. Like a mechanical robot, it is guided by algorithmic rules of behavior – *if this happens, do that: if that happens, do this*. But instead of clanking around a laboratory room bumping into walls, software robots are programs that maneuver through cyberspace, bouncing off of communications protocols and operating systems....Mailbots filter electronic mail, preventing junk mail and spam advertising from clogging up our online mailboxes. Chatterbots carry on whimsical conversations in online, real-time text environments, such as chat rooms or MUDs. Cancelbots seek out unwanted expression and erase it from electronic bulletin boards. Gamebots populate computer game environments with believable characters and wily foes. Web robots explore the hyperlinked reality of cyberspace, mapping out and indexing the vast quantities of information available throughout the World Wide Web.
>
> (Leonard, 1997: 7–8)

Leonard calls bots 'the first indigenous species of cyberspace' (Leonard, 1997: 8) and notes they have three characteristics. They have personality, offer some aspect of human behaviour or have been anthropomorphised in some way. They are autonomous and operate without direct human supervision. Finally, they usually perform a service, even if it is only comic relief (Leonard, 1997: 11). For example, take the AutoNomy tool for searching the Web. This takes the form of cartoon dogs that appear on the screen and howl with boredom if left with nothing to do for too long. Once they are trained by inputting a number of sentences, they rush off into the Web searching for relevant information. As they search small animations of the dogs run on the screen: a dog may sit begging to be let in (signifying they are waiting to access a Web page); they may have their snout to the ground, digging furiously (on the scent of something); or one may return with a bone in its mouth (found something!) (Leonard, 1997: 78–9). As Haraway claimed, our machines have become disturbingly lively, as we sit inert in front of the screen. From both directions – life entering cyberspace and cyberspace producing life – it appears as if the dream of everything becoming information is just around the corner, with individual desires for empowerment alongside powerful software companies and government initiatives speeding up its arrival.

Information is dreamt of as the magic component of the new age that is dawning at the beginning of the third millennium. Information codes constitute both nature and culture. Everything and everyone is controlled or constituted by information codes. But humans can program information codes, which means humans can control everything. Information in the imaginary rests on this dualism of the thing that constitutes and the thing that can be constituted. Cyberspace, cyborgs, humanity, cultures and nature are all constituted by information but they all create information as well. The duality of maker/made allows a deep tension at the heart of cyberspace's imaginary, where rather than a final resting state on which the dreams of cyborgs and immortality can be firmly built, there appears a process that continually empowers and disempowers, supports and orders, controls and obeys. This can be seen in some of the great slogans of cyberspace.

What is information? Not a state of rest, but a constant motion of creation and control at the heart of dreams for a perfect world through cyberspace. It comes as no surprise then to find that information is the subject of some of the great maxims of cyberspace. The most powerful and famous of these is the one credited to Stewart Brand: 'information wants to be free'. Countless nooks and crannies of cyberspace beat to this particular drum. The strangeness of 'information' wanting anything at all makes perfect sense here at the heart of the utopian side of cyberspace's imaginary, because it expresses the belief that information is out there beyond humans and creates all that there is. Brand's slogan is often theorised using biologist Richard Dawkins' concept of the meme, which argues that ideas are self-replicating patterns of information that multiply across populations. Memes make ideas into elements of the natural world, subject to the same evolutionary patterns that genes are subject to. For example, Barlow argues pieces of information

> are life-forms in every respect but a basis in the carbon atom. They self-reproduce, they interact with their surroundings and adapt to them, they mutate, they persist. Like any other life-form they evolve to fill out the possibility spaces of their local environments, which are in this case the surrounding belief systems and cultures of their hosts, namely, us.
>
> Indeed, the sociobiologists like Dawkins make a plausible case that carbon-based life-forms are information as well, that, as the chicken is the egg's way of making another egg, the entire biological spectacle is just the DNA molecule's means of copying out more information strings exactly like itself.
>
> (Barlow, 1996b: 159)

Memes and 'information wanting to be free' are two sides of the same coin, the belief that information codes are alive and govern everything. But there is a second slogan, heard perhaps less frequently than Brand's, yet nonetheless also heard often, that cuts across Brand's and is also, curiously, held by many who passionately believe information wants to be free.[6]

'Information is alienated experience' is the slogan credited to virtual reality pioneer Jaron Lanier (Brockman, 1996: 170). Alienated experience means that information is an expression of someone's work or life. Information here is not a natural thing but an expression from somebody that has been concretised at some time into an object. When discussing technopower, this process was analysed as the way human input creates objects that are then detached and appear to be independent, while in fact being made up of someone's prior work. Reification[7] is the closest term for Lanier's expression. Reification is the process by which humans take their creations to be objects independent of human life and forget their objects have social origins. The human work of creating information is alienated, made foreign, from the human creator and thereby appears as a self-sufficient thing. When the human genome has given up all its secrets we can expect it to become a thing – in fact, the thing that governs human life – but it is a human creation. It is information made by humans working in a vast project. Operating systems like Windows 95/98 or the hideously complex software that runs the Space Shuttle are written by humans but experienced as things. With Lanier's slogan, the flip side of the heavenly hopes in cyberspace's imaginary re-emerges and information becomes something made by humans. If information is the experience, creativity and work of humans that exists apart from those humans, then information can be formed by humans. Everything is governed by information codes and humans create information codes. The two slogans come together in the two fundamental tenets of visionary hope for cyberspace to reveal a third that can be understood in two different ways:

1   Information wants to be free.
2   Information is alienated experience.
3   Alienated experience wants to be free.

  3a   Humanity wants to be free.
  3b   I want to be free.

Our alienated expressions want to be free, which can only mean that the expressions we alienate are expressions of our desire to be free. Given that free alienated expression, as information codes, underlies everything then the combined slogans can be decoded to reveal our inherent desire to be free by merging into the substance that constitutes us. By creating the knowledge that we are information, we are freed from ourselves and merge with all others in a pure world. Some people hope that cyberspace will lead to a community of mind. Teilhard de Chardin's Omega Point is most commonly invoked to explain this goal. McLuhan first developed this connection between de Chardin's mysticism and the effects of new electronic media and it has been taken up by many (Dery, 1996: 45–9). *Wired* magazine's editor Louis Rosetto argued 'society is organised by a "hive-mind consensus" that allows humanity to evolve into ever higher forms, perhaps even fulfilling McLuhan's prophecy to 'make of the entire globe, and of the human family, a single consciousness' (cited in Dery, 1996: 47). It is fitting that John Perry Barlow again appears here, this time not in the guise of cowboy or cyber-civil libertarian but as the graduate in comparative religion that he also is.

> And I looked at the net as being the Great Work of the present...the highest expression of the culture of this era....At a certain point it suddenly dawned on me, I had a very crystalline perception, that this was precisely what he [Teilhard de Chardin] had been talking about. That the point of all evolution to this stage is to create the collective organism of mind. That's what Teilhard would say. I have some other things to say in addition to that. But that's the best way I can sum up his work. It's about creating a consciousness so profound that it will make good company for God himself. Or itself.
>
> (Barlow, 1994a)

Many of those who seek inspiration from Donna Haraway's socialist–feminist myth of the cyborg can be interpreted as seeking a materialist version of this hope for utopia. Sandoval sees the cyborg as the way to join feminists, alienated white males and the Third World together in a movement that will overthrow the oppressors. Lurking behind such desires is the materialists' utopia of a world without oppression, in which truly egalitarian life becomes possible. The cyborg metaphor, and the importance of information codes that it invokes, offers tools for realising this ambition, in its own way as grandiose as the hope of a fully realised pantheism:

> certain dualisms have been persistent in Western traditions; they have all been systemic to the logics and practices of domination of women, people of colour, nature, workers, animals – in short, domination of all constituted as others, whose task is to mirror the self....Cyborg imagery can suggest a way out of the maze of dualisms in which we have explained our bodies and our tools to ourselves. This is a dream not of a common language, but of a powerful infidel heteroglossia. It is an imagination of a feminist speaking in tongues to strike fear into the circuits of the supersavers of the new right. It means both building and destroying machines, identities, categories, relationships, space stories. Though both are bound in the spiral dance, I would rather be a cyborg than a goddess.
>
> (Haraway, 1991: 177, 181)

Whether as mystical godhood or the material revolution of oppression, the tensions and forces in the heavenly side of cyberspace's imaginary lead towards utopia. Coursing through cyberspace's imaginary are these powerful dreams, each of which appears to be in various stages of implementation. Cyberspace offers the chance that utopia is coming, even as you read. The imaginary offers those with virtual lives the hope that they are creating the essentially better world, as they labour on the intricacies of online life. Of course, few recognise in its entirety the tensions and implications that have been outlined as the heavenly imaginary of cyberspace. It is also easy to feel that the rhapsodies of Barlow and Haraway are, in their very different ways, both distant from the reality of corporate interests in cyberspace, where we expect imagination to be filled with dollar signs rather than gods or social revolutions. However, this is the richest of the rich, Bill Gates, talking 'The vision that really got Microsoft going – a computer on every desk and in every home' (Gates, cited in Brockman, 1996: 96) and this is not just a vision of Microsoft software on every desk and in every home but also a social vision of the power of computers revolutionising people's lives. Gates is less likely to be believed than Barlow or Haraway when he discusses a social vision, simply because it will be assumed it is all a secret ploy to make money, but there is no reason to think he is being hypocritical[8] and so he takes part in cyberspace's imaginary.

But with Microsoft comes the dark side. Many fear Microsoft and the vision of a Microsoft-powered computer on every desk and in every home is to some a fearful vision of social control through software code. In the blink of an eye, the hope of computer power on every desk can become the fear of control by large corporations in the nightmare of a deeply divided world:

> As Bill Gates cheerfully admits, the economic success of a cybernetic economy depends crucially upon 'total participation' in a digitised and fully networked landscape whose 'pervasiveness is part of the design'. Those who choose to disconnect will automatically be marginalised....If a technology becomes like an umbilical cord – when you cannot unplug or opt out without threatening your survival (economically or otherwise) – then you are truly a captive of that system.
>
> (Brown, 1997: 143)

Cyberspace's imaginary is two sided: in every dream home a heartache.

...and hell

Or should that be, every dream home is heartache? For some, the fantasies of immortality and omnipotence are themselves to be feared. They are not the Great Work of humanity but an expression of the psychopathology of modern life. Les Levidow points to the role of technology in the Gulf War, in particular the way watching it on screens the world over subtly drew people into the glamour of high-tech weapons. Film of smart bombs finding the right door or the correct exhaust shaft entices populations into both forgetting what the bomb's purpose is and celebrating the fact that it can be done:

The Gulf War illustrates the role of high-tech systems in mass psychopathology. A paranoid rationality expressed in terms of the machine-like self combines an omnipotent fantasy of self-control with fear and aggression directed against the emotional and bodily limitations of mere mortals...computer systems can seduce us into a participatory paranoia, turn our selves into social and emotional cripples, and extend a commodity-type reification far beyond market relations, to our very sense of who we are. This dynamic refutes the naïve hopes of those who have idealized electronic information – as an instrument of participatory democracy, as a social prosthesis, or even as resistance to the commodity form.

Electronic information, rather, operates as ideology, contributing and accelerating the development of a paranoiac environment.

(Levidow, 1994: 327)

The heaven built around everything becoming information is, for Levidow, really driven by hate and fear for the body and mortality. This hate is expressed through electronic information in the cyborg soldier, massacring in the desert, and the cyborg individual, buying their self-identity from rampant capitalism. All the hope contained in the imaginary's heaven is mere ideology, promoting this paranoid personal and social form that serves the interests only of the already powerful. The doom-sayers of cyberspace are as common as the utopians: Brown believes democracy is threatened, Slouka that day-to-day personal interaction is in danger and Robins that communication at a distance will destroy our obligation to live with those who are physically close (Brown, 1997; Slouka, 1995; Robins, 1997). There is a fantasy of doom that is every bit as strong as collectively imagined liberation.

MYTHS OF THE ELECTRONIC FRONTIER 9: TOTAL SURVEILLANCE OR THE COMING OF THE SUPERPANOPTICON

Imagine you are never hidden, never in private. Imagine everything you do is watched and recorded by 'them'. Imagine that you never know if this perfect record of your life is ever examined – all you know is that it could be. How would you act? Do you act differently driving your car if you see a police car travelling behind you? Do you, perhaps, slow down and indicate just that little bit earlier? What if your driving were recorded all the time? It would be as if a police car were permanently on your tail but you would never know if the police actually examined your driving. Would you drive differently?

Imagine the following system. Every person has a unique digital signature. This signature is attached to all financial transactions. If you buy something it is recorded with your signature because money is now electronic and even paying for the newspaper generates a little electronic footprint. The state also uses this signature to mark your tax records, your education history and any other contact you have with it. Alongside the continual recording of every minute interaction are a number of systems that automatically trigger investigation. The government possesses a deposit tracking system that can access all individual bank accounts and has linked these to monitoring programs that track money flows and issue alerts if atypical flows occur. If someone suddenly shifts from receiving unemployment payments to banking large sums of money, the system automatically issues an alert and their records are gathered. These alerts are in turn networked to criminal records, to all state services and to other financial databases and these, in turn, also use computerised methods for issuing alerts if preset patterns of use are not met. All vehicles are fitted with sensors that allow cars, trucks or bikes to be tracked from satellites in real time. The vehicle registration database is networked to other databases. When an alert is issued, all your vehicles are automatically located and monitored. Individual stores keep track of purchases by logging everything bought and attaching digital signatures to the records. These databases are also connected to the network of other databases and also use programs to detect unusual buying patterns. Finally, digital signatures are attached to a number of unique personal identifiers: retinal scan, facial heat image, DNA profile and, perhaps, even an old-fashioned fingerprint. Closed-circuit television cameras (CCTVs) cover all major public ways and most offices, shops and businesses also use cameras that are connected to the CCTV network. Cameras are sophisticated enough to identify a person by either retinal scan or facial heat image, without the subject knowing this has occurred. The scan or image can be compared with a database to identify the individual and cameras can automatically search for an individual the database has alerted them to. Once an alert is signalled, not only are your vehicles located but as soon as you step into the view of the cameras that cover all but the loneliest areas of society, you can be found as well. Are you receiving help from a relative who has become rich or have you begun a life of crime? What explains the change in your banking habits from unemployment to riches? All the information has been collected, you have been found and are watched. The answer will be known to the police before you are even aware you are under surveillance, because the possibility of surveillance has been embedded in normal, daily life. If you are legitimate, it will be as if no investigation ever happened because you will never know you were under suspicion, but if you are not legitimate the first you will know is when you are arrested and admit your guilt – after all, the evidence will be massive and conclusive. After some time, courts will fall into disuse because justice will become a matter of mechanically applying a sentence to an accusation that is never contested because evidence is irrefutable. Perhaps pleas of not guilty will carry an extra penalty for the waste of time and money they will cause.

All the elements of this system are being built or are available for use. It amounts to total surveillance (Lyon, 1994; Clark, 1994; Kimery, 1993; Davies, 1996).

Always being under the threat of surveillance but never knowing whether you are actually being watched creates a society where being seen by 'authorities' is the norm. Every action someone takes must include consciousness of the possibility that it will be watched. The first point of this nightmare is total visibility, at all times and in all places. The distinction between public and private will become one between places in which we are visible and ones in which we are invisible. But it will be at most a deeply circumscribed invisibility, with every touch of the electronic domain – logging on to the Web, using the telephone – shining light into the private realm. The second element is that any action out of the norm triggers investigation. Anything unusual is prima-facie evidence of guilt and demands an inquiry. The norms are programmed into databases and consist of the norms of agencies seeking out illicit behaviour as interpreted by programmers into software code. Transgressing any of these cyberspatial norms brings investigation and the marshalling of surveillance. In this system files need not be kept but can be generated automatically from comprehensive databases as soon as a need for investigation is found. Cyberspace constructs and keeps a file on all of us, a distributed file located in a number of dispersed databases that need only be constituted as one file when a preprogrammed alert is issued.

The ultimate nightmare of cyberspace, the moral of this myth of the electronic frontier, is that in cyberspace virtually everything about you can be made visible, without you knowing. It is a moral that says privacy is precious and cyberspace is giving our privacy away without our knowledge. Cyberspace is the ultimate system of surveillance, the ultimate tool for repression and the nightmare of totalitarian societies in which not only is everything watched and recorded but any action considered out of the normal is a reason for investigation. The ghosts of all liberal democratic societies return here and in virtual whispers repeat the fear known as 1984 and Big Brother.[9]

The fear of a virtually driven totalitarian or police state draws inspiration from an aspect of Michel Foucault's work that has not yet been discussed. Foucault developed not only a general theory of the analytics of power, which was briefly outlined in Chapter 1, but also a number of theories of the nature of really existing forms of power. In particular, he analysed the emergence of modern forms of power in the nineteenth century in relation to penal practices and he called this form of power disciplinary power. The details of his theory are not necessary here,[10] but the overall characterisation of disciplinary power is relevant. Foucault attempted to answer the question, why do people act in cohesive ways? Why do students turn up to class and sit quietly? How do patients know how to act in hospitals or workers in a factory? He traced the historical path of the common disciplines that society relies on and argued that a particular form of power makes sense of these different patterns. The general form of this power is explained through the panopticon. The panopticon was an invention of nineteenth-century thinker Jeremy Bentham who tried to create the perfect prison. It consisted, in plan, of a round, hollow building with only a tower at its centre. The outside wall was one cell thick, so that the outside window of each cell allowed light in and the inside window faced the inner tower. This meant every occupant of every cell was isolated from each other but became a silhouette to the central tower:

> All that is needed, then, is to place a supervisor in a central tower and to shut up in each cell a madman, a patient, a condemned man, a worker or a schoolboy. By the effect of backlighting, one can observe from the tower, standing out precisely against the light, the small captive shadows in the cells of the periphery. They are like so many cages, so many small theatres, in which each actor is alone, perfectly individualised and constantly visible. The panoptic mechanism arranges spatial unities that make it possible to see constantly and to recognise immediately....Full lighting and the eye of a supervisor capture better than darkness, which ultimately protected. Visibility is a trap.
>
> (Foucault, 1977: 200)

Bentham also imagined supervision of the supervisors by the public passing the panopticon, through a system of mirrored images of the supervisors reflected outside the prison. Everyone watching someone, who is being watched and watching someone else. Foucault argued this form of power spreads the panoptic mechanism throughout society, realised in different ways but with similar basic principles in all institutions of modern societies – schools, factories, prisons, hospitals, asylums, universities and so on. The coming of cyberspace seems to many to offer even greater possibilities for panoptic mechanisms to make more corners of society visible:

> Today's 'circuits of communication' and the databases they generate consti-
> tute a Superpanopticon, a system of surveillance without walls, windows,
> towers or guards.
>
> (Poster, 1990: 93)

The nightmare of cyberspace is the creation of Poster's Superpanopticon, offering almost unimaginable possibilities for social control. As with cyberspace's heaven, the Superpanopticon seems to be emerging before us with startling speed, driven by technology that also constitutes cyberspace. These technologies come from three directions: hellish cyborgs, the accumulation of minutiae and the fear of cyberspace. Briefly examining each in turn allows the full fear and flavour of the Superpanopticon to be established. In each case something that was thought to underpin the hope for utopia is reversed to reveal its role in creating dystopia. Techno-hopes crumble into techno-fears with a simple shift of perspective.

Superpanopticon: cyborgs, minutiae and fear of cyberspace

As already argued, cyborgs underpin many hopes for cyberspace. Benign cyborgs surround us: 15,000 people world-wide have had microchips inserted in their skulls that are connected to thin probes buried deep in their brain and fed by platinum wires laced underneath the skull and in this way have had their hearing restored. What could be greater evidence of hope than this god-like power to make the deaf hear (Davies, 1996: 1)? How many people have artificial hips, pacemakers, or newly implanted corneas? Nearly every day seems to bring a new cyborg that corrects some human deficiency. However, implanting microchips in the brain may have other uses. Some pets have already been implanted with a tiny chip that records information about them – their home, owner, medical history – that ensures stray dogs can be returned to their owners. Implanting similar chips is being considered for humans; children and those suffering dementia are likely candidates whose home and medical characteristics might need to be read by someone. Once tracking devices can be included in the identity chip, then lost or abducted children may become a thing of the past; no matter where they have been taken someone with an implant could be tracked. With prisons overflowing in many Western countries the next step seems simple enough: implant non-dangerous prisoners and ensure they remain effectively under house arrest in their own homes. The UK and US governments have experimented with electronic tagging, finding problems when the tag was easily removed by prisoners, but a deeply implanted chip would need surgery to remove. Or, why not provide chips for everyone with some medical condition and in the case of an emergency paramedics will have immediate access to vital information? Insurance companies can be relied upon to ensure compliance here, with those refusing chips receiving either higher insurance premiums or a refusal to supply insurance altogether. Many countries have, are setting up or are considering national identification systems; why not finish off this problem once and for all by requiring the implanting of identity chips that can be tracked? The steps from curing deafness to total surveillance are not as long as might be imagined and many have already been taken (Davies, 1996: 57–77).

A supermarket offers you a 'loyal customer' card. In return for some personal information, the supermarket will give you a swipe card, record your purchases and when you have spent a certain amount you receive some money back. For nothing but the transaction of some information, you obtain cheaper supermarket shopping. Soon the supermarket thoughtfully installs smart shopping trolleys. You place your loyal customer swipe card in a slot on the trolley; it reads your habitual purchases and then alerts you if you pass by something you normally buy. You can also take a moment to tick a list of products, feed it into the trolley and the trolley can guide you around the store. No more frustrating searches for dried yeast – the trolley knows where it is. A series of small steps involve nothing on your part but giving information and gain you both ease of shopping and free goods. However, soon you start receiving junk mail that seems to target a certain type of buyer. You realise that your olive oil, rocket and parmesan buying habits have marked you out as a certain sort of consumer. Your consumption habits have been absorbed through the loyal customer scheme and categorised, a virtual you is followed by the supermarket computers, and anyone who buys the information from them. Changes in your virtual consumer are registered as soon as shifts in your buying habits occur. It seems more annoying than anything and, if annoying enough, you start calling the supermarket to request that they do not sell on your personal details, or consider going to a different supermarket and refusing their loyal customer card, a sadder but wiser informational consumer. But then your credit card is refused one day; sadly you have forgotten to pay your bill for some time and it has been suspended. This information is attached to your record and your future use of credit cards in this supermarket comes under a cloud. You find that mysteriously other supermarkets, even from different companies, also know about your transgression and you are dealt with suspiciously whichever supermarket you go to. You realise, of course, that supermarkets not only sell information but share information they would all like to have, such as who is a bad credit risk. No matter that your credit company and you are in accord because you have paid your bill, the supermarkets are applying their own rules based on their own information. The only light side is that your junk mail now turns to offers of loans or advice for those 'in financial trouble'. All this seems at one level trivial, but at another the constitution of a virtual consumer out of your purchase records means you are effectively traded to others and explored for further consumption possibilities. When the credit card problems happen, you begin to wonder more whether this level of information in private hands is a good thing and begin to worry even more when you hear that government and private corporations are beginning to share information. From what seemed like a nice payback from a supermarket to a loyal customer, only small, seemingly insignificant steps lead to worries about surveillance. You realise that mundane and insignificant moments can be accumulated into virtual selves that can be manipulated in the search for government control and private profit. Minutiae can create the Superpanopticon (Lyon, 1994: 136–57; Clark, 1994).

A third fear haunts cyberspace's imaginary, the fear that society has become too dependent on cyberspace. Here the fear is that all the various powers that individuals gain in cyberspace can be used for evil purposes; identity fluidity allows harassment or censorship-evading technology means children can access all manner of information from pornography to bomb-making instructions. This fear has been seen most clearly in the already discussed encryption wars. Again the story starts benignly. The development of public key encryption allows the creation of secure communications that can support individuals against large corporations and facilitate widespread secure distribution of information. The mathematics of encryption claims that the war between coder and decoder is being won in favour of secrecy. This does not, however, reassure governments and particularly their security agencies. Governments point to the use of secret communications by a number of deeply fearful figures: international terrorists, drug pushers, organised crime and paedophiles. The director of the FBI told the US Senate Judiciary Committee that 'uncrackable encryption will allow drug lords, spies, terrorists and even violent gangs to communicate about their crimes and their conspiracies with impunity' (cited in Campbell, 1997b: 3). Dark rumours are heard of encrypted files on a computer used by one of the World Trade Center bombers, as are accounts of paedophiles using encryption to pass child pornography or to keep lists of liaisons secret. Society seems to be suddenly threatened by hordes of demons from the darkest reaches of our nightmares and encryption, that necessary adjunct to online commerce, is the source of them. The fear encryption engenders tears in two directions: are we more scared of governments having the automated ability to read our online communications; or is the prospect of these appalling demons having secure communication more frightening? No choice is a good choice here: either another building block in the total surveillance society or our darkest fears of drugs, gangs, child abusers and terrorists laughing securely in their encrypted halls (Barth and Smith, 1997; Campbell, 1997a; 1997b; Vesely, 1997; Ludlow, 1996: 173–250).

In all three of these nightmares, further technological elements of the dystopian side of cyberspace's imaginary could be discussed. For example, what significance does it have that in the UK public records have been privatised so that a US firm, whose aim is profit, has control of British people's personal details? Is that frightening or just a business transaction or both (Davies, 1997)? Or perhaps the fact that the small town of King's Lynn in Norfolk, UK, led the world in the implementation of surveillance of public space through CCTV. At present over a hundred powerful, remote-controlled cameras (that can read a cigarette packet at 100 metres and work at night) watch all of the city centre, housing estates, sports grounds, car parks and industrial estates. Originally installed to deter burglary and theft, the system operators acknowledge it is largely used to monitor anti-social behaviour and minor offences (fighting, evading parking meters, drunkenness, litter, urinating in public). The council's CCTV project director notes: 'What it comes down to is there's a perception of crime, a fear of crime, rather than actual crime' (cited in Davies, 1995: 61). Or there is the fact that a bank deposit tracking system has been designed for the USA that can access all 388 million individual bank accounts, costed at $12.5 million (Kimery, 1993).

Fear itself

No further scare tactics are probably necessary because the fears of cyberspace are the flip side of the hopes and nearly everything that was discussed in the previous section exploring cyberspace's utopia could be repeated as cyberspace's dystopia. Immortality in silicon? Many probably feel queasy at the very idea, of what will be lost when the connection between mind and body is severed for a connection between mind and machine. Many probably agree with the Dixie Flatliner in Gibson's *Neuromancer*, whose demand is that he be erased. The ability to reverse utopia into dystopia is to be expected because lurking underneath cyberspace's imagined hell is the same equation fuelling cyberspace's heaven: everything becomes information. The vision of total surveillance is one in which all the minor movements of our lives can be converted into information that can be organised and communicated. Once every little element of life leaves a digital footprint then the possibility of the Superpanopticon looms over us.

> Surveillance, as described here, concerns the mundane, the ordinary, taken-for-granted world of getting money from a bank machine, making a phone call, applying for sickness benefits, driving a car, using a credit card, receiving junk mail, picking up books from a library, or crossing a border on trips abroad. In each case mentioned, computers record our transactions, check against other known details, ensure that we and not others are billed or paid, store bits of our biographies, or assess our financial, legal or national standing. Each time we do one of these things we actually or potentially leave a trace of our doings. Computers and their associated communications systems now mediate all these kinds of relationships; to participate in modern society is to be under surveillance.
>
> (Lyon, 1994: 4)

The two key components of this fear are first, as Lyon argues, the fact of being under constant surveillance and, second, that acting differently to some predefined norm is evidence of guilt deserving investigation. It is not just that all the information is collected but that it is constantly cross-checked to produce the new information that this person does not match the expectations that have been programmed into databases. For example, in the USA you have to report every transaction involving sums of more than $10,000 to the Inland Revenue Service. A system was set up that triggered an alert if a series of $9,900 transactions were made. In one case, the result of this definition of people deserving closer surveillance was the identification of someone who turned out to be a drug dealer (Kimery, 1993). The fear is of a world where our actions are accountable to norms we often do not know about and which trigger investigations. The fear of the Superpanopticon is of a world in which deviance from the norm is already guilt. The fear is of a world where we must all keep to the straight and narrow and we are all, all the time, being watched. Visibility is constant, because we constantly leave behind information that can be collected and processed through cyberspace. We are all trapped. Once everything becomes information, the Superpanopticon flickers to life.

Cyberspace's imaginary

Cyberspace's utopia and dystopia stem from the awed realisation that everything is controlled by information codes that can be manipulated, transmitted and recombined through cyberspace. Certain particular visions are then collectively imagined and provide some of the unifying thoughts that allow individuals in cyberspace to recognise each other as members of the same community. *Wired* magazine even has a phrase that recurs when its writers analyse whether somebody understands the implications of cyberspace (though *Wired*'s general definition of understanding cyberspace seems to be agreeing with *Wired*'s understanding of cyberspace). *Wired* writers ask if he or she 'gets it'.[11] It is these community-building devices, often less obvious than in *Wired*, that result from the collective imagination of cyberspace. The imagined utopian or dystopian possibilities coalesce around either hopes or fears that are structured as the belief that immortality and omnipotence are within human grasp or that total control of all individuals by totalitarian states has become a possibility. Such troubling or confident thoughts create a sense of urgency because the technology that creates these possibilities always seems to have been invented or is on the point of being implemented The fantasies peopling cyberspace's imaginary motivate all sorts of behaviour in virtual beings.

In the preceding outline of cyberspace's imaginary, science fiction has been deliberately put to one side to stress how these fantasies seem like unvarnished reality, or nearly created reality, which explains the fanatical energy that at times discussions of cyberspace and its possibilities generate. But, of course, the exploration of possibilities is one of the greatest strengths of science fiction and nearly all of the elements of cyberspace's imaginary that have been discussed can be found explored in cyberpunk. The importance established in Chapter 2 of recognising both the visionary force of cyberpunk and the engineering feats of computer networks simply needs to be reiterated here. Any quick examination either of relevant science fiction, or of the brief analyses in Chapter 2, will establish the importance of fiction in fuelling the collective imagination of cyberspace. To complete this analysis, it only remains to outline briefly the nature of this form of power and then to move on, in the next chapter, to summarise the interrelations between the three forms of power that constitute cyberpower as a whole.

Many different people constitute cyberspace's imaginary by investing some thought in the possibilities cyberspace offers, both good and bad. Once these thoughts become recognised as collective ones, then a power to mobilise human energy and direct it in certain ways begins to be felt. Commonly realised knowledge creates certain powers between people. As outlined, cyberspace's imaginary tends to bifurcate between an ultimate good and ultimate bad but it is not this content that is crucial to the analysis of the imaginary (as opposed to living within its grip). The importance of the imaginary is that it constitutes a community through collective imaginings. The power of cyberspace's imaginary does not predestine either the liberation of individuals, as cyberpower as a possession seems to, or the subjection and domination of communities, as cyberpower as a knowledge/power matrix seems to. Rather, the power of the imaginary is that a community comes to see itself as a community, not as a disparate set of individuals. The power produced by cyberspace's imaginary is, then, close to that outlined by Barnes, in which the question of power is the question of social order and not repression or liberation. Both the previously analysed circuits of power point towards inherent forces for liberation or repression. At the level of the individual, there seems to be a libertarian force driving back the state and corporations in favour of freely created and maintained virtual communities. At the level of the social, technopower seems to be constituting individuals in ways that subject them to the power of newly emerging online elites. But at the level of the imaginary we find both these possibilities in hyperbolic form, seemingly pointing us with dramatic urgency to the potential for cyberspace either finally to liberate us in the most profound way possible or finally (and totally) to repress us. However, by entering whichever parts of these hyperboles we do, we participate in the real power of the imaginary to bind communities and produce powerful individual commitments to collective causes. In the imaginary, we are in the presence of communities in creation. In cyberspace's imaginary, techno-utopias and techno-dystopias dazzle people and in those moments of bedazzlement people become aware of, and often passionately committed to, their virtual communities.

Just as the collective imagination of many nations drives them to seek their destiny, manifest or otherwise, the collective imagination of cyberspace drives people to argue, implement, design, struggle and ultimately create different

versions of cyberspace. The importance of imaginaries is not in their relationship to reality, in the sense of whether their dreams and nightmares can be
made into reality, but in the way collectively held fantasies bond people into
communities and, simultaneously, drive them to try to realise their fantasies.
The temptation is to think of imaginaries as providing models or blueprints to
the future, when their effect is to build communities and inspire loyalty,
commitment and hard work in the present. Cyberspace's imaginary does all
these things and, in doing so, constitutes a third circuit of power coursing
through the virtual lands. The imaginary binds the virtual social order. The
imaginary creates the possibility of virtual community.

Chapter 7

Cyberpower

Key concepts

Cyberpower

Cyberpower is the form of power that structures culture and politics in cyberspace and on the Internet. It consists of three interrelated regions: the individual, the social and the imaginary. Cyberpower of the individual consists of avatars, virtual hierarchies and informational space and results in cyberpolitics. Power here appears as the possession of individuals. Cyberpower of the social is structured by the technopower spiral and the informational space of flows and results in the virtual elite. Power here appears as forms of domination. Cyberpower of the imaginary consists of the utopia and dystopia that make up the virtual imaginary. Power here appears as the constituent of social order. All three regions are needed to map cyberpower in total and no region is dominant over any other.

Introduction

Power is the condition and limit of politics, culture and authority. Power seeps through and around all forms of politics and subjectivity, at times bringing opposites into conflict in a way that reinforces the fundamental flow of power, just as the opposition between Barlow's mysticism and Haraway's materialism reinforces the heaven in cyberspace's imaginary. Power concerns not immediately obvious forms of politics, culture and authority but the structures that condition and limit these three. Power is pre- and post-politics, pre- and post-culture and pre- and post-authority. Cyberpower reveals the underlying workings of lives, societies and dreams in cyberspace. A certain complex form of power can now be seen careering through the virtual lands and it explains why conflict and consensus tend to occur around certain distinctive issues. All that remains to complete the definition of cyberpower is to link its three levels together and outline the outstanding, overarching issue of politics, culture and authority that results from cyberpower. To do this the three levels will first be summarised and then their relations established.

When the individual is the starting point for analysis of life in cyberspace, power as the possession of individuals emerges as the compelling experience of cyberspace. This is understandable because the constant experience of virtual lives is of individuals passing through the screen to become avatars who then construct societies. This is not a misguided perception, it is not somehow false knowledge of cyberspace, rather it is the accurately understood experience of many. From this flows the most often analysed aspects of cyberspace: identity fluidity, anti-hierarchism, informational spaces and the way these underpin a politics strung across the two axes of access to cyberspace and rights in cyberspace. Yet unease with such an individualistic basis for cybersocieties is sometimes felt. Are the strongly felt commitments people have really just for the individuals they meet? Or is there also a commitment to cybersociety as something more than a collection of individuals? Is there a commitment not just to the collective experiences individuals construct but also to the fact of collective experience? Is there a commitment to the common spaces that may need to be defended on behalf of individuals who have never been met, who have not helped create that common space but whose right to come and exist there needs to be asserted? Sometimes an allegiance is felt first and foremost to society and not to individuals. From this perspective, a very different power appears.

What makes individuals in cyberspace possible? Certain forms of technology make them possible, certain wires, code and computers. All such artefacts of technoscience are part of a process by which pieces of technology are constructed according to certain social values but then appear as things for use. The way this oscillation between social values and technological things is structured creates a form of power that is crucial in a realm that only exists because of this oscillation. The particular structure of technopower in cyberspace is an ongoing spiral in which the amount of information available causes an information overload that is answered by the creation of new techno-logical tools, that in turn produce new forms of overload, again calling for more tools. Offline societies also increasingly depend on and are affected by these tools because part of cyberspace functions as an informational space of flows that provides essential services to newly emerging informational socio-economies. Life in cyberspace and meatspace is ever more dependent on ever more complex forms of technology that structure the possible actions individ-uals take. Greater freedom of action is available to technologically adept individuals and, given the ever increasing complexity of cyberspace's tech-nology, this means that an elite based on expertise or the control of expertise increasingly dominates the fabric of cyberspace and the informational space of flows. Power distributes individuals and their capacities for action across cyberspace according to their place in networks of experts and technology and, in doing so, constitutes a cyber-elite that dominates the possible choices indi-viduals have in cyberspace.

Around these two levels of power flows power as the constituent of social order. This occurs in cyberspace through the collective imagination individuals construct that allows them to recognise people they have never, and will never, meet as members of the same virtual community. The hopes and fears that constitute this collective imagination are expressed as a heaven of immortality and omnipotence counterposed to a hell of total surveillance and perfect totalitarian weapons. Even though the technology to create either of these always appears to be almost ready, and so demands urgency and commitment from members of the virtual community, the essential purpose of the collective imagination or imaginary is not to create heaven and/or hell but through the mutual recognition of these hopes and fears to create the cybercommunity. These are the three levels or circuits of cyberpower; the final question is, how do they relate to each other?

Relations between three types of cyberpower

The first place to start is a dynamic between cyberpower of the individual and the social that has already been identified. The connection is two way, with pressures from each feeding into the other. From cyberpower of the individual comes the cyberpolitics of greater access and the defence of online rights. When power is a possession that individuals use against oppressions and institutions, it seems important to extend that power. Those who believe in the liberatory power of cyberspace not only defend their powers within cyberspace but extend those powers to others. Yet this commitment also feeds the spiral of technopower by committing more and more people to use the information that constitutes cyberspace's power for the individual, thereby putting them on the path to information overload and the demand for further elaboration of technology to solve overload. The exercise of power as a possession by the individual leads to demands for new technology that drives further spirals of technopower, elaborating the power of an expertise-based elite while also providing new ways of exercising the power of individuals. The result is that the extension of power as a possession and power as structured relations of domination occurs simultaneously. For example, the use of email to gain knowledge that empowers or to construct inclusive decision making can lead to demands for better email programs. People may want to filter their mail so that an urgent message is clearly marked, ensuring even decisions that need to be made quickly can be communicated widely. People may need more sophisticated means of storing emails on various topics so that the knowledge they are gathering remains accessible. Such obvious demands for extra tools lead to further complexity in the technological infrastructure of cyberspace and augment the power of a technically based cyber-elite which designs and controls email programs. But these demands also lead to more easily used and more powerful tools for individuals, such as better email programs. The cyberpower of individuals and that of the elite here extend and contract together. Perhaps the clearest example of this is Sun Microsystems' claim that by eviscerating the desktop computer, because it is too complex and unnecessarily powerful, and replacing it with simpler computers connected to a network, the user is both empowered to have the software they need when they need it and removed from the complexities of installing and maintaining their own software because all complex work will be done by a 'trained professional' (Brockman, 1996: 211). Sun offers to free the computer world from the dominance of Microsoft and Intel, to create simpler and more useful tools for individuals and to extend the power of the expertise-based elite into what once was the hard drive sitting on your desk. Sun's vision of the future sits directly on the connection between individual and social cyberpowers, simultaneously offering individual empowerment and elite domination.

How can elites and individuals gain power at the same time and through connected mechanisms? The answer to this question deepens the understanding of the connection between individual empowerment and elite domination because the connection does not demand that both occur simultaneously. The connection between individual and social cyberpowers does not merge them or ensure any reconciliation. Rather, the connection is the point at which the two create effects in each other. The individual demand for greater mastery of cyberspace leads to the demand for new tools. Once developed, these new tools immediately sink into the fabric of cyberspace, becoming things enabling individuals and their powers, but in doing so they create a more complex cyberspace that needs greater expertise to manipulate. The echo of individual empowerment in cyberspace is the elaboration of cyberspace's technopower and the technopower elite. The condition of this elaboration is, however, the delivery of new tools to individuals who then also have enhanced abilities to act, as long as they are willing to depend on the new fabric of cyberspace. The two levels agitate each other, forever creating different permutations of dominance between elites and individuals and forever tending to deal with separate spheres of cyberspace. Individual empowerment occurs when the technology that creates cyberspace is taken as a given to be used. Elite domination occurs when the technology that creates cyberspace is manipulated and reconstructed. Individuals exist in cyberspace by using the tools that depend on a technological infrastructure controlled by an elite, but that technological infrastructure exists to provide the tools that individuals use for empowerment. It is a continually developing relationship that affects two powers with fundamentally different natures.

The elaborate dance between individual empowerment and elite domination helps explain the sense so many have that cyberspace is a continually changing place that can barely be analysed because, by tomorrow, it will be different. Many feel that online time is somehow speeded up and that events and fundamental changes pass in a blur, where shifts of similar magnitude in offline life take time to become established. This perception can be understood as a result of the ceaseless process of individuals' struggling to make use of the vast resources of cyberspace in ways that then demand the renovation of cyberspace's substance by the few who wield the necessary expertise to remake the constituents of online life. This is the fundamental dynamic between the cyber-powers of the individual and the social. It is also a dynamic driven forward by the third level of cyberpower.

Cyberspace's collective imagination works through hopes and fears and, in doing so, inhabits all corners of individual and social cyberpower. The dreams of the imaginary may often appear as imaginative froth bubbling on top of real individuals and societies but they work to bind individuals and societies together through imagined communities. As cyberpower courses through the individual and the social in cyberspace and inhabits the ever changing relations between them, it is everywhere infused with a collective imagination that prompts people to recognise themselves as inhabitants of a particular space. Inspired with horror or optimism, sometimes at the same time, people recognise themselves and others as having similar dreams or nightmares and in those moments of recognition also realise they are now members, citizens even, of cyberspace. While the content of these dreams and hopes can appear as fantastic as the wildest ravings of techno-utopians and dystopians, the process of engaging with hopes and fears creates shared languages, makes explicit assumptions and allows the articulation of a 'virtual we'. These dreams and nightmares also drive people ever onward by constantly appearing to be on the verge of realisation. Individuals and groups are engaged, first, by their awareness that they are part of a collective and, second, by the expectation that the collective might offer salvation or damnation within a very short time. Creating this urgency, this passion, further propels the changes that are already being driven by the connection between individual and social cyberpowers. The ceaseless rearticulation of the abilities of the cyber-elite and of individuals is further impassioned by the expectation that time is short before virtual heavens or hells will appear. In this way, the imaginary does not so much connect to the individual and the social as permeate them. Cyberpower of the imaginary inhabits the cyberpowers of the individual and the social, underpinning both through moments when common citizenship of cyberspace is recognised and driving both forward through evangelical imaginings.

Having separated the three levels of cyberpower and defined their interrelations, many will find it tempting to discern a dominant or fundamental level within cyberpower, to ask which level determines in the first or last instance. It is tempting, perhaps, to see the powers individuals can take up in cyberspace as, in the end, able to construct social structures to the dictates of individuals and in this way subordinate technopower to individual power. Many of the libertarian strands of cybercultures implicitly take this position, arguing that the determined defence of individual liberty serves cybersocieties best. After all, individuals are real and social structures are abstractions; elites cannot 'want' but Bill Gates or Kevin Mitnick can and as long as individuals are free to 'want' then cybersocieties will conform to their desires. It will also be tempting to dismiss any such primacy of the individual as idealist fantasy. Individuals never exist in isolation, even in cyberspace. The simple fact that even libertarians have to use similar computers and similar software to enter cyberspace, and these technologies are controlled and determined by corporations, governments and other institutions, means that the virtual individual is always having their nature predetermined. Do you want to change gender? Well don't try it via email when your address is John.Male@aol.com, but go to a MUD where you can hide your male marker of John and become Joanna. The two different places in cyberspace made by email or MUDs only allow certain types of individuality. And an elite based on expertise and the control of expertise controls all such predeterminations of individuality. These, some may want to believe, are the fundamental facts of cyberspace; it is another arena in which the privileged gain power over the underprivileged, yet here the privileged control even the gender, name or identity any individual might want. Then again, some might see all these concerns for primacy within cyberspace as small thinking at the turn of the millennium, as so many little rockets and explosions to fascinate those who cannot see that the destruction and reinvention of humanity is occurring. Is godhood around the corner? Will cyborgs rise up finally to unite the disparate strengths of the oppressed in the revolution? Are truly totalitarian societies finally being created? Those who cannot see that these are the sorts of questions that cyberspace poses are simply missing the greatest mutation of humanity, of life on Earth, since humans first walked the Earth. The only importance of individual powers or elite domination is their role in these fundamental transformations. Three sets of arguments easily come to mind, each of which demonstrates the primacy of one level of cyberpower over the others, and it is not that these arguments are each fundamentally wrong, rather all three are both right and wrong. Articulating them together shows how they do not escape each other, how each dominates and is subordinated to each other and that cyberpower is only understood when its full, undetermined complexity is allowed. The temptation for many will be to simplify the complexity of cyberpower; there will be an almost irresistible refusal to allow cyberpower its full intricacy and its fundamental multiplicity of direction, but all arguments and evidence point to the co-dependence of all three levels of cyberpower and not to any one level's independence.

The totality of cyberpower is these three levels and their connections. Taken together they provide a complex map of the dominant structures and trends of life in cyberspace. However, as with any map, this cartography of power does not provide an experiential picture. It does not recount this author's exploits online, follow the history of a famous corner of cyberspace or record growing confidence or anxiety with cyberspace. Cyberpower is not perceptible from any one person's journey in online life because all such journeys are constrained by the day-to-day lived reality such authors ground their work in. Cyberpower is never experienced as separated levels of the individual, the social and the imaginary or as the connections between them. Cyberpower is an abstract representation of the forces at work in cyberspace and is experienced by individuals in complex, confused moments. While many different adventures, technologies and people have appeared during the analysis of cyberpower, cyberpower cannot be represented solely through these moments. Cyberpower must be distilled from the many and varied experiences available in cyberspace, until it appears as an abstraction of life online. When people are online they experience emails, text-based worlds and conversations and all-singing, all-dancing Web pages, all in the blur of a normal virtual life. Cyberpower is a chart of the forces and tensions that underpin the blur that is a lived virtual life and it can never be grasped through any simple, single perception, but must be leached out of the richness of cyberspace with arguments, examples, statistics and many people's experiences. This should be no surprise. It is the normal process by which a theory that can never grasp the full complexity of a single moment in a single person's life somehow tells us essential, constitutive facts about that moment for that person. Cyberpower is the theory of the virtual life.

The first war of cyberspace: elites and grassroots

Cyberpower allows a complex understanding of the different relations of force and their different foundations in cyberspace. All three forms of power will continue to circulate and complicate each other, with no one form having any obvious way of becoming the primary form of power. This does not, however, mean that there is no overall conclusion about the effects of cyberpower on cyberspace up to 1998, it simply means that these conclusions are about the results of cyberpower. And a similar story has emerged from cyberpower at the level of the individual and the social, a struggle between elites and grassroots. In both levels, though in different ways, cyberpower underpins a conflict between ordinary users creating and controlling their virtual communities and elites controlling the conditions that allow virtual communities. The analysis of cyberpower points to cyberspace having been constituted out of conflicts around the rights of individual users, the grassroots, or the authority of software coders, corporate managers, systems operators and hardware designers, the elite, over the nature of virtual life.

Shifts between the grassroots and elites can be seen in almost any history of any corner of cyberspace. For example, nearly all MUDs experience a conflict between the users who argue about some aspect of MUD life and the wizards who control the code that determines the possible forms of MUD life. The myth of cyberrape includes a striking example of this, with wizards deciding to give up decision-making power and instead enforce democracy through software code that allowed ballots. Battles around electronic mail have been felt, particularly through the encryption wars that will determine whether secure electronic mail will one day be available to users or whether governments will insist on the right to peek into anybody's email. Internet civil rights activists, like John Perry Barlow or Esther Dyson, have called for users of the Internet to be left alone to work out their own forms of governance. Such calls have almost no hope of succeeding, if only because the importance of the informational space of flows to offline socio-economies means offline interests cannot be disentangled from online services, but they mark the demands of users of cyberspace to be left in peace in their world. Corporations are struggling to redefine cyberspace according to a paradigm most suitable to their interests and ideologies. Microsoft's goal of a computer in every home and on every desk was conceived as a personal computer running Microsoft software, but Sun Microsystems argues for the power of the network, using Sun software, to run dumber terminals in people's homes, allowing the ordinary user to be shepherded by professionals. Such corporations have wide scope for action within technopower because they draw vast numbers of experts into large projects. But experts can also come together co-operatively to create software like Linux, distributing it for free and placing the power to construct cyberspace back into the hands of those who cannot hire thousands of programmers. Or the hacker can absorb truly extraordinary amounts of information and make themselves master of existing networks, solely with the power of their expertise and a second-hand computer. All across cyberspace, in different ways according to the peculiar rules of different corners of the virtual lands, conflicts are played out between the grassroots and the elites.

The ideology of libertarianism can be expected to play an important role in these ongoing battles because it speaks both to individuals and to the cyber-elite. At the level of the individual, libertarianism connects to the powers individuals gain to construct their communities. Individuals feel that they create their own communities and the attractions of an ideology that places individual liberty at its core seem obvious. No government or state is needed in a frontier society that allows individuals to create and participate in communities as they wish. The technopower elite will also feel attractions to libertarianism because of its close relationship to the free market. As a class, the technopower elite can justify its control over the fabric of cyberspace by pointing out it was gained within an equal contest on the level playing field of a free market:

> the online market must be understood in relation to, at least, two related markets. The first is the market of ideas. Given wide and virtually universal exchange of ideas, the online community simply takes up those that work without any need for some intervening bureaucracy or government. The second market is the market of goods. Exchanging software is an economic activity whether this is realised, for example, as it is in Cygnus Support...by giving away software but asking for payment to support it or, like the famed game Doom, by giving away a limited version of a programme to entice people to buy the full version or even, as in much shareware, by giving away a full version of the programme but asking for payment if it is used. Placing a software package online seems equivalent to owning a factory and distribution system, because once online that package can be copied again and again. For both goods and ideas, themselves nearly indistinguishable in

a product like software, the net provides open competition, because barriers to entry are very low, and near perfect information for consumers, because products can be freely tested (what better information is there about a product than using it?) and results of these tests can be widely disseminated. Unlike many markets, the net fulfils some of the essential criteria of a self-regulating, productive free market. Though distinguishable the two markets of goods and ideas are not entirely distinct. As Barlow says 'Class struggle is really an industrial manifestation. You've got capital and you've got labour, well in this instance the labour is the capital. It changes the whole equation.' The labour to produce ideas and embody them either in software packages or in web-sites and documents that appear online automatically produces the capital investment of products that can be tested in the anarchy of the net.

(Jordan, 1998)

The greater freedom of action that spirals of technopower produce for those who command technical expertise can be constantly justified as the result of individual liberty as played out in the free markets of goods and ideas. Libertarianism becomes an online ideology that can emphasise either individual liberty, speaking to individuals and their powers, or that cyberspace produces the best possible outcomes because these outcomes are tested through free markets, speaking to the elite as a justification for its growing control. Libertarianism on the net has at its core a doubly articulated concept that fuses individual liberty with free markets, allowing the one ideology to speak to both the elite and the grassroots. This does not mean libertarianism will be universally celebrated on the net; some will claim to see a trick that promises individuals' liberty but delivers power to an elite which will exploit them. Barbrook and Cameron attack the proponents of cyberspace's libertarianism:

they are passionate advocates of what appears to be an impeccably libertarian form of politics – they want information technologies to be used to create a new 'Jeffersonian democracy' where all individuals will be able to express themselves freely within cyberspace.

However, by championing this seemingly admirable ideal, these techno-boosters are at the same time reproducing some of the most atavistic features of American society, especially those derived from the bitter legacy of slavery. Their utopian vision...depends upon a wilful blindness toward the other – much less positive – features of life on the West Coast: racism, poverty and environmental degradation...each member of the 'virtual class' is promised the opportunity to become a successful high-tech entrepreneur. Information technologies, so the argument goes, empower the individual, enhance personal freedom, and radically reduce the power of the nation-state. Existing political and legal power structures will whither away to be replaced by unfettered interactions between autonomous individuals and their software.

(Barbrook and Cameron, 1997: 45, 53)

Barbrook and Cameron, and others, see individual powers as only a smoke-screen through which the cyber-elite is attempting to impose its will, for its advantage and in ways that repeat the inglorious US history of slavery, racism, poverty and pollution (Barbrook and Cameron, 1997; Hudson, 1997: 173–259; Kroker and Weinstein, 1994). Within the perspective of the social such arguments can make sense; libertarianism can be seen as the ideology of a technopower elite which increasingly controls the possibilities for life in cyberspace. But cyberpower tells us this is not the whole story and we can also expect celebrations of libertarianism. Louis Rosetto is the editor in chief of *Wired*, one of the homes of cyberspace libertarianism, and argues:

the question is no longer what sort of statists we should be supporting: Republicans or Democrats, communists or fascists. The question really is what sort of libertarians we should be supporting. There is no alternative to a world that's out of control. Central power not only doesn't work, it is not even possible any more.

(Cited in Hudson, 1997: 173)

Speaking from the cyberpower of the individual, Rosetto points to power in cyberspace as the distributed possession of individuals who have and need their liberty to exercise their powers. When *Wired* reported its survey of digital citizens, the second result it printed was that 95 per cent of superconnected people have a lot or some confidence in free markets and 90 per cent of connected people have the same, figures that drop to 70 per cent for the semi- or disconnected (Katz, 1997b: 71).[1] *Wired*, as it shows in numerous articles, is committed to the twins of individual liberty and free markets (Editors, 1996; Borsook, 1996). The strength of libertarian beliefs in online life surprises some people, but from the perspective of cyberpower it is a uniquely equipped ideology for the battles around grassroots and elites in cyberspace because it allows each side to translate its demands and beliefs into language acceptable to the other. Libertarianism is the language through which virtual individuals and the cyber-elite play out their alliances and conflicts. The ongoing battles between grassroots and elites, battles that will fragment both sides into coalitions and oppositions, can be articulated through libertarian rhetoric.

At present, there appears to be no clear direction to these conflicts, with the interconnection between the grassroots and the elite being played out again and again. Elites seemingly in control through their ability to set the conditions for life are contradicted by users who find powers to act in new and unimagined ways. The overall conclusion can only be that cyberspace has so far seen these battles and can expect more. Perhaps increasing numbers of users will draw governments into more and more restrictive legislation, though the powers of cyberspace to evade censorship will continue. Perhaps the emergence of widespread, safe online shopping will create such profits in cyberspace that corporations will flock there in ever greater numbers and will come to dominate the preconditions of virtual lives, though users have continually sought information and contact with each other ahead of shopping opportunities. Perhaps through virtual reality and consciousnesses loaded onto silicon cyberspace will become a heavenly paradise, though once loaded into cyberspace our every thought and emotion will be registered in software code making heavenly cyberhosts subject to total and complete surveillance. Perhaps the informational space of flows will become so important to restructured socio-economies that uncertainty in cyberspace will become unthinkable, though the power of the informational space of flows is built in part on the powers individuals gain in cyberspace. All these 'perhaps', and more besides, are possible. There is no reason why the battle of grassroots and elites cannot be decided one way or another. However, the view from cyberpower in 1998 was of an ongoing struggle and the likelihood that it will be ongoing. Cyberpower points not to the ultimate dominance of elites, though it clearly identifies the burgeoning power of elites, nor does it predict the libertarian ideal of individual empowerment, though it makes conspicuous the ongoing creation of powers for individuals in cyberspace. Cyberpower points to these processes continuing, driven by dreams and nightmares. When examining cyberpower we must always be aware of the roar of battle and the complex conflicts that define virtual lives, elites and dreams.

Notes

1 Power and cyberspace

1 This is John Perry Barlow's famous question.
2 It should be stressed that the following three theories of power are offered as useful tools for examining cyberspace. A discussion that defines the 'real' nature of power would take too much space and is not appropriate in this context, even if such a question could be definitively answered. Comparison of the three theories will be offered but all three will be taken forward into virtuality. Of course, all three have a certain validity even if they also disagree. The issue will ultimately be: do they contribute to a valid and consistent concept of cyberpower? Not: does this introductory outline solve the long-standing problem of the nature of power? For discussion of power see Barnes (1988), Clegg (1989), Lukes (1986).
3 Techno music was in fact criminalised in the United Kingdom in the early 1990s. The Criminal Justice Act defined and criminalised 'music wholly or predominantly characterised by the emission of a succession of repetitive beats' (Huq, 1998).
4 This example and the theory being outlined below are derived from the work of British sociologist Barry Barnes. For the example, see Barnes (1988: 56 and 59).
5 It should be stressed that this approach does not invalidate Barnes' or Weber's analyses nor does it mean Barnes or Weber could not study inequalities; rather it begins from a different question to produce a different theory of power.

2 Cyberspace and the matrix

1 It is an often-noted irony that Gibson's classic of cyberpunk literature was written on an old-fashioned, manual typewriter (Bukatman, 1993b).
2 The following account of cyberpunk science fiction is indebted to Bukatman's *Terminal Identity*.
3 To pursue cyberpunk science fiction, the three obvious places to start are Sterling (1985), McCaffery (1991b) and Bukatman (1993a).
4 Steven Levy traced the meaning of 'hacker' to its beginnings among early computer pioneers, people who were willing to 'hack' technological solutions. Hacker has since come to refer largely to unauthorised computer intruders, who use a computer and communications network to enter and control computers (Levy, 1984; Jordan and Taylor, 1998).
5 ROM in current usage refers to read-only memory, that is a CD-ROM is a CD that can be read but not recorded on.
6 The history of the first networks until the emergence of the Internet is well told in Hafner and Lyons (1996), but no single detailed history of developments since then is available. Hudson (1997) provides a polemical and somewhat sketchy overview.

Relevant documents will be indicated as the story is told. For a compressed and more technically minded version see Minoli (1997).

7 See John Gilmore's home page at http://www.cygnus.com/~gnu.

8 You will find this myth in many places, though the claim about nuclear war should be receding in the face of Hafner and Lyons (1996) (see next paragraph). Try Sterling (1993), Castells (1997: 351), Rheingold (1994: 7, 74), Hudson (1997: 14–16).

9 Though it is unclear exactly what happened, the master database did in fact fail in 1997, not catastrophically but disabling a significant part of the Internet (Bellos, 1997: 5; Diamond, 1998).

10 BBSs are individual computers, usually desktop personal computers, which allow other computer users to dial in using telephone lines. By instructing my computer to dial a certain telephone number, I gain access to a system running on someone else's computer. A BBS costs the expense of a home computer, the time and effort to set the system up (software often being free), the cost of telephone calls to connect (which are incurred by the person dialling up the BBS and not the BBS system operator). In FidoNet, the BBS owner incurs the telephone cost of uploading email or echomail from their BBS. The only charges a FidoNet BBS owner is allowed to make is to cover these phone costs.

11 AT&T's nature as a corporation changed in the 1980s and it made efforts to recover UNIX. By the 1990s, it had succeeded and was free to charge for copies of UNIX, which it proceeded to do. This lead to the Free Software Foundation's attempt to generate an operating system like UNIX that did not include any AT&T code and could therefore be distributed free (Freedman and Mann, 1997: 73). See end of Chapter 4 for a brief description of this effort.

12 There have been seven top-level domain names, six for types of organisations and one for geography. The organisational ones were: .com for commercial organisations, .edu for educational, .gov for civilian government, .mil for US Department of Defense, .net for network administrative organisations and .org for other organisations. Geographic addresses have developed world-wide, such as .uk for the UK, .us for USA, .au for Australia, .fr for France and so on. Lower levels of addresses are then organised by administrations for particular networks. For example, within the top-level domain .uk addresses with .ac are part of the academic network, meaning that uel.ac.uk identifies the university uel (University of East London) as a member of the UK academic network (Quarterman, 1990: 110–12; Hakala and Rickard, 1996; Minoli, 1997: 45). In 1997 and 1998, discussions were being conducted about problems in DNS due to the enormous growth in the Internet and the possibility that IP numbers would simply run out, combined with an end to the contract for administering the DNS. Though the number of names is infinite, the number of numbers is not. Plans are ongoing to create a number of new top-level domain names to relieve this looming problem (Diamond, 1998; Kahin and Keller, 1997: 107–270).

13 A computer may maintain a certain address itself or look elsewhere on a close-by network; however, after a period of time it will make a request to the central DNS. DNS was maintained by the National Science Foundation in the USA in the 1980s and early 1990s but was contracted out to a private company called Network Solutions Inc. in 1993 which runs the InterNIC server. As part of the revision of domain names a new contract was being discussed through 1997 and into 1998 (Diamond, 1998).

14 Again there are several different ways of naming the World-Wide Web; for convenience I will use Web to stand for WWW or World-wide Web.

15 For example, the opening lines of an otherwise perceptive article about the dominance of men on the Internet are 'Make no mistake about it, the Internet is male

territory. Considering its roots are sunk deep in academia and the military–industrial complex, that's hardly surprising' (Wylie, 1995: 3). The Internet's roots *are* in academia and the military–industrial complex but the effect of networks like Usenet or FidoNet is here ignored in favour of an overly simplistic reading of cyberspace's history. This does not mean Wylie is necessarily incorrect in seeing the Internet as male territory or in arguing that misogyny is related to a military past, but it does mean she overly simplifies the relationship between the net's history and its nature.

16 The nature and limitations of any country-based analysis of host counts are discussed later when analysing the distribution of Internet hosts across the world.

17 Even as this is written in 1998 further attempts at censorship, of various types, are being made in the USA. For current news on the USA, see the newsletters 'EFFector' from EFF (http://www.eff.org) and/or 'Policy Post' from the Centre for Democracy and Technology (http://www.cdt.org). Both these sites also offer links to other important civil rights activists and organisations. For elsewhere in the world there are no obvious centres of information. However, try http://www.community.co.uk for the UK and links to Europe.

18 Which can be found at http://www.mids.org.

19 For the evidence of increasing speed see http://www.mids.org/weather/pingstats. The Internet Weather Report that Mids produces is also very interesting and traces the concentration of data usage via the Internet as it moves around the world.

20 Network Wizards and the host count can be found at http://www.nw.com. Lottor and the company he works for, Network Wizards, altered the method for counting hosts for the January 1998 host count and provided estimates for host numbers back to January 1995. They found that owing to changes in the Internet their original method was underestimating host numbers by as much as a quarter. This introduces a discontinuity into the host count figures. I have used figures produced according to the old and the new methods because the old method provides a long time-line and can be taken as accurate until the last two or three years. For current figures, the new method should be used.

21 Network Wizards use a computer command called 'ping' to test a sample of all hosts to see how many are actually attached to the Internet at any one time. Ping simply sends a message to an IP number that is then returned to the originating computer if the target is active. A count conducted in July 1998 was analysed too late to be included in the graphs, but has been noted in the text.

22 Network Wizards' data indicated there were 4,228,207 hosts in the USA at the time of the 1995 surveys.

23 These percentages are from the new method Network Wizards use for generating host counts and must be treated with caution as figures for 1995, 1996 and 1997 are estimates.

24 See http://www.cc.gatech.edu/gvu for a copy of the graph of NSFNET packet traffic.

25 Difficulties with the following figures need to be noted and are two-fold; though these problems do not undermine the usefulness of the figures they do mean the results need to be treated with care. First, there is no guarantee that a computer with a host name ending in .uk is actually located in the UK. A name may be registered but that does not mean the computer using it has to reside within the indicated national boundary. Second, the largest domain names are .com, .edu and .net and provide no indication of their national origin. In July 1998, these three domain names made up 74 per cent of all hosts, with all seven international domain names taking up 83 per cent of all hosts. The first of these problems needs simply to be noted as a limitation of the following figures; the disparities demonstrated below are so vast as some switching of domain names from their referent nation would most likely make little difference. For the second problem, Quarterman has provided a breakdown of all seven top-level domains according to country and the figures

supplied by Lottor have been accordingly redistributed. Quarterman's figures are incomplete but only for very small numbers of hosts; however this does produce some insignificant differences in figures between the numbers of hosts (Quarterman, 1997).

26 It is due to run again in late 1997 and biannually after that. By the time this text appears the results of further surveys should be available at http://www.cc.gatech.edu/gvu.

27 References are not given for each measure: O'Reilly survey refers to ORA (1995); Find/SVP refers to Find/SVP (1995; 1997); first GVU refers to Pitkow and Recker (1994a); second GVU refers to Pitkow and Recker (1994b); third GVU refers to Pitkow and Kehoe (1995a); fourth GVU refers to Pitkow and Kehoe (1995b); fifth GVU refers to Pitkow and Kehoe (1996a); sixth GVU refers to Pitkow and Kehoe (1996b); and seventh GVU refers to Pitkow and Kehoe (1997). All GVU surveys are copyright, 1994, 1995, 1996, 1997 Georgia Tech Research Corporation. All rights reserved.

28 For the November 1997 survey the return for the category 'Searching for Personal Information' was taken as a measure for 'browsing', because browsing was not measured in 1997.

29 For material related to Philcat see Rheingold (1994) and Hafner (1997).

3 The virtual individual

1 As just noted there are a number of names for these virtual spaces. However, for simplicity MUDs will be used from here on for all such spaces. MUDs originally stood for Multi-User Dungeons but now more often refers to Multi-User Dimensions (Stone, 1995: 68–70; Turkle, 1995: 11–14).

2 Commands differ on different MUDs. The commands here are used consistently so that the reader of this book only has to understand one MUD!

3 The myth of Julie, Joan, Sanford and Alex is retold in many places. The two that seem to have done most to create the myth disagree whether Julie was called Joan and Sanford Alex. See Stone (1995), Van Gelder (1991) and Turkle (1995). Turkle follows Van Gelder in calling Julie Joan and Sanford Alex.

4 Anonymous emails and postings are possible but are not the majority. The following examples of email addresses are (mainly) fictional, though they conform to the standards for email addresses.

5 IRC stand for Internet Relay Chat. This is a program that allows users to create shared spaces in which real-time conversations can occur. This means people's comments appear on screen as soon (connections permitting) as they press the send button. Channel names are given following the # symbol, such as #hackers, #gaysex and so on.

6 It is not being assumed that individuals in offline life have one coherent, centred, unified identity. Where the singular 'identity' is used it should be taken to indicate that maybe one identity of an individual's identities is relevant. To explore and establish the nature of identity as multiple or singular is beyond the scope of this text but it should be noted that the present account works whether multiple or singular identities are assumed for non-virtual selves. See Turkle (1995) for these arguments in detail.

7 See http://www.cygnus.com/~gnu.

8 Non-electronic sources also attempted to flow around these blockages, chiefly by people travelling over the border to the USA to buy newspapers. Of course, this is a far more difficult action for most Canadians than the Internet potentially allows (Shade, 1996: 20).

9 ISDN stands for Integrated Services Digital Network and it provides a much faster connection than most modems but usually at greater cost.

10 Mike Godwin is staff counsel for the cyberspace civil rights organisation the Electronic Frontier Foundation and has been closely involved in some of the more sensational of hacker cases (Sterling, 1994; Godwin, 1998).

11 Technically, it is the CPU and motherboard, which is the board on which the CPU sits and which allows all the other devices such as hard drive, monitor, etc., to connect to each other.

12 For example, from 1990 to 1993 the cost of memory did not drop but increased by 10 per cent a year. Memory takes up around 13 per cent of the price of a personal computer and over this time began to slow down the constant drop in price or rise in power of personal computers. However, by 1996 memory prices were dropping again and Moore's law was again governing personal computers (Manners, 1996).

13 There is a wide range of data on the Rimm episode. The following account draws on a number of sources, in particular Platt (1997) and documents in the archives at http://www.eff.org or http://www.ethics.ubc.ca/papers/cyberporn.html. Mike Godwin has written the definitive civil libertarian and activist account; it is probably the best place to start (Godwin, 1998).

14 Images can be posted on Usenet as text that, when processed with the correct software, produces a picture.

15 It is possible that 'obscenity' would simply have moved out of the USA but remained in cyberspace, in this way neutralising the legislation. The fact that a large part of cyberspace originates in the USA, as outlined in the previous chapter, means this cyberspatial answer (flowing around censorship) might not have been successful.

16 Discussions of these events and their meaning have been widespread; the place to begin is Rheingold (1994: 32–7).

4 The virtual social I

1 And there still is, as far as I am aware. Try MUD guide Mudconnector for an up-to-date location (http://www.mudconnector.com).

2 On some systems, toading is not virtual death but simply some transformation such as having an avatar's self-description changed to something loathsome. This is how toading received its name, as in some places it was common to change a self-description to that of a smelly, warty toad. An avatar would then have to live with this self-description for some time, with everyone they encountered knowing they had been for some reason toaded. However, toading now often means the more serious penalty of virtual execution.

3 The LambdaMOO rules, including this quote, were logged in early 1997.

4 The normal description of an avatar when the offline user is not logged on is that it is asleep. This means Dr.Jest could wake at any time and has not been toaded; it just so happens that whoever 'plays' Dr.Jest has stopped doing so.

5 As will be discussed at length below, it should not be assumed that technology is asocial or independent of human values. Arguing that power in MUDs is technically based does not mean it is not dependent on human decisions or values, only that these decisions and values are embedded in technology.

6 As with the other myths, the tale of Mr_Bungle crops up all over cyberspace. The canonical source is Dibbell (1994), particularly as an electronic version was released over the net. Dibbell's own discussion of the fate of his original article is interesting for its account of the spreading of one of the myths of the electronic frontier (Dibbell, 1994: 257–61) This retelling relies on Dibbell (1994), Quittner (1994a) and Curtis (1992).

7 And can be found at http://whoa.femail.com.

8 Many analyses or stories about harassment begin from spectacular examples, creating a sense of drama and even panic about online harassment, but there is no authoritative survey of its nature or extent. Chelmick conducted the only survey I am aware of, but unfortunately it has methodological limitations. First, it had only sixty respondents. Second, a number of respondents were found by advertising on a Web site dedicated to fighting online harassment, perhaps biasing the survey towards those who have suffered harassment and were seeking help from the Web site. Third, the survey asked only a general question that did not distinguish sexual from any other form of harassment. However, as the only figures available they are worth quoting, as long as these limitations are kept firmly in mind. Chelmick found that nearly 80 per cent of female respondents felt they had been harassed in chat rooms compared with 20 per cent of men, that nearly 70 per cent of women felt harassed in MUDs compared with 10 per cent of men and that nearly 40 per cent of women felt harassed in newsgroups or online asynchronous debates compared with 20 per cent of men (Chelmick 1997).

9 The following account of technopower is heavily indebted to both the sociology of scientific knowledge and technology and to politicised readings of epistemology. The work of Barry Barnes is the simplest emblem of this connection, as he is both a theorist of power and a sociologist of knowledge. The work that underpins the following theory of technopower is too broad to be summarised but can be indicated by the following: Barnes (1988), Harding (1991), Haraway (1991; 1997), Latour (1987), Knorr-Cetina and Mulkay (1983), Aronowitz et al. (1996).

10 This is true even where software creates software, such as experiments with evolutionary software. The results of software that creates software may sometimes be unexpected and surprising, but those results come from choices humans have made to create and release the software.

11 This is a simplified version to help establish the point clearly that, for example, leaves aside the emergence of Gopher as an aid to navigating cyberspace. The more complicated story is indicated in Chapter 2.

12 And this may well be true, though Chase denies this in the article and claims that users will be able to choose to have Netscape Navigator rather than Internet Explorer; though he does not explain what will happen if Internet Explorer disappears into Windows 98. The situation at present is further muddied by US government investigation into Microsoft for restrictive trade practices. Microsoft has suffered several investigations and it is unclear what effect its trial at the end of 1998 (or any others that follow) will have.

13 It should be noted that all through this discussion, it is being assumed that Microsoft or some other corporation will be able to deliver the technology to fulfil its aims. This is to ensure a clear focus on issues of technopower. But such achievements have not always been the case with Microsoft, which suffered delays to the launch of Windows 95 and in September 1997 announced a three-month delay to the launch of Windows 98. On the other hand, when Windows 95 was released it sold far more copies than expected and extended Microsoft's dominance of personal computer operating systems (Anon., 1997; Wallace, 1997: 279 and *passim*).

14 In mid-1997, 128-bit encryption was the length thought to be unbreakable. The National Security Agency in the USA has reportedly kept the Data Encryption Standard in the USA to 56 bits to ensure it can crack encrypted mail (Campbell, 1997a; 1997b). In fact, encryption appears to be winning through larger keys that effectively prevent any real possibility of decryption. While the mathematical complexity of this argument is not needed here, its conclusion is relevant because 'Decoding computer-generated messages is fast becoming impossible' (Libicki, 1995a; Loen, 1993).

15 Public and private keys can be generated using the RSA algorithm (Campbell, 1997a; 1997b).

16 One component of the rejection of strong encryption was that in the USA it was designated as restricted munitions and as such could not be transported across US borders, just as privately taking a Stealth bomber out of the country might be frowned upon. France had also outlawed the use of strong encryption (Barth and Smith, 1997: 284–6). However, given the global nature of the net, the US initiative has failed to keep the encryption genie in the bottle. It has also slowed down the emergence of safe financial transactions online, something that has led to leading Internet corporations lobbying alongside civil rights groups for liberalisation of encryption laws.

17 Clipper failed, partly for technical reasons, but a reformed proposal, the Digital Telephony Act, was passed. This mandated the insertion of tapping into the US communication infrastructure but by early 1998 funds have not been committed to implement such a system (though some commercial communications companies have been implementing it as part of informal co-operation with law enforcement).

18 The battle over the infrastructure rocked back and forth in 1997, with veteran Internet libertarian John Gilmore claiming '1997 may be the year we finally win the crypto wars' (Gilmore, cited in Lappin, 1997), partly because a long-standing court case between the US government and an exporter of encryption ended with a resounding defeat for the government – encryption code was declared a form of speech protected by the constitutional right to free speech – and partly because a bill appeared to be passing through the US legislatures that would protect a citizen's rights to encryption (Lappin, 1997). Within a few months this bill, the Security and Freedom though Encryption Act, or SAFE, had been attacked by representatives of the FBI, the National Security Agency, the Drug Enforcement Agency and the Commerce Department, resulting in amendments that reversed the intent of the legislation by removing the right to sell strong encryption and replacing it with a ban on US citizens using strong encryption within the USA. After this Gilmore's hopes look less likely (Campbell, 1997a; 1997b; Vesely, 1997). Germany, the main competitor to the USA in developing encryption software, has refused to develop proposals similar to the USA despite pressure. The UK Labour Party was (before its election as government in 1997) opposed to the trusted third-party scheme. The European Union has decided against supporting any key escrow systems and argued for widespread, freely available strong encryption. Japan seemed to be developing expertise in cryptography as a strategy for gaining commercial opportunities in the emerging global net. And, neatly side-stepping such problems, Netscape has joined with ex-Russian security software engineers to develop strong encryption outside the USA (Barth and Smith, 1997; Campbell, 1997a; 1997b; Vesely, 1997; Ludlow, 1996: 173–250).

19 It is important to reiterate here that these myths seek to draw out the moral of a story that is widely retold on the net. I have indicated below whether some of the mythic elements of Mitnick's story are true or not, simply because Mitnick has suffered and is suffering jail for computer intrusions he did not necessarily commit. It does not diminish Mitnick's myth to note when his story seems untrue or uncertain and, unlike any of the other myths, it seems important not to indulge in the hyperbole surrounding a myth that might be helping to condemn a man to jail. For a more sympathetic treatment of Mitnick than many, which also does not hide his intrusions and their painful effects, see Littman (1996).

20 One of the ironies of the IP spoofing attack is that it led almost directly to Mitnick but it still does not seem certain that Mitnick conducted the attack on Shimomura. It is clear Mitnick was working with someone, who either might have coded sections

of the attack leaving Mitnick to run the code or might have conducted the attack either by themselves or in conjunction with Mitnick.

21 The Mitnick story and myth is most easily explored by reading together two accounts of his capture in 1995, see Shimomura (1995) and Littman (1996). This account is developed from these two sources as well as Littman (1997), Hafner and Markoff (1991), Goodell (1996) and Platt (1997). Littman (1996) and Platt (1997) allow an exploration of the demonisation of Mitnick. See Jordan and Taylor (1998) for an investigation of hacking communities. See Stoll (1989), Sterling (1992), Quittner and Slattala (1995) and Freedman and Mann (1997) for other accounts of hackers.

5 The virtual social II

1 This tripartite division of agricultural, industrial and informational is too simple but forms a useful basis for beginning discussion. I will use the broad labels industrial and informational to designate the two sides of the broad socio-economic transition that is under discussion.

2 If anyone wishes to take up the nature of the information age, the work of Castells, particularly his three-volume work *The Information Age*, is a complex and well-grounded place to start. In the following section, key points are appropriately referenced, but it should also be noted that the section as a whole draws on a wide range of sources. The key sources are Castells (1989, 1996, 1997), Hirst and Thompson (1996), Lash and Urry (1987, 1994), Harvey (1989), Castells and Hall (1994), Graham and Marvin (1996), Webster (1995). I have also attempted to draw on the most up-to-date sources, leaving aside the more prescient and visionary attempts to explain the information society. For these forebears look to the varying ideologies in Alvin Toffler's *The Third Wave*, Ernest Mandel's *Late Capitalism*, Daniel Bell's *The Coming of Post-Industrial Society* and Alain Touraine's *The Post-Industrial Society*.

3 There are innumerable ways of dividing the world up for analysis and it would undoubtedly be possible to choose different categories than I have and create a useful result. However, the point is not to explore exhaustively all the different categories that might be used to analyse socio-economies but to pick out the ones that most clearly identify the roles played by cyberspace. Hopefully the following analysis makes clear why production, consumption and politics are appropriate to this task.

4 This is not meant to be an exhaustive or technically detailed account of capital, a subject worth many books to itself. Instead, it attempts to stay at as simple a level as possible while still conveying the central trends for cyberspace, capital and information societies.

5 USA, Japan, Germany, France, Italy, UK and Canada.

6 This comment is not meant to hide the fact that economic migration of various types often results in harsh exploitation of immigrants. It simply notes that it is a minor component of informational socio-economies (Lash and Urry, 1994: 171–92).

7 These figures are part of those presented in Chapter 2 concerning the international division of Internet hosts.

8 The top 1 per cent of household incomes in the USA grew by 49.8 per cent between 1980 and 1987, the top 10 per cent grew by 14.8 per cent, while the bottom 10 per cent *shrunk* by 14.8 per cent (Perkin, 1996: 192). With the exception of the UK, which has reaped similar 'benefits' as the USA from a commitment to Reaganite/Thatcherite socio-economic policies, Europe has generated less dramatic shifts in inequality but has still generated significant areas of deprivation (Lash and Urry, 1994: 157–60).

9 See Castells for a discussion of productivity in informational socio-economies and the difficulties of measuring and defining it (Castells, 1996: 66–92).

10 The USA and Japan exhibited the greatest increases of 3 and 4.1 per cent in manufacturing production, respectively, with the UK not far behind. France and Germany, by contrast, lagged with 2.4 and 1.5 per cent increases respectively (Castells, 1996: 78–9).

11 North American Free Trade Area, including the USA, Canada and Mexico.

12 The one area in which cyberspace appears to be participating in change, which has not been covered, is war and the military. This is a complicated and confused topic that simply cannot fit into the present space. See Gray (1997), Shukman (1995), de Landa (1991), Libicki (1995a; 1995b) and Jones and Sessions (1993).

13 The following analysis borrows terms from Castells but does not use the same concept. The space of flows here analysed is the one cyberspace creates, not the one Castells argues is fundamental to the Information Age.

14 A rise that is under threat in 1998, with the collapse of East Asian currencies, the near bankruptcy of South Korea and Indonesia and the possible beginnings of the collapse of the Japanese banking system.

15 It is arguable that the highway has overtaken the frontier as the dominant metaphor for cyberspace and images of infobahn's and superhighways are common. However, the frontier remains the founding metaphor and, so far, the most influential.

16 Shimomura is supposed to have said catching Mitnick was a 'matter of honour' and one of his chief complaints about the attack on him was that it cost him time on the skiing slopes. Unfortunately his Eastern-sounding name led many into overblown samurai metaphors, rather than the Wyatt Earp role a frontier metaphor might have offered him.

17 These stories occur in a large number of places. See Sterling (1992), EFF Web site http://www.eff.org; Sardar (1996), Ravetz and Sardar (1996), Miller (1995), Brook and Boal (1995). For interpretations of the Wild West see Brown (1994) and Cronon *et al.* (1992). For Barlow and Fena's comments on frontiers and EFF see Barlow (1996a), Fena (1996), Jordan (1998).

6 The virtual imaginary

1 Collective imagination is Benedict Anderson's term (see below), while imaginary is from the work of Jacques Lacan where it refers to, in short, the relationship between the ego and its images (and is contrasted with the symbolic and the real). Lacan's theory is too complex to be explained here without a long digression, but I have retained his term alongside Anderson's to indicate the erotic and fantasy dimensions of a community's relationship between its desires and its images that may be underplayed in Anderson. For a brief account of Lacan's theory see Sheridan (1977: 279–80).

2 EFF is now a membership organisation, though the membership has no say in policy. Rather, membership is an indication of support for the policies decided by EFF's Board. The Board decides membership of the Board.

3 In addition to the sources cited in the myth see the following. For accounts of the desire for immortality see Moravec (1988), Minsky (1986), Dery (1996), Hudson (1997) and Hayles (1993). For the collapse of life and computer systems see Kelly (1994). For the Extropians see Hudson (1997: 115–20) and http://www.c2.net/arkuat/extr/. And for a vigorous, at times hysterical, attack on the idea that the mind could dominate the body or reality, see Slouka (1995).

4 It is, of course, chess master Gary Kasparov's famous comment that he became frightened in the second game of his contest against the computer program Deep Blue

when he saw, for the first time, signs of intelligence in his non-human opponent. Kasparov lost the contest.

5 For a beginning try the Human Genome Project Web site at http://www.ornl.gov/ TechResources/Human_Genome, Marks (1994), Lewontin (1994) and Kevles and Hood (1992).

6 Despite believing that information is a life-form, Barlow also considers Lanier's slogan to be 'the most important thing anybody ever said to me in defining my digital mission' (Barlow, cited in Brockman, 1996: 170).

7 The Marxist concept of reification is one of the richest sources for this type of analysis, though rarely invoked in these contexts (Sayer, 1979; Haraway, 1997: 43).

8 Especially as his social vision involves using more and more Microsoft software. Profit and social liberation go hand in hand in Gates's part of the imaginary.

9 Many sources explore these possibilities. See Poster (1990) for a theoretical view, Lyon (1994), and Davies (1996) for the introductions to the reality. In October 1998 a local authority in London (Newham) introduced CCTV that can identify faces, a system already operating in parts of the USA. It was also confirmed that the US secret services, in conjunction with some other nation-states, were recording and examining *all* data, telephone and fax, in Europe and elsewhere, aiming specifically at non-military targets (this is the Echelon project) (Wright, 1998).

10 For such details see innumerable commentaries on Foucault or, better, Foucault (1977).

11 The subheading for an interview in *Wired* with the Deputy Secretary of the Treasury in the USA reads 'Fortunately for the New Economy, Larry Summers – Clinton's point man on trade and international finance – not only gets it, he's actually being helpful' (Heilemann, 1997: 53).

7 Cyberpower

1 The superconnected exchange emails at least three days a week and use a laptop, cell phone, beeper and home computer. The connected exchange email at least three days a week but only use three of the following four: laptop, cell phone, beeper and home computer. The semiconnected use at least one of the technologies already mentioned, but not more than four. And the disconnected use none. For the initial survey 1,000 were interviewed, with 444 being further interviewed. The survey does not state how many of the superconnected and connected were interviewed, making it difficult to judge the legitimacy of the survey's results.

Glossary

ARPA Advance Research Projects Agency, Department of Defense, USA.

ARPANET First large-scale, distributed, packet-switching network of computers.

ASCII American Standard Code for Information Interchange, set of roman language characters often used as standard in cyberspace's technology.

ASCII art Pictures drawn using ASCII characters, such as @} for a rose

AT&T Once national US telecommunications monopoly, opened to competition in 1984.

avatar Online identity.

Barlovian cyberspace Cyberspace understood as whatever currently exists on computer networks.

BBN Bolt Beranek and Newman, firm that built ARPANET.

BBS Bulletin Board Service, usually personal computers using phone lines.

bots Autonomous software programs let loose in cyberspace to conduct (mundane) online jobs.

browser Software program that allows the Web to be viewed, such as Navigator, Mosaic or Internet Explorer.

CCTV Closed Circuit Television cameras.

CDA Communications Decency Act, US legislation to censor the Internet.

CDT Center for Democracy and Technology, online civil rights organisation.

CERN Physics laboratory where the Web was invented.

Clipper chip Chip US government once wanted to embed in telecommunications devices that allowed encryption but created a secret decoding ability for government.

CompuServe   An ISP.

CPU   Central Processing Unit.

DARPA   Defense Advance Research Projects Agency, Department of Defense, USA. Successor to ARPA.

DEC   Digital Equipment Corporation.

DNS   Domain Name Server, system of creating and administering Internet names and numbers.

download   Taking a file, picture, document or whatever from a network and loading it 'down' to your computer.

EFF   Electronic Frontier Foundation, online civil rights organisation.

emoticons   Pictures drawn with ASCII characters to indicate user's emotional state, such as :-) for smiling or =:-0 for screaming with hair standing on end (read them sideways).

FidoNet   World-wide network of bulletin boards, connected via telephone lines.

Find/SVP   Company that conducts surveys of the Internet.

Gopher   System for organising the Internet's resources that utilises branching menus.

GUI   Graphical User Interface, presenting applications that run on a computer as a combination of graphics and text.

GVU   Graphic, Visualisation and Usability Centre, conducts regular surveys of Web users.

handle   Online name, usually different to offline name and often fanciful, such as Phiber Optick.

hardware   Machinery that makes up computer systems and networks.

HTML   Hypertext Markup Language, the language that converts documents and pictures into hypertext Web pages.

HTTP   Hypertext Transfer Protocol, protocol that defines how documents on the Web are connected.

IBM   International Business Machines.

Internet   Global, distributed, packet-switching computer network connecting machines utilising the Internet Protocol.

IP, Internet Protocol, IP/TCP   Protocol that defines how computers who wish to connect to the Internet can do so.

IRC Internet Relay Chat, allows real-time online chat over the Internet.

IRC channel Particular IRC group, usually dedicated to specific topic such as #gaysex or #hackers.

ISP Internet Service Provider, company that offers connections to the Internet, usually paid.

Java Computer language created by Sun Microsystems.

key escrow Placing encryption keys in escrow so that law enforcement or government can demand they be turned over when necessary.

kill file List of addresses from which a user does not want to receive newsgroup posts or other communications.

LambdaMOO A MUD.

LAN Local Area Network, computer network restricted to a local area.

Listserv Email list that allows discussion by automatically emailing all posts to participants.

matrix Computer networks, defined by John Quarterman as all computers who can exchange email.

MUDs, MUSHES, MUCKs and MOOs Virtual worlds, usually created out of text and allowing multiple users.

NAFTA North American Free Trade Agreement, a free trade zone created between the USA, Canada and Mexico.

NCSA National Center for Supercomputing Applications, where the first widespread GUI Web browser was created.

newbie New Internet or cyberspace user.

newsgroups Particular online discussion group, usually Usenet and usually dedicated to specific topic such as rec.pets.cats (cats) or alt.tasteless (tastelessness).

NSFNet National Science Foundation Network, successor to ARPANET. Backbone network connecting supercomputer centres.

ORA O'Reilly and Associates, company that conducts surveys of the Internet.

Parc Palo Alto Research Center, run by Xerox Corporation.

search engine Mechanism for searching the Web.

software Instructions (code) written by humans to make computers 'do' things.

sysadmin System administrator, person administering a computer system.

sysop   System operator, person administering a computer system.

TCP   Transmission Control Protocol, see IP.

toading   Turning a user's self-description into something loathsome or destroying an avatar.

top-level domain name   Final letters of email or Web address that identify mail or address as part of one of six international groups or a nation.

UNIX   Computer language commonly used to control computers that are part of cyberspace.

upload   Taking a file, picture, document or whatever from your own computer and loading it onto a network.

URL   Universal Resource Locator, the string of characters that defines the location of a resource on the Web.

Usenet   World-wide computer conferencing system, contains the 'alt.' news-groups.

UUCP   UNIX to UNIX Copy Protocol, facility in UNIX to copy files to other UNIX computers.

VR   Virtual Reality.

WAN   Wide Area Network, computer network of regional size (somewhere between a LAN and a global network).

WELL   Whole Earth 'Lectronic Link, influential BBS (now Web-based).

Win95/98 or Windows   Operating systems created by Microsoft Corporation for personal computers.

WWW, World-Wide Web, the Web   Information organised on the Internet that utilises URL and HTML to create hypertext.

Bibliography

Anderson, B. (1991) *Imagined Communities*, second edition, London: Verso.

Anon. (1997) 'Microfile', *Guardian OnLine Supplement* 18 September: 13.

Aronowitz, S., Martinsons, B. and Menser, M. (eds) (1996) *Technoscience and Cyberculture*, London: Routledge.

Audit Commission (1990) 'Survey of Computer Fraud and Abuse', Audit Commission.

Bagguely, P. (1995) 'Protest, Poverty and Power: a case study of the anti-poll tax movement', *Sociological Review* 43(4): 693–719.

Baker, S. (1994) 'Don't Worry Be Happy: why clipper is good for you', *Wired USA* 2.06: 100, 132–3.

Balsamo, A. (1993) 'Feminism for the Incurably Informed', in Dery, M. (ed.) *Flame Wars: the discourse of cyberculture*, Durham, NC: Duke University Press, pp. 681–712.

Barbrook, R. and Cameron, A. (1997) 'The Californian Ideology', *Science as Culture* 26: 44–72.

Barlow, J.P. (1990) 'Crime and Puzzlement', *Whole Earth Review* 44–57, available at http://www.eff.org/pub/Publications/.

Barlow, J.P. (1994a) 'John Perry Barlow Interview', available at http://www.eff.org/~barlow/library.html .

Barlow, J.P. (1994b) 'Stopping the Information Railroad', paper given at the USENIX Conference, San Francisco, California, January 17.

Barlow, J.P. (1996a) 'Interview with Tim Jordan', unpublished.

Barlow, J.P. (1996b) 'Selling Wine without Bottles: the economy of mind on the global net', in Leeson, L. (ed.) (1996) *Clicking In: hot links to a digital culture*, Seattle: Bar Press, pp. 148–72, also available at http://www.eff.org/~barlow/library.html.

Barlow, J.P. (1996c) 'A Declaration of the Independence of Cyberspace', available at http://www.eff.org/~barlow/library.html.

Barlow, J.P. (1998) 'Africa Rising: everything you know about Africa is wrong', *Wired USA* 6.01: 143–58.

Barme, G. and Ye, S. (1997) 'The Great Firewall of China', *Wired USA* 5.06: 138–51, 182.

Barnes, B. (1988) *The Nature of Power*, Cambridge: Polity.

Barnes, B. (1995) *The Elements of Social Theory*, London: UCL Press.

Barrett, J. (1996) 'Killing Time: the new frontiers of cyberspace capitalism', in Strate, L., Jacobson, R. and Gibson, S. (eds) *Communication and Cyberspace: social interaction in an electronic environment*, Creskill, NJ: Hampton Press, pp. 155–65.

Barth, R. and Smith, C. (1997) 'International Regulation of Encryption: technology will drive policy', in Kahin, B. and Neeson, C. (eds) *Borders in Cyberspace: information policy and the Global Information Infrastructure*, Cambridge, MA: MIT Press, pp. 283–99.

Baym, N. (1995) 'The Emergence of Community in Computer-Mediated Communication', in Jones, S. (ed.) *Cybersociety: computer-mediated communication and community*, London: Sage.

Bear, G. (1985) 'Petra', in Sterling, B. (ed.) *Mirrorshades: the cyberpunk anthology*, New York: Arbor House, pp. 105–24.

Bell, D. (1973) *The Coming of Post-Industrial Society: a venture in social forecasting*, Harmondsworth: Penguin.

Bellos, A. (1997) 'Error Unravels World Wide Web', *Guardian* 19 July: 5.

Bender, G. and Druckrey, T. (eds) (1994) *Culture on the Brink: ideologies of technology*, Seattle: Bay Press.

Benedikt, M. (1991a) 'Introduction', in Benedikt, M. (ed.) *Cyberspace: the first steps*, Cambridge, MA: MIT Press, pp. 1–25.

Benedikt, M. (1991b) 'Cyberspace: some proposals', in Benedikt, M. (ed.) *Cyberspace: the first steps*, Cambridge, MA: MIT Press, pp. 119–224.

Benedikt, M. (ed.) (1991c) *Cyberspace: the first steps*, Cambridge, MA: MIT Press.

Berger, M. and Borer, D. (1997a) 'Introduction: The Rise of East Asia; critical visions of the Pacific Century', in Berger, M. and Borer, D. (eds) *The Rise of East Asia: critical visions of the pacific century*, London: Routledge, pp. 1–36.

Berger, M. and Borer, D. (eds) (1997b) *The Rise of East Asia: critical visions of the pacific century*, London: Routledge.

Berners-Lee, T. (1996) 'The World Wide Web: past, present and future', available at http://www.w3.org/people/berners_lee/1996.

Berners-Lee, T. and Cailliau, R. (1989) 'World Wide Web: proposals for a hypertext project', available at http://www.w3.org/pub/WWW.

Borsook, P. (1996) 'The Memoirs of a Token: an aging Berkeley feminist examines *Wired*', in Cherny, L. and Weise, E. (eds) *Wired_Women: gender and new realities in cyberspace*, Seattle: Seal Press, pp. 56–72.

Bourbonnais, J. and Yergau, F. (1996) 'Languages on the Internet', paper given at INET 96, available at http://www.isoc.org/conferences/inet96.

Boutin, P. (1998) 'Pushover?', *Wired USA* 6.03: 86.

Bowers, S. (1997) 'Clock Idea is a Chip of the Old Block', *Guardian* 6 August: 4.

Branscomb, A. (1993) 'Jurisdictional Quandries for Global Networks', in Harasim, L. (ed.) *Global Networks: computers and international communication*, Cambridge, MA: MIT Press , pp. 83–104.

Branwyn, G. (1993) 'Compu-sex: erotica for cybernauts', in Dery, M. (ed.) *Flame Wars: the discourse of cyberculture*, Durham, NC: Duke University Press, pp. 779–91.

Brenner, A. and Metson, B. (1994) 'Paul and Karla Hit the Net', *Wired USA* 2.04: 28–9.

Brockman, J. (1996) *Digerati: encounters with the cyber elite*, San Francisco: Hardwired.

Brook, J. and Boal, I. (eds) (1995) *Resisting the Virtual Life: the culture and politics of information*, San Francisco: City Lights Books.

Brown, D. (1994) *The American West*, New York: Simon & Schuster.

Brown, D. (1997) *Cybertrends: chaos, power and accountability in the information age*, London: Viking.

Bukatman, S. (1993a) *Terminal Identity: the virtual subject in post-modern science fiction*, Durham, NC: Duke University Press.

Bukatman, S. (1993b) 'Gibson's Typewriter', in Dery, M. (ed.) *Flamewars: the discourse of cyberculture*, Durham, NC: Duke University Press, pp. 627–46.

Burkhalter, B. (1998) 'Reading Race Online: discovering racial identity in Usenet discussions', in Kollock, P. and Smith, M. (eds) *Communities in Cyberspace*, London: Routledge.

Burrows, R. (1997) 'Virtual Culture, Urban Social Polarisation and Social Science Fiction', in, Loader, D. (ed.) *The Governance of Cyberspace: politics, technology and global restructuring*, London: Routledge, pp. 38–45.

Burrows, R. and Featherstone, M. (eds) (1995) *Cyberspace, Cyberbodies, Cyberpunk: cultures of technological embodiment*, London: Sage.

Bush, V. (1945) 'As We May Think', *The Atlantic Monthly* 196(1): 101–8, also available at http://www.isg.sfu.ca/~duchier/misc/vbush/.

Campbell, D. (1997a) 'Screw the Internet', *Guardian OnLine Supplement* 18 September: 1–3.

Campbell, D. (1997b) 'Europe Spikes Spook's E-mail Eavesdrop Bid', *Guardian OnLine Supplement* 16 October: 3.

Casey, C. (1996) *The Hill on the Net: Congress enters the Information Age*, Boston: Academic Press.

Castells, M. (1989) *The Informational City: information technology, economic restructuring and the urban-regional process*, Oxford: Blackwell.

Castells, M. (1996) *The Rise of the Network Society: the information age*, vol. 1, Oxford: Blackwell.

Castells, M. (1997) *The Power of Identity: the information age*, vol. 2, Oxford: Blackwell.

Castells, M. and Hall, P. (1994) *Technopoles of the World: the making of 21st Century Industrial Complexes*, London: Routledge.

Chapman, M. (1993) 'Taming the Computer', in Dery, M. (ed.) *Flame Wars: the discourse of cyberculture*, Durham, NC: Duke University Press, pp. 827–49.

Chelmick, S. (1997) 'The Old Boy Network? A study in the prevalence of sexual harassment and gender discrimination in cyberspace', BA Honours Dissertation, Social Science, University of East London.

Cherny, L. and Weise, E. (eds) (1996) *Wired_Women: gender and new realities in cyberspace*, Seattle: Seal Press.

Clark, N. (1995) 'Rear-view Mirrorshades: the recursive generation of the cyberbody', in Featherstone, M. and Burrows, R. (eds) *Cyberspace, Cyberbodies, Cyberpunks: cultures of technological embodiment*, London: Sage, pp. 113–33.

Clark, R. (1994) 'The Digital Persona and Its Application to Data Surveillance', *The Information Society* 10 (2): 77–92.

Clegg, S. (1989) *Frameworks of Power*, London: Sage.

Clough, B. and Mungo, P. (1992) *Approaching Zero: data crime and the computer underworld*, London: Faber & Faber.

Conley, V. (ed.) (1993) *Rethinking Technologies*, London: University of Minnesota Press.

Coupland, D. (1995) *Microserfs*, London: HarperCollins.

Cronon, W., Miles, G. and Gitlin, J. (eds) (1992) *Under an Open Sky: rethinking America's Western Past*, London: W.W. Norton.

Curtis, P. (1992) 'Mudding: social phenomena in text-based virtual realities', *Intertek* 3.3: 26–34.

Davies, S. (1995) 'Welcome Home Big Brother', *Wired UK* 1.02: 58–63, 110.

Davies, S. (1996) *Big Brother: Britain's web of surveillance and the new technological order*, London: Macmillan.

Davies, S. (1997) 'Big Brother Plc', *Wired UK* 2.10: 59–62, 87–90.

Davis, M. (1992) *Beyond Blade Runner: Urban Control, The Ecology of Fear*, New York: Open Media.

deamon9/route/infinity (1996) 'IP-Spoofing Demystified', *Phrack* 7(48), also available at http://www.geocities.com/CapeCanaveral/3498/.

De Landa, M. (1991) *War in the Age of Intelligent Machines*, New York: Zone Books.

Denning, P. (ed.) (1990) *Computers Under Attack: intruders, worms and viruses*, New York: Addison-Wesley.

Dery, M. (1993a) 'Flame Wars', in Dery, M. (ed.) *Flame Wars: the discourse of cyberculture*, Durham, NC: Duke University Press, pp. 559–68.

Dery, M. (1993b) 'Black to the Future: interviews with Samuel R. Delany, Greg Tate and Tricia Rose', in Dery, M. (ed.) *Flame Wars: the discourse of cyberculture*, Durham, NC: Duke University Press, pp. 735–78.

Dery, M. (ed.) (1993c) *Flame Wars: the discourse of cyberculture* (special edition of *South Atlantic Quarterly* 92(4)), Durham, NC: Duke University Press.

Dery, M. (ed.) (1994) *Flame Wars: the discourse of cyberculture*, Durham, NC: Duke University Press.

Dery, M. (1996) *Escape Velocity: cyberculture at the end of the century*, New York: Grove Press.

Diamond, D. (1998) 'Whose Internet Is It, Anyway?', *Wired US* 6.04: 172–7, 187–95.

Dibbell, J. (1994) 'A Rape in Cyberspace: or, how an evil clown, a Haitian trickster spirit, two wizards, and a cast of dozens turned a database into a society', in Dery, M. (ed.) *Flame Wars: the discourse of cyberculture*, Durham, NC: Duke University Press, pp. 237–61.

Donath, J. (1998) 'Identity and Deception in the Virtual Community', in Kollock, P. and Smith, M. (eds) *Communities in Cyberspace*, London: Routledge.

Doob, A. and Greenspan, E. (eds) (1985) *Perspectives in Criminal Law*, Aurora, Ontario: Canada Law Books.

Dreyfus, H. and Rabinow, P. (1983) *Michel Foucault: beyond structuralism and hermeneutics*, second edition, Chicago: Chicago University Press.

Dreyfus, S. (1997) *Underground: tales of hacking, madness and obsession on the electronic frontier*, Kew: Mandarin.

Dunlop, C. and Kling, R. (eds) (1991) *Computerisation and Controversy: value conflicts and social choices*, Boston: Academic Press.

Editors (1996) 'The Wired Manifesto for the Digital Society', *Wired UK* 2.10: 42–7.

Edwards, P. (1996) *The Closed World: computers and the politics of discourse in Cold War America*, Cambridge, MA: MIT Press.

EFF (1995) 'German Government Pushes Blockage of Netherlands Web Sites', available at http://www.eff.org.

EFF (1996) 'Singapore Government Curtails Online Freedoms', available at http://www.eff.org.

Fanon, F. (1986) *Black Skin, White Masks*, London: Pluto Press.

Farmer, F. and Morningstar, C. (1991) 'The Lessons of Lucasfilms' Habitat', in Benedikt, M. (ed.) *Cyberspace: the first steps*, Cambridge, MA: MIT Press, pp. 273–302.

Featherstone, M. and Burrows, R. (1995a) 'Cultures of Technological Embodiment', in Featherstone, M. and Burrows, R. (eds) *Cyberspace, Cyberbodies, Cyberpunks: cultures of technological embodiment*, London: Sage, pp. 1–19.

Featherstone, M. and Burrows, R. (eds) (1995b) *Cyberspace, Cyberbodies, Cyberpunks: cultures of technological embodiment*, London: Sage.

Felten, E., Balfanz, D., Dean, D. and Wallack, D. (1996) 'Web-Spoofing: an Internet con game', Technical Report 540–96, Department of Computer Science, Princeton University, also at http://www.cs.princeton.edu/sip.

Fena, L. (1996) 'Interview with Tim Jordan', unpublished.

FidoNet (1989) *FidoNet Policy Document: version 4.07*, available at http://www.fidonet.org.

Find/SVP (1995) *American Internet User Survey 1995*, available at http://www.findsvp.com.

Find/SVP (1997) *American Internet User Survey 1997*, available at http://www.findsvp.com.

Foucault, M. (1977) *Discipline and Punish: the birth of the prison*, Harmondsworth: Penguin.

Foucault, M. (1979) *History of Sexuality Volume 1: an introduction*, Harmondsworth: Penguin.

Foucault, M. (1983) 'The Subject and Power', in Dreyfus, H. and Rabinow, P. *Michel Foucault: beyond structuralism and hermeneutics*, second edition, Chicago: Chicago University Press, pp. 208–26.

Foucault, M. (1991) *Remarks on Marx: conversations with Duccio Trombadori*, New York: Semiotext(e).

Freedman, D. and Mann, C. (1997) *At Large: the strange case of the world's biggest Internet invasion*, New York: Simon & Schuster.

Friedan, J. (1991) 'Invested Interests: the politics of national economic policies in a world of global finance', *International Organisation* 45(5): 425–51.

Gabilando, J. (1995) 'Postcolonial Cyborgs: subjectivity in the age of cybernetic reproduction', in Gray, C.H. (ed.) *The Cyborg Handbook*, London: Routledge, pp. 423–32.

Garfinkel, S., Stallman, R. and Kapor, M. (1996) 'Why Patents are Bad for Software', in Ludlow, P. (ed.) *High Noon on the Electronic Frontier*, Cambridge, MA: MIT Press, pp. 35–46.

Gates, B. (1995) *The Road Ahead: with N. Myhrvold and P. Rhinearson*, New York: Viking.

Gellner, E. (1964) *Thought and Change*, London: Wiedenfeld & Nicholson.

Gerth, H. and Wright Mills, C. (eds) (1952) *From Max Weber*, London: Routledge.

Gibson, W. (1984) *Neuromancer*, London: Grafton Books.

Gibson, W. (1986a) *Count Zero*, New York: Ace Books.

Gibson, W. (1986b) *Burning Chrome*, London: Victor Gollancz.

Gibson, W. (1988) *Mona Lisa Overdrive*, London: Victor Gollancz.

Gibson, W. (1993) *Virtual Light*, London: Viking.

Gibson, W. and Sterling, B. (1991) *The Difference Engine*, London: Victor Gollancz.

Giese, M. (1996) 'From ARPAnet to the Internet: a cultural clash and its implications in framing the debate on the information superhighway', in Strate, L., Jacobson, R. and

Gibson, S. (eds) *Communication and Cyberspace: social interaction in an electronic environment*, Creskill, NJ: Hampton Press, pp. 123–41.

Gilboa, N. (1996) 'Elites, Lamers, Narcs and Whores: exploring the computer underground', in Cherny, L. and Weise, E. (eds) *Wired_Women: gender and new realities in cyberspace*, Seattle: Seal Press, pp. 98–113.

Gilmore, J. (1996) 'Interview with Tim Jordan', unpublished manuscript.

Godwin, M. (1991) 'The Electronic Frontier Foundation and Virtual Communities', available at http://www.eff.org/pub/Publications/.

Godwin, M. (1996) 'Interview with Tim Jordan', unpublished manuscript.

Godwin, M. (1997) 'Free Speech 1, Censorship 0: looking beyond the CDA victory', *Wired USA* 5.09: 94.

Godwin, M. (1998) *Cyber Rights*, New York: Random House.

Goldstein, E. (1993) 'Hacker Testimony to House Sub-committee Largely Unheard', *Computer Underground Digest* 5.43.

Goodell, J. (1996) *The Cyberthief and the Samurai: the true story of Kevin Mitnick and the man who hunted him down*, New York: Dell.

Gow, D. and Norton-Taylor, R. (1996) 'Surfing Superhighwaymen', *Guardian* 7 December: 28.

Graham, S. and Marvin, S. (1996) *Telecommunications and the City: electronic spaces, urban places*, London: Routledge.

Gray, C.H. (ed.) (1995) *The Cyborg Handbook*, London: Routledge.

Gray, C.H. (1997) *Postmodern War: the new politics of conflict*, London: Routledge.

Gray, M. (1996) 'Web Wanderer and Web Growth', available at http://www.mit.edu:8001/people/mkgray/mkgray.html.

Grebb, M. (1997) 'Net Congestion Talks Clogged', available at http://www.netizen.com.

Gromov, G. (1995) The Road and Crossroads of Internet's History, available at http://www.internetvalley.com/.

Hafner, K. (1997) 'The World's Most Influential Online Community (and it's not AOL): the epic saga of the Well', *Wired US* 5.05: 98–142.

Hafner, K. and Lyon, M. (1996) *Where Wizards Stay Up Late: the origins of the Internet*, New York: Simon & Schuster.

Hafner, K. and Markoff, J. (1991) *Cyberpunk: outlaws and hackers on the computer frontier*, London: Corgi.

Hakala, D. and Rickard, J. (1996) 'A Domain by any other Name!', *Boardwatch* 10(10), also available at http://www.boardwatch.com/.

Hall, S. and Jacques, M. (eds) (1989) *New Times: the changing face of politics in the 1990s*, London: Lawrence & Wishart.

Harasim, L. (ed.) (1993) *Global Networks: computers and international communication*, Cambridge, MA: MIT Press .

Haraway, D. (1991) *Simians, Cyborgs and Women: the reinvention of nature*, London: Free Association Books.

Haraway, D. (1995) 'Foreward: cyborgs and symbionts; living together in the new world order', in Gray, C.H. (ed.) *The Cyborg Handbook*, London: Routledge, pp. xi–xx.

Haraway, D. (1997) *Modest_Witness@Second_Millennium.FemaleMan©_Meets_Oncomouse™ feminism and technoscience*, London: Routledge.

Harding, S. (1991) *Whose Science? Whose Knowledge? Thinking from women's lives*, Milton Keynes: Open University Press.

Hardman, E. (1995) 'Hardware of the Future: man or mouse?', *Guardian: Online Supplement* 14 December: 4.

Hardy, H. (1993) 'The History of the Net', Master's Thesis, Grand Valley State University, also available at ftp://ftp.ocean.ic.net/pub/doc/.

Harvey, D. (1989) *The Condition of Postmodernity: an enquiry into the origins of cultural change*, Oxford: Blackwell.

Hayles, N.K. (1993) 'The Seductions of Cyberspace', in Conley, V. (ed.) *Rethinking Technologies*, London: University of Minnesota Press, pp. 173–90.

Heilemann, J. (1997) 'The Integrationists vs. The Separatists', *Wired USA* 5.07: 53–6, 182–7.

Held, D. (1995) *Democracy and the Global Order*, Cambridge: Polity.

Hertz, J.C. (1994) *Surfing on the Internet: a net-head's adventures online*, London: Abacus.

Hiltz, S. and Turroff, M. (1985) 'Structuring Computer-Mediated Communication to Avoid Information Overload', *Communications of the ACM* 28(7): 680–9.

Hiltz, S. and Turroff, M. (1993) *Network Nation: human communication via computers*, Cambridge, MA: MIT Press.

Holland, S. (1995) 'Descartes Goes to Hollywood: mind, body and gender in contemporary cyborg cinema', in Featherstone, M. and Burrows, R. (eds) *Cyberspace, Cyberbodies, Cyberpunks: cultures of technological embodiment*, London: Sage, pp. 157–74.

Hirst, P. and Thompson, G. (1996) *Globalization in Question: the international economy and the possibilities of governance*, Cambridge: Polity.

Hudson, D. (1997) *Rewired*, Indianapolis: Macmillan Technical Publishing.

Huq, R. (1998) 'The Right to Rave: opposition to the Criminal Justice and Public Order Act 1994', in Jordan, T. and Lent, A. (eds) *Storming the Millennium: the new politics of change*, London: Lawrence & Wishart.

Hyman, A. (1982) *Charles Babbage: pioneer of the computer*, Oxford: Oxford University Press.

Intel (1998) 'History of the Microprocessor', available at http://www.intel.com/intel/museum/25anniv/index.htm.

Ito, M. (1997) 'Virtuality Embodied: the reality of fantasy in a Multi-User Dungeon', in Porter, D. (ed) *Internet Culture*, London: Routledge, pp. 87–110.

Jacobs, K. (1990) 'Design for an Unreal World', *Metropolis* 10(2): 40–3, 65–77.

Jerman-Blazic, B. (1996) 'Europe and the International Character Sets: strategy of implementation and development of networked services', paper given at INET 96, available at http://www.isoc.org/conferences/inet96.

Jones, C. and Sessions, S. (1993) 'Interoperability: a Desert Storm case study', McNair Paper 18, Institute for National Strategic Studies, National Defense University, USA, available at http://www.ndu.edu/ndu/inss/.

Jones, S. (1995a) 'Introduction: from where to who knows?', in Jones, S. (ed.) *Cybersociety: computer-mediated communication and community*, London: Sage, pp. 1–9.

Jones, S. (1995b) 'Understanding Community in the Information Age', in Jones, S. (ed.) *Cybersociety: computer-mediated communication and community*, London: Sage, pp. 10–35.

Jones, S. (ed.) (1995c) *Cybersociety: computer-mediated communication and community*, London: Sage.

Jones, S. (ed.) (1997) *Virtual Culture: identity and communication in cybersociety*, London: Sage.

Jordan, T. (1995) 'The Unity of Social Movements', *Sociological Review* 43(4): 675–92.

Jordan, T. (1998) 'New Space? New Politics: cyberpolitics and the Electronic Frontier Foundation', in Jordan, T. and Lent, A. (eds) *Storming the Millennium: the new politics of change*, London: Lawrence & Wishart.

Jordan, T. and Lent, A. (eds) (1998) *Storming the Millennium: the new politics of change*, London: Lawrence & Wishart.

Jordan, T. and Taylor, P. (1998) 'A Sociology of Hackers', *Sociological Review* 46(4): 675–93.

Kahin, B. and Keller, J. (eds) (1997) *Coordinating the Internet*, Cambridge, MA: MIT Press.

Kahin, B. and Nesson, C. (eds) (1997) *Borders in Cyberspace: information policy and the Global Information Infrastructure*, Cambridge, MA: MIT Press.

Katz, J. (1997a) 'Birth of a Digital Nation', *Wired USA* 5.04: 49–52, 184–91.

Katz, J. (1997b) 'The Digital Citizen', *Wired USA* 5.12, 68–82, 274–5.

Keller, L (1988) 'Machismo and the Hacker Mentality: some personal observations and speculations', paper presented to *WiC (Women in Computing) Conference*.

Kelly, K. (1994) *Out of Control: the new biology of machines*, London: Fourth Estate.

Kelly, K. and Wolf, G. (1997) 'Push! Kiss your Browser Goodbye: the radical future of media beyond the Web', *Wired UK* 3.03: 69–81.

Kevles, D. and Hood, L. (eds) (1992) *The Code of Codes: scientific and social issues in the Human Genome Project*, Cambridge, MA: Harvard University Press.

Kimery, A. (1993) 'Big Brother Wants to Look Into Your Bank Account', *Wired USA* 1.06: 90–3, 134.

Knorr-Cetina, K. and Mulkay, M. (1983) *Science Observed: perspectives on the social study of science*, London: Sage.

Kollock, P. and Smith, M. (eds) (1998) *Communities in Cyberspace*, London: Routledge.

Kroker, A. and Weinstein, M. (1994) *Data Trash: the theory of the virtual class*, Montreal: New World Perspectives.

Lacan, J. (1977) *The Four Fundamental Concepts of Psycho-Analysis*, Harmondsworth: Penguin.

Lacoue-Labarthe, P. and Nancy, J.-L. (1997) *Retreating the Political*, London: Routledge.

Landsberg, A. (1995) 'Prosthetic Memories: Total Recall and Blade Runner', in Featherstone, M. and Burrows, R. (eds) *Cyberspace, Cyberbodies, Cyberpunks: cultures of technological embodiment*, Londond: Sage, pp. 175–89.

Lappin, T. (1997) 'Winning the Crypto Wars: why John Gilmore believes things are going our way', *Wired USA* 5.05: 94.

Lash, S. and Urry, J. (1987) *The End of Organised Capitalism*, Cambridge: Polity.

Lash, S. and Urry, J. (1994) *Economies of Signs and Spaces*, London: Sage.

Latour, B. (1987) *Science in Action: how to follow scientists and engineers through society*, Milton Keynes: Open University Press.

Lea, M. (ed.) (1992) *Contexts of Computer-Mediated Communication*, London: Harvester Wheatsheaf.

Lee, E. (1997) *The Labour Movement and the Internet: the new internationalism*, London: Pluto Press.

Lee, J. (1996) 'Charting the Codes of Cyberspace: a rhetoric of electronic mail', in Strate, L., Jacobson, R. and Gibson, S. (eds) *Communication and Cyberspace: social interaction in an electronic environment*, Creskill, NJ: Hampton Press, pp. 275–96.

Leeson, L. (ed.) (1996) *Clicking In: hot links to a digital culture*, Seattle: Bar Press.

Lefebvre, H. (1991) *The Production of Space*, Oxford: Blackwell.

Leonard, A. (1997) *Bots: the origin of new species*, San Francisco: Hardwired.

Levidow, L. (1991) 'Women Who Make the Chips', *Science as Culture* 2(1): 103–24.

Levidow, L. (1994) 'The Gulf Massacre as Paranoid Rationality', in Bender, G. and Druckrey, T. (eds) *Culture on the Brink: ideologies of technology*, Seattle: Bay Press, pp. 317–27.

Levinson, P. (1997) *The Soft Edge: a natural history and future of the information revolution*, London: Routledge.

Levy, S. (1984) *Hackers: heroes of the computer revolution*, London: Penguin.

Lewontin, R. (1994) 'The Dream of the Human Genome', in Bender, G. and Druckrey, T. (eds) *Culture on the Brink: ideologies of technology*, Seattle: Bay Press, pp. 107–28.

Leyden, P. (1997) 'Moore's Law Repealed, sort of', *Wired USA* 5.05: 166–7.

Libicki, M. (1995a) 'What is Information Warfare?', Institute for National Strategic Studies, National Defense University, available at http://www.ndu.edu/ndu/inss/.

Libicki, M. (1995b) 'The Mesh and the Net: speculations on armed conflict in a time of free silicon; second edition', McNair Paper No 28, Institute for National Strategic Studies, National Defense University, available at http://www.ndu.edu/ndu/inss/.

Littman, J. (1996) *The Fugitive Game: online with Kevin Mitnick, the inside story of the great cyberchase*, Boston: Little, Brown.

Littman, J. (1997) *The Watchman: the twisted life and crimes of serial hacker Kevin Poulsen*, Boston: Little, Brown.

Loader, D. (ed.) (1997) *The Governance of Cyberspace: politics, technology and global restructuring*, London: Routledge.

Loen, L. (1993) 'Hiding Data in Plain Sight: some key questions about cryptography', *EFFector Online* 4.05, available at http://www.eff.org.

Lottor, M. (1992) *Internet Growth 1981–1991*, Network Working Group, Request for Comment 1296.

Ludlow, P. (ed.) (1996) *High Noon on the Electronic Frontier*, Cambridge, MA: MIT Press.

Lukes, S. (ed.) (1986) *Power: readings in social and political theory*, Oxford: Blackwell.

Lyon, D. (1994) *The Electronic Eye: the rise of the surveillance society*, Cambridge: Polity.

Lyotard, J.-F. (1988) *The Differend: phrases in dispute*, Manchester: Manchester University Press.

Macauley, W. and Gordo-Lobez, A. (1995) 'From Cognitive Psychologies to Mythologies: advancing cyborg textualities for a narrative of resistance', in Gray, C.H. (ed.) *The Cyborg Handbook*, London: Routledge, pp. 433–44.

McCaffery, L. (1991a) 'An Interview with William Gibson', in McCaffery, L. (ed.) *Storming the Reality Studio: a casebook of cyberpunk and postmodern science fiction*, Durham, NC: Duke University Pres, pp. 263–87.

McCaffery, L. (ed.) (1991b) *Storming the Reality Studio: a casebook of cyberpunk and postmodern science fiction*, Durham, NC: Duke University Press.

McCandlish, S. (1995) 'Interview for NetGuide Magazine', available at http://www.eff.org/~mech/scritt.

McCandlish, S. (1996) 'Interview with Tim Jordan', unpublished manuscript.

McChesney, J. (1997) 'Is Microsoft's Brad Chase Aiming to Own your Desktop?', available at http://www.hotwired.com.

MacKinnon, R. (1995) 'Searching for the Leviathan on Usenet', in Jones, S. (ed.) *Cybersociety: computer-mediated communication and community*, London: Sage, pp. 112–37 .

McLuhan, M. (1995) *Essential McLuhan: edited by E. McLuhan and F. Zingrone*, London: Routledge.

McRae, S. (1996) 'Coming Apart at the Seams: sex, text and the virtual body', in Cherny, L. and Weise, E. (eds) *Wired_Women: gender and new realities in cyberspace*, Seattle: Seal Press, pp. 242–64.

Maes, P. (1994) 'Agents that Reduce Work and Information Overload', available at http://pattie.www.media.mit.edu/people/pattie/CACM-94.

Maes, P. (1996) 'Artificial Life meets Entertainment: lifelike autonomous agents', in Leeson, L. (ed.) *Clicking In: hot links to a digital culture*, Seattle: Bar Press, pp. 210–21 .

Mandel, E. (1975) *Late Capitalism*, London: Verso.

Manners, D. (1996) 'Memories are Made of This', *Guardian Online Supplement* 14 March: 2.

Markoff, J. (1993) 'A Free and Simple Computer Link', *New York Times (late edition – final)* 12 December, also available at http://www.crs4.it/~zip/markoff.html.

Marks, J. (1994) 'The Human Genome Project: a challenge in biological technology', in Bender, G. and Druckrey, T. (eds) *Culture on the Brink: ideologies of technology*, Seattle: Bay Press, pp. 99–106.

Mason, R. (1993) 'Computer Conferencing and the New Europe', in Harasim, L. (ed.) *Global Networks: computers and international communication*, Cambridge, MA: MIT Press, pp. 199–220.

Meyer, G. and Thomas, J (1989) 'The Baudy World of the Byte: a post-modernist interpretation of the Computer Underground', paper presented at the American Society of Criminology annual meeting, Reno, November.

Miller, L. (1995) 'Women and Children First: gender and the settling of the electronic frontier', in Boal, I. and Brook, J. (eds) *Resisting the Virtual Life: the culture and politics of information*, San Francisco: City Lights Books, pp. 49–57.

Miller, S. (1996) 'Hacker takes over Labour's cyberspace', *Guardian* 10 December: 1.

Minoli, D. (1997) *Internet and Intranet Engineering: technologies, protocols, and applications*, New York: McGraw-Hill.

Minsky, M. (1986) *The Society of Mind*, New York: Simon & Schuster.

Mitchell, W. (1996) *City of Bits: space, place and the infobahn*, Cambridge, MA: MIT Press.

Mommsen, W. (1989) *The Political and Social Theory of Max Weber*, Cambridge: Polity.

Moody, G. (1997) 'The Greatest OS That (N)ever Was', *Wired USA* 5.08: 122–5, 154–64.

Moravec, H. (1988) *Mind Children: the future of robot and human intelligence*, Cambridge, MA: Harvard University Press.

Mort, F. (1996) *Cultures of Consumption: masculinities and social space in late twentieth century Britain*, London: Routledge.

Mosco, V. and Wasko, M. (eds) (1988) *The Political Economy of Information*, Madison,WI: University of Wisconsin Press.

NCC (1991) *Survey of Security Breaches*, Manchester: National Computing Centre.

Network Wizards 'Host Count', available at http://www.nw.com .

Nietzsche, F. (1983) *Untimely Meditations*, Cambridge: Cambridge University Press.

NOP (1995) 'Press release for NOP Internet Survey', available at http://www.nopres.co.uk.

NUA (1997) 'How Many Online?', *NUA Internet Review* 12 November, available at http://www.nua.ie/surveys/how_many_online.html.

O'Brien, J. (1998) 'Writing the Body: gender (re)production in online interaction', in Kollock, P. and Smith, M. (eds) *Communities in Cyberspace*, London: Routledge.

ORA (1995) *Defining the Internet Opportunity: Internet user survey*, available at http://www.ora.com/research.

Parks, B. (1997) 'Where Computers Go to Die', *Wired USA* 5.07: 146–51, 180–1.

Pearce, F. (1996) 'Greenpeace: mindbombing the media', *Wired UK* 2.05: 49–53, 87–8.

Perkin, H. (1996) *The Third Revolution: professional elites in the modern world*, London: Routledge.

Pitkow, J. and Recker, M. (1994a) *Results from the First World-Wide Web User Survey*, available at http://www.cc.gatech.edu/gvu.

Pitkow, J. and Recker, M. (1994b) *Using the Web as a Survey Tool: Results from the Second World-Wide Web User Survey*, available at http://www.cc.gatech.edu/gvu.

Pitkow, J. and Kehoe, C. (1995a) *GVU's Third WWW User Survey*, available at http://www.cc.gatech.edu/gvu.

Pitkow, J. and Kehoe, C. (1995b) *GVU's Fourth WWW User Survey*, available at http://www.cc.gatech.edu/gvu.

Pitkow, J. and Kehoe, C. (1996a) *GVU's Fifth WWW User Survey*, available at http://www.cc.gatech.edu/gvu.

Pitkow, J. and Kehoe, C. (1996b) *GVU's Sixth WWW User Survey*, available at http://www.cc.gatech.edu/gvu.

Pitkow, J. and Kehoe, C. (1997) *GVU's Seventh WWW User Survey*, available at http://www.cc.gatech.edu/gvu.

Pitkow, J., Kehoe, C., Morton, K., Zou, L., Read, W. and Rossignac, J. (1998) *GVU's Eighth WWW User Survey*, available at http://www.cc.gatech.edu.gvu.

Platt, C. (1997) *Anarchy Online: net.sex and net.crime*, New York: HarperCollins.

Porter, D. (ed.) (1997) *Internet Culture*, London: Routledge.

Poster, M. (1990) *The Mode of Information: poststructuralism and social context*, Cambridge: Polity.

Poster, M. (1995) *The Second Media Age*, Cambridge: Polity.

Quarterman, J. (1990) *The Matrix: computer networks and conferencing systems worldwide*, Bedford: Digital Press.

Quarterman, J. (1993) 'The Global Matrix of Minds', in Harasim, L. (ed.) *Global Networks: computers and international communication*, Cambridge, MA: MIT Press, pp. 35–56.

Quarterman, J. (1997) 'Is COM Primarily U.S. or International?', *Matrix News* 7(8): 8–10.

Quarterman, J. (1998) 'Internet Economics 101: why is it so slow?', *Matrix News* 8(1): 10–12.

Quittner, J. (1994a) 'Johnny Manhattan meets the Furrymuckers', *Wired USA* 2.03: 92–7, 138.

Quittner, J. (1994b) 'The War between alt.tasteless and rec.pets.cats', Wired USA 2.05: 46–53.

Quittner, J. (1994c) 'The Merry Pranksters Go to Washington', Wired USA 2.06: 77–81, 128–31.

Quittner, J. (1998) 'Netscape's Survival Kit', Wired USA 6.04: 154–8, 182–4.

Quittner, J. and Slatalla, M. (1995) Masters of Deception: the gang that ruled cyberspace, London: Vintage.

Rafferty, K. and Tran, M. (1996) 'A Hard Drive When the Chips are Down', Guardian Online Supplement 14 March: 2–3.

Rapaport, R. (1995) 'Muse: we learn through experience', Wired UK 1.06: 74–7, 108.

Ravetz, J. and Sardar, Z. (eds) (1996) Cyberfutures: culture and politics on the information superhighway, London: Pluto.

Rawlins, G. (1996) Moths to the Flame: the seductions of computer technology, Cambridge, MA: MIT Press.

Reid, E. (1995) 'Virtual Worlds: culture and imagination', in Jones, S. (ed.) Cybersociety: computer-mediated communication and community, London: Sage, pp. 164–83.

Reid, E. (1998) 'Hierarchy and Power: social control in cyberspace', in Kollock, P. and Smith, M. (eds) Communities in Cyberspace, London: Routledge.

Reid, R. (1997) 'Real Revolution', Wired USA 5.10: 122–7, 174–88.

Rheingold, H. (1991) Virtual Reality, London: Secker & Warburg.

Rheingold, H. (1994) The Virtual Community: surfing the Internet, London: Minerva.

Rickard, J. (1995) 'The Internet by the Numbers: 9.1 million users can't be wrong', Boardwatch 9(12), also available at http://www.boardwatch.com.

Rickard, J. (1996a) 'Microsoft, The Internet and BILLGATUS OF BORG' , Boardwatch 10(5), also available at http://www.boardwatch.com/.

Rickard, J. (1996b) 'Netscape vs Microsoft: the battle continues', Boardwatch 10(7), also available at http://www.boardwatch.com/.

Riddell, R. (1997) 'Doom Goes to War: the Marines are looking for a few good games', Wired USA 5.04: 114–18, 164–6.

RIPE, 'European Host Count', available at http://www.ripe.net .

Robins, K. (1994) 'The Haunted Screen', in Bender, G. and Druckrey, T. (eds) Culture on the Brink: ideologies of technology, Seattle: Bay Press, pp. 303–15.

Robins, K. (1997) 'The New Communications Geography and the Politics of Optimism', Soundings 5: 191–202.

Rose, F. (1998) 'The Televisionspace Race', Wired USA 6.04: 148–52, 181–2.

Ross, A. (1991) Strange Weather, London: Verso.

Rosteck, T. (1994) 'Computer Hackers: rebels with a cause', Honours Thesis, Concordia University, Montreal, also at http://www.geocities.com/CapeCanaveral/3498/.

Rucker, R., Sirius, R. and Mu, Q. (1992) Mondo 2000 Users' Guide to the New Edge, New York: HarperCollins.

Rushkoff, D. (1997) 'The plug that was waiting to be pulled', Guardian Online Supplement 24 July: 11.

Sagan, D. (1995) 'Sex, Lies and Cyberspace: online, no one knows you're a dog or a male or a 13-year old girl', Wired USA 3.01: 78–84.

Sale, K. (1995) Rebels Against the Future: the Luddites and their war on the Industrial Revolution, lessons for the computer age, London: Quartet Books.

Sandoval, C. (1995) 'New Sciences: cyborg feminism and the methodology of the oppressed', in Gray, C.H. (ed.) *The Cyborg Handbook*, London: Routledge, pp. 407–22.

Sardar, Z. (1996) 'alt.civilizations.faq: cyberspace as the darker side of the West', in Ravetz, J. and Sardar, Z. (eds) *Cyberfutures: culture and politics on the information super-highway*, London: Pluto, pp. 14–41.

Sassen, S. (1991) *The Global City: New York, London, Tokyo*, Princeton NJ: Princeton University Press.

Sayer, D. (1979) *Marx's Method: ideology, science and critique in Capital*, Brighton: Harvester.

Schiller, H. (1996) *Information Inequality: the deepening social crisis in America*, London: Routledge.

Schofield, J. (1996) 'A Tiny Sliver Not to be Sneezed At', *Guardian Online Supplement* 31 October: 2–3.

Schofield, J. (1997) 'Between a Rock and a Hardware Place', *Guardian Online Supplement* 1 May: 2–3.

Schwartz, P. and Leyden, P. (1997) 'The Long Boom: the history of the future 1980–2020, *Wired USA* 5.07: 115–29, 168–73.

Seiger, J. (1996) 'Interview with Tim Jordan', unpublished.

Shade, L. (1996) 'Is There Free Speech on the Net? Censorship and the global information infrastructure', in Shields, R. (ed.) *Cultures of Internet: virtual space, real histories, living bodies*, London: Sage, pp. 11–32.

Shapard, J. (1993) 'Islands in the (Data)Stream: language, character codes, and electronic isolation in Japan', in Harasim, L. (ed.) *Global Networks: computers and international communication*, Cambridge, MA: MIT Press, pp. 255–69.

Shearing, C. and Stenning, P. (1985) 'From the Panopticon to Disney World: the development of discipline', in Doob, A. and Greenspan, E. (eds) *Perspectives in Criminal Law*, Aurora, Ontario: Canada Law Books, pp. 335–49.

Shenk, D. (1997) *Data Smog: surviving the information age*, San Francisco: HarperEdge.

Sheridan, A. (1977) 'Translator's Note', in Lacan, J. *The Four Fundamental Concepts of Psycho-Analysis*, Harmondsworth: Penguin, pp. 277–82.

Shields, R.(ed.) (1996a) *Cultures of Internet: virtual space, real histories, living bodies*, London: Sage.

Shields, R. (1996b) 'Introduction: virtual space, real histories, living bodies', in Shields, R. (ed.) *Cultures of Internet: virtual space, real histories, living bodies*, London: Sage, pp. 1–10.

Shimomura, T. (1995) *Takedown: the pursuit and capture of Kevin Mitnick, the world's most notorious cybercriminal – by the man who did it*, with John Markoff, London: Secker & Warburg.

Shukman, D. (1995) *The Sorceror's Challenge: fears and hopes for the weapons of the next millennium*, London: Hodder & Stoughton.

Slouka, M. (1995) *War of the Worlds: the assault on reality*, London: Abacus.

Sowa, F. (1996a) 'Meltdown or Monopolisitc Power Play?', *Boardwatch* 10(9), also available at http://www.boardwatch.com/.

Sowa, F. (1996b) 'Back to the Future', *Boardwatch* 10(11), also available at http://www.boardwatch.com/.

Spafford, E. (1990) 'Are Computer Hacker Break-Ins Ethical?', Princeton University Technical Report, CSD-TR-994, Princeton.

Spertus, E. (1991) 'Why are there so few female computer scientists?', unpublished paper, MIT.

Spertus, E. (1996) 'Social and Technical Means for Fighting On-Line Harassment', paper presented at Virtue and Virtuality: gender, law and cyberspace Conference, MIT, available at http://www.mit.edu.

Springer, C. (1993) 'Sex, Memories and Angry Women', in Dery, M. (ed.) *Flame Wars: the discourse of cyberculture*, Durham, NC: Duke University Press, pp. 713–33.

Sproull, L. and Kiesler, S. (1986) 'Reducing Social Context Cues: electronic mail in organisational communication', *Management Science* 32(11): 1492–1512.

Sproull, L. and Kiesler, S. (1993) 'Computers, Networks and Work', in Harasim, L. (ed.) *Global Networks: computers and international communication*, Cambridge, MA: MIT Press, pp. 105–20.

Stanley, C. (1995) 'Teenage Kicks: urban narratives of dissent not deviance', *Crime, Law and Social Change* 23: 91–119.

Steinberg, S. (1996) 'Seek and Ye Shall Find (Maybe)', *Wired UK* 2.05: 61–6, 99–103.

Stephenson, N. (1992) *Snow Crash*, London: Penguin.

Sterling, B. (ed.) (1985) *Mirrorshades: the cyberpunk anthology*, New York, Arbor House.

Sterling, B. (1988) *Islands in the Net*, New York: Ace Books.

Sterling, B. (1992) *The Hacker Crackdown: law and disorder on the electronic frontier*, London: Viking.

Sterling, B. (1993) 'Short History of the Internet', *The Magazine of Fantasy and Science Fiction* February: 4–5.

Sterling, B. (1994) 'The Hacker Crackdown three years later', only published electronically, available at http://www.uel.ac.uk/research/nprg.

Stoll, C. (1989) *The Cuckoo's Egg: tracking a spy through the maze of counter-espionage*, New York: Simon & Schuster.

Stoll, C. (1995) *Silicon Snake Oil: second thoughts on the information highway*, London: Macmillan.

Stone, A.R. (1995) *The War of Desire and Technology at the Close of the Mechanical Age*, Cambridge, MA: MIT Press.

Strate, L., Jacobson, R. and Gibson, S. (eds) (1996) *Communication and Cyberspace: social interaction in an electronic environment*, Creskill, NJ: Hampton Press.

Stross, R. (1996) *The Microsoft Way*, New York: Addison-Wesley.

Stroud, F. (1996) 'Battle of the Browsers', *Boardwatch* 10(3), also available at http://www.boardwatch.com/.

Taylor, P. (1993) 'Hackers: a case-study of the social shaping of computing', PhD dissertation, University of Edinburgh.

Tepper, M. (1997) 'Usenet Communities and the Cultural Politics of Information', in Porter, D. (ed.) *Internet Culture*, London: Routledge, pp. 39–54.

Thomas, J. (1990) 'Review of The Cuckoo's Egg', *Computer Underground Digest* 1.06.

Thompsen, P. (1996) 'What's Fuelling the Flames in Cyberspace: a social influence model', in Strate, L., Jacobson, R. and Gibson, S. (eds) *Communication and Cyberspace: social interaction in an electronic environment*, Creskill, NJ: Hampton Press, pp. 297–315.

Toffler, A. (1980) *The Third Wave*, New York: Collins.

Tomas, D. (1991) 'Old Rituals for New Space: rites de passage and William Gibson's cultural model of cyberspace', in Benedikt, M. (ed.) (1992) *Cyberspace: the first steps*, Cambridge, MA: MIT Press, pp. 31–48.

Touraine, A. (1971) *The Post-Industrial Society: tomorrow's social history; classes, conflicts and culture in the programmed society*, New York: Wildwood House.

Travis, A. (1997) 'Net Porn to get a X-rating', *Guardian* 30 June: 5.

Tsagarousianou, R., Tambini, D. and Bryan, C. (eds) (1998) *Cyberdemocracy: technology, cities and civic networks*, London: Routledge.

Turkle, S. (1995) *The Second Self: computers and the human spirit*, London: Granada.

Van Bakel, R. (1996) 'How Good People Helped Make Bad Law', *Wired UK* 2.02: 38–46.

Van Gelder, L. (1991) 'The Strange Case of the Electronic Lover', in Dunlop, C. and Kling, R. (eds) *Computerisation and Controversy: value conflicts and social choices*, Boston: Academic Press, pp. 365–81.

Vesely, R. (1997) 'The Generation Gap', *Wired USA* 5.10: 53–6, 207.

3W (1994) 'How Big is the Web?', *3W: global networking newsletter* 3: 32.

Walby, S. (1990) *Theorizing Patriarchy*, Oxford: Blackwell.

Wallace, J. (1996) *Hard Drive: Bill Gates and the making of the Microsoft Empire*, New York: John Wiley.

Wallace, J. (1997) *Overdrive: Bill Gates and the race to control cyberspace*, New York: John Wiley.

WarRoom (1996) '1996 Information Systems Security Survey', WarRoom Research, LLC, available at http://www.infowar.com/.

Weber, M. (1952) 'Class, Status, Party', from Gerth, H. and C. Wright Mills (eds) *From Max Weber*, London: Routledge, pp.180–95.

Weber, M. (1986) 'Domination by Economic Power and by Authority', in Lukes, S. (ed.) *Power: readings in social and political theory*, Oxford: Blackwell.

Webster, F. (1995) *Theories of the Information Society*, London: Routledge.

Wilson, K. (1988) *Technologies of Control: the new interactive media for the home*, Madison, WI: University of Wisconsin Press.

Wolf, B. (1994) 'The Second Phase of the Revolution has begun', *Wired USA* 2.10: 116–21, 150–2.

Wresch, W. (1996) *Disconnected: haves and have-nots in the Information Age*, Piscataway, NJ: Rutgers University Press.

Wright, S. (1998) *An Appraisal of Technologies of Political Control: Scientific and Technological Options Assessment Working Document (Consultation Version)*, Luxembourg: Directorate General for Research European Parliament, available at http://www.jya.com/atpc.htm.

Wylie, M. (1995) 'No Place for Women: Internet is flawed model for the Infobahn', *Digital Media* 4(8): 3–6.

Yong, K.Y., Wee, T.T., Govindasamy, N. and Chee, L.T. (1996) 'Multiple Language Support Over the World Wide Web', paper given at INET 96, available at http://www.isoc.org/conferences/inet96.

Zeltser, L. (1995) *The World Wide Web: origins and beyond*, available at http://www.seas.upenn.edu/~lzeltser/WWW.

Zuboff, S. (1988) *In the Age of Smart Machines: the future of work and power*, Oxford: Heinemann.

Index